The Psychedelic Origin of Religion

Matthew Lawrence Weintrub
יונה

God is Love
Aho Mitákuye Oyás'iŋ
בָּרוּךְ הַשֵּׁם

ISBN: 9798373191289

2022/5782 by Matthew Weintrub

Words of Gratitude

Thank you, thank you, thank you to all the seekers, scholars and researchers who came before me. Thank you for questioning "the truth" and pursuing it for yourself. I'm grateful for your lives. Thank you for guiding me to the truth for this book is not possible without your life. The scholars cited herein spent lifetimes examining ancient myths, folklore, and art to articulate the key role of psychedelic sacraments in ancient cultures from Vedic Brahmins to the Greeks, Christian mystics and many more. Thank you to Jerry and Julie Brown, Brian Muraresku, Herbert Bruce Puryear, Elaine Pagels, Meggan Watterson, Carl Ruck, Chris Bennett, R. Gordon Wasson, Harry Rozenberg, Mike Crowley, David Brooks, Laura Barringer, Scot McKnight, Claudio Naranjo and all the others who I didn't name for creating a path for me to walk down. Your light has helped me immensely and I owe you a debt of gratitude. I hope our paths cross soon in this world or the next.

Thank you to all my friends and my family, your love and friendship is the greatest gift of my life and makes me feel alive. Thank you to my parents for my life. I pray that you all have a good day, a joyful year and a good life filled with love and blessings. And lastly thank you, thank you, thank you to Great Mystery, Great Spirit, the Angels and the Ancestors who guided me and frankly did most of the hard lifting to compose this book. I'm grateful to be of service.

Table of Contents

Disclaimer

DISCLAIMER: The information provided in this book is for educational and informational purposes only. It is not intended to be a substitute for professional medical advice, diagnosis, or treatment. I do not encourage or support the reckless use of psychedelics or any other substances outside of safe, sacred ceremonial spaces. The use of psychedelics can be associated with risk and should be approached with caution, especially in individuals with a history of mental health issues, individuals currently receiving pharmaceutical treatment for mental health issues or individuals with a family history of such conditions. It is important to carefully research the potential risks and benefits of using psychedelics and to always use these substances under the guidance of a trained healer, facilitator or medical professional. I have dedicate my life to spread the good word of natural psychedelic medicine but I also believe nothing should be encouraged absolutely. Life is all about balance. Act wisely. God Bless You.

Introduction

I've spent my whole life seeking answers to the questions: why am I here, where do I come from and why is the world so upside down? On my journey, God gave me many blessings: a good family, good health and a strong relationship with jail. I spent the ages of 17 to 23 becoming intimate with the justice system because I was healing myself with natural medicine - like psychedelics and marijuana. Medicines that today are mostly legal or close to it.

At 19 I faced up to 10 years in jail. To avoid prison, I did what I was told. I peed in front of my probation officer and I passed all my drug tests. I straightened up and I became very "successful." By 2019, I had it all: a million-dollar penthouse condo in San Francisco, a high six-figure corporate job, a corporate expense account, a beautiful girlfriend, and a fun group of friends. However, inside I was miserable AF. One night I was crying alone in my condo overlooking the Bay and I knew something had to change.

Luckily, I heard the call of Grandmother Ayahuasca. Ayahuasca contains the DMT molecule, which scientists call the Spirit Molecule because of its potential to help one see God. I knew at that moment I needed to seek Ayahuasca. In the fall of 2019, I traveled to Cuenca, Ecuador, to participate in my first ayahuasca retreat where I intended to discover my life's purpose because whatever I was doing wasn't it.

Well guess what? That time I spent on the mountain and the blessings I received from God during those the indigenous-led ceremonies were some of the greatest gifts of my life. The first two ceremonies, Grandmother Ayahuasca and Grandfather San Pedro taught me the lesson of goodness. I learned how much loved me.

And how I needed to become a better person, brother, son, cousin, lover, and friend. I realized I wasn't ready to understand my true purpose because I had so much healing to do in my life. Fast forward to the third ceremony took place in the temazcal, a sweat lodge. Indigenous sweat ceremonies typically last for many hours and take place in domed, circular lodges where rocks that have been heated in a fire for hours are brought into the lodge and cooled with water. Sweat lodge ceremonies have four rounds. Each round of the sweat is dedicated to one of the sacred directions, and the spirits and elements of that direction are honored in prayer by those hosting the ceremony. The conductor splashes water on the grandfather stones to create steam and fill the lodge with heat; as one sweats, impurities are taken from all the bodies. The conductor is also responsible for controlling the energies within the lodge and keeping the participants safe while they are spiritually open and vulnerable.

Before we started this ceremony, we were offered the gift of taking cups of Ayahuasca and San Pedro. Naturally, I drank to my hearts' content. Growing up in the Texas heat, I thought this ceremony would be a piece of cake. By the third round, I could barely catch my breath. I laid down, and soon, I drifted out of my body where I met with what I best describe as the Angels, Spirits, and Ancestors in the vastness of space. In this space, I was shown my past lives. Once I kinda understood what was going on the ancestors asked me: "Hey kid, what do you want?"

I said, "I wish to learn how I could best be of service to my family, my brothers, and sisters."

They asked, "Are you sure this is what you want?"

I responded, "Yes, of course."

They asked, "Would you be willing to give your life to help others?"

I responded, "Yes, of course."

They said, "Ok. Good luck! Be careful what you wish for."

I laughed. The Ancestors are not without a sense of humor. They proceeded to share with me many visions and instructions on how to fulfill my wish. Their message was this:

1. Write and share the teachings on the science of psychedelics and reincarnation.
2. Work to share the medicine plants with all the people.
3. Make relations with the tribes of the North and the South.
4. Create a platform dedicated to healing the forests and the oceans.

It is a great joy of my life to share with you these teachings which involve learning about the true origins of religion, the story of the master plant teachers and the true eucharist of Christ.

CHAPTER 1:

The Psuedo Spiritual Age

When you look at the world today, what do you see? What kind of problems do we face, and why do we face them? Do you feel like the world is becoming better or worse? Are we living our lives in a good and sustainable way? Are we building a better world for our children? Please take a moment to reflect.

I want to share some sobering facts with you:

- The world is on the precipice of an environmental catastrophe.
- Climate scientists warn us that we must maintain warming below 1.5°C, but our current CO_2 emissions exceed that threshold.
- From transport and housing to food production and fashion, our current civilization is driving climate and ecological breakdown.
- The obesity epidemic is now a leading cause of death.
- There is a global mental health epidemic, and 1 in 4 Americans report a mental health disorder.
- Western healthcare prioritizes profit over healing people.

We live in an age where everything around us feels fake. We live in a fake culture where we practice fake religions. We live in a fake society with politicians but no real leaders. We consume fake processed food, which damages our health. We have a fake healthcare system to profit from keeping us sick. We breathe dirty air, which we pollute because we only value money. We drink unclean water - water which is now causing cancer. The world is but a mirror of what is happening inside of us. And we - humanity - have become rotten, barren, and corrupted. And so our home and our shared world have also turned rotten, barren, and corrupted.

I used to think the top environmental problems facing the world were global warming, environmental degradation, and ecosystem collapse and that we scientists would fix those problems with enough science. But I was wrong. The real problem is not those three items but greed, selfishness, and apathy. And for that, we need a spiritual and cultural transformation. As scientists, we don't know how to do that.

- Gus Speith, Founder National
Resources Defense Council

Why does it feel like everything is falling apart? Why are we doing this? Why are we complacent with living this way?

I feel it is because we have forgotten the roots of religion. We are in a moment of collective spiritual crisis. People, especially young people, are abandoning institutional religion because it's synthetic. 30% of progressive liberals - an identity shared by most Americans - no longer believe in God[1]. And less than 50% Of U.S. adults belong to a religious community[2]. 40% of millennials don't identify with any faith whatsoever[3].

NEWS

Number of Americans who believe in God dips to new low: Gallup

BY CHLOE FOLMAR - 06/17/22 7:35 AM ET

I'm one of those people. I am disillusioned with religion because these organizations no longer speak to the truth of our reality. The point of spirituality is unity, yet modern religion spends its time dividing us. That's because these institutions of religion have sanitized, censored, and banned the truth. For thousands of years, they have been guilty of lying to humanity about how our religions first begin. In doing so, these institutions shall reap the karma of what they sowed. These organizations masquerade as religion. They are destined to lose their connection to their congregants, Earth, and God.

I believe that we forget so that we can remember. Humanity has forgotten the origins of religion. It's why religions are not healthy. It's why we are not healthy. If you are not healthy, you are not happy. If you are not happy, you are diseased. This is a negative prefix; it means not or none. Ease means a feeling of comfort, relaxation, and contentment. When we say we are dis-eased, we are not feeling good inside. The dis-ease of our hearts, minds, bodies, and souls is causing us to suffer until we remember the truth of psychedelics.

CHAPTER 2:

The Psychedelic Origin
of Religion

I'm grateful for the spiritual crisis we face as a human family because I choose to see this moment as an opportunity to change—an opportunity to be the change I wish to see in the world. I wished to change how I understood religion. I spent time with the archaeological evidence and the scientific evidence. Seek, and you shall find, the Bible says. So I sought, and I found a psychedelic origin of religion.

For thousands of years, religion was a way for our ancestors to better understand the relationships between us, the earth, the universe, and why we are here. However, it did not occur in a building made by man's hands. The way of our ancestors, the root of religion, began in the forests, rivers, deserts, and sanctuary of Mother Earth. We made relationships with the members of our tribe and all of life through shamanic ceremonies using psychedelic sacraments.

> *God does not reside in a holy book. Whether it's the Bible or the Qur'an, the mystics have never found God by reading about God. There is no class, no lecture, and no sermon that will ever bring you closer to God. Because there is, in fact, absolutely nothing you could ever learn about God. For the mystics, the only way to know God is to experience God.*
>
> - Brian Muraresku, The Immortality Key

The world's religions share a common heritage of psychedelics and shamanism. Christianity, Hinduism, Buddhism, Judaism, and Islam - all find their origins in shamanism. Psychedelics are classified as Entheogens. Entheogen means a psychedelic substance one takes to communicate with God or Consciousness for spiritual purposes. Psychedelics allow us to access the Kingdom of Heaven, the God within. The indigenous people have known this for thousands of years because they still worship similarly. Today scientific research can explain that connection. Science and archeology can explain how psychedelics and shamanic practices gave birth to modern religion in both Eastern and Western civilizations.

I'm grateful for the research of the many scholars who questioned what they were told and pursued the truth. My research is built on the shoulders of these giants, and my heart goes out to them. Scholars examined ancient myths, folklore, and art to articulate the key role of natural sacraments in ancient cultures, from Vedic Brahmins to the Greeks, Christian mystics, Manicheans, and many more.

Shamanism: The World's Religion

Shamanism traces its origins back to the age of hunter-gatherer societies. It is a religious practice involving interaction with the world of spirit through altered states of consciousness. There are many ways to alter one's consciousness. The mystical Sufis of Islam practice the whirling dervish. The San people of Botswana conduct a trance dance - an indigenous ritual that uses rhythmic dancing and hyperventilation to achieve altered states. Buddhist, Hindu, and Christian monks practice meditation to elevate their consciousness in hopes of realizing nirvana. The tribes of North and South America use a combination of the psychedelic sacrament, fasting, and dancing to raise their consciousness. New-age spiritualists teach astral projection, where practitioners learn to use the dream state to access the astral realm. Altering consciousness is so common we find examples of it in every culture and religion! These acts of shamanism seek a divine, mystical connection with the field of information that is best called Spirit, God, Consciousness, Allah, Brahma, Christ, or All that is and All that will be.

Shamanic Cave Art

The oldest archeological evidence linking humans and psychedelics comes to us from 7,000-10,000 years ago from art in the Paleolithic age from Tassili, Algeria cave paintings depicting Psilocybe mairei mushrooms[11]. The U.S. Forest Service acknowledges Tassili as "the oldest known petroglyph depicting the use of psychoactive mushrooms," adding the postulate that "the mushrooms depicted on the 'mushroom shaman' are Psilocybe mushrooms"[22].

Cave art like Tassili's suggests that such instrumental uses of hallucinogenic plants — as vital parts of rituals, for example — may stretch back to 10,000 BC (the Neolithic era), when last the Sahara desert was a relatively verdant savanna rather than the vast expanse of sand we know today[33].

Cave murals found in Spain dating to around 6000 BC appear to depict Mushrooms' use in religious rituals - which would be the oldest evidence of their use in Europe[44]. The Selva Pascuala cave mural near the town of Villar del Humo has a bull in the center, but researchers from America and Mexico focus on a row of 13 small mushroom-like objects.

Brian Akers at Pasco-Hernando Community College in Florida and Gaston Guzman at the Ecological Institute of Xalapa in Mexico say they believe the objects are Psilocybe hispanica[55], local fungi with hallucinogenic properties[66].

FIGURE 3. The bee-faced mushroom shaman of Tassili-n-Ajjer. Drawing by Kat Harrison-McKenna. From O. T. Oss and O. N. Oeric. Psilocybin: The Magic Mushroom Grower's Guide, 1986, p. 71. From the original in Jean-Dominique ajoux, The Rock Paintings of the Tassili (New York: World Publishing, 1963). 71.

FOOD OF THE GODS

In this Algerian cave painting from 4700 BC, we can see mushrooms merging with the head of a human-like entity. Its body is covered in a fractal-like pattern that will be familiar to those who have taken psychedelics before. The theme of mushroom-headed people seems to be near universal. Moving north to chilly Siberia, we find cave art made by nomadic whale hunters.

These 2000-year-old petroglyphs are in a region so far north that it can only be reached by helicopter. The closest town is Pevek, around 5,555 km east of Moscow. Russian experts have dubbed the depicted figures 'fly agaric people', named after the variety of psychedelic mushrooms in the region. Since little is known about the artists who created the art, any speculation on the artists' message is mere speculation[77].

Stonehenge

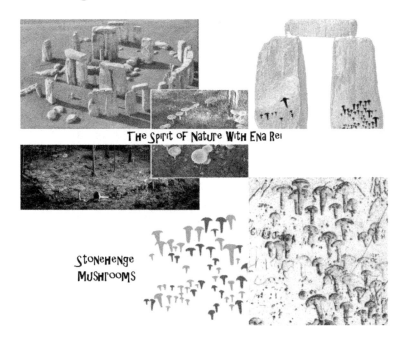

THe Spirit oF Nature WitH ENa Rei

ȘtoNeHeNge MuSHrooMS

Laser scanning has revealed 72 undiscovered Bronze Age carvings on five of Stonehenge's giant stones, the new images found on the monument, which were originally built in the third millennium BCE as a solar temple, portray mushrooms (you can make out mushroom caps and veil in many of the petroglyphs on the monuments)[88].

> *"Stonehenge is unique... Immense and still, it seems beyond man, beyond mortality; in its presence, within those silent circles, one feels the great past all around."*

According to Nicklas Failla, author of "The Origins of Religion," spores that fall to the ground from a mushroom cap will often form a circular network of mycelium beneath the ground, and over time as mushrooms grow from these mycelium rings, the rings will grow out as the mycelium ages. So the size of the ring indicates the age of the mycelium patch, similar to the rings in a tree's trunk. It just so happens that one of the largest fairy rings in the world surrounds the megalithic monument of Stonehenge.

Gobekli Tepe

Turkey's stunning Gobekli Tepe temple predates Stonehenge by at least 6,000 years and is considered the world's oldest temple. It predates the literate civilizations of Egypt, Sumer, India, and Crete. It is interesting to note that many of the strange t-shaped carved pillars at Göbekli Tepe in the Anatolia region of Turkey—founded in the 10th millennium BCE and currently believed to be the oldest 'city' in the world — certainly resemble mushrooms.

Mushroom Pillars of Gobekli Tepe

Not only do we see pillars shaped like a mushroom, but upon closer observation of the pillar on the right, we see there is also a representation of various animals, particularly cattle, which was always associated with many mushroom-based religions of the past.

For example, magic mushrooms are often found growing on cattle dung. Plant-based psychedelics have been used for thousands of years for holistic healing and the evidence spans the entire world.

CHAPTER 3:

Psychedelics in Ancient India

S everal historical urban centers — Mesopotamia, Egypt, Indus Valley, China, etc. — claim to be the cradle of all civilizations in human history. Historians rarely consider the Indus Valley civilization, but they should because early humans lived in northern India 80,000 years ago[1].

The Cult of Soma

Indian civilization is home to the world's oldest and largest religious text: the Rig Veda. Astronomical references and Indian tradition in the Rig Veda suggest a date of 6000 BCE. One must also consider that for much of the time, the Vedas were not written down but were transmitted orally. Tradition says that there is no author of the Vedas. The book could easily be 15,000 years old based on various calculations.

The Rig Veda contains 1000 Hymns, containing over 10,000 verses divided into ten books. Soma is mentioned in almost every one of the thousand Hymns as the preferred drink of both Gods and men. The Soma beverage is considered the most precious liquid in the universe and therefore was an indispensable aspect of all Vedic rituals, used in sacrifices to all gods.

The effects of the Soma drink should capture one's attention: one who consumes it could connect with the bliss of all existence and the source of the universe. The legend states that through Soma, man could grant immortality and become God.

The consumption of Soma by ordinary humans is attested in Vedic rituals. Modern researchers agree that ancient Indians and Iranians used a drink containing a psychoactive substance. The debate is about the drink's identity and how it affected the consciousness of those who consumed it. The descendants of the ancient Hindus and Zoroastrians continue to perform their age-old rituals. However, the identity of the plant from which Soma was extracted or fermented was lost.

The Origins of Soma

In 2009, while digging at a deep burial chamber in the forests of Mongolia, a Russian-Mongolian expedition from the Institute of Archaeology and Ethnography, Siberian Branch of the Russian Academy of Sciences (SB RAS) discovered embroidered woolen textiles dating back two millennia. Although the archaeologists' work is not yet complete, the first fragments restored have revealed some stunning facts. The fragments of the textile found were parts of a carpet composed of several cloths of dark-red woolen fabric. It had made quite a journey – the cloth was spun in Syria or Palestine, embroidered in north-western India, and ended up in Mongolia. The discovery is nothing less than miraculous because of its improbability[2].

"Finding it 2000 years later is a pure chance; its amazingly good condition is almost a miracle. How it made its way to the grave of a person it was not meant for will long, if not forever, remain a mystery," said Natalia V. Polosmak, Chief Researcher, SB RAS

To the left of the altar is the king (priest), who is holding a
mushroom over the fire. Opposite him is a warrior in a jacket
with a "tail" and a belted quiver

The embroidery depicts an ancient Zoroastrian ceremony centered around a mushroom. In the middle of the composition, to the left of the altar, is the king or priest, who is dressed in a smart, long, embroidered kaftan gaping open at the bottom[3]. He is focused on the mushroom in his hands. Polosmak says the "divine mushroom" resembles the well-known psychoactive species psilocybe cubensis. "The weight of evidence suggests that soma, the ancient ritual drink, has been prepared from the mushrooms of family Strophariaceae, which contains the unique nervous system stimulator psilocybin."

A priest with the divine mushroom in his hand. Drawn from the carpet by Ye. Shumakova. The "divine mushroom" embroidered on the carpet resembles Psilocybe cubensis in its habit, shape of the cap, and stitches along the cap margin that look like radial folding or veil remnant. Dark inclusions on the stalk may depict the annulus that blackens because of falling spores. The mushrooms of genus Psilocybe, like many other species of family Strophariaceae, contain the psychoactive substance psilocybin. On the left is a king/priest with a mushroom in his hand. Drawing of the carpet by Ye. Shumakova. On the right is the fruit body of P. cubensis, grown on elephant dung (India). From: (Stamets, 1996). In the center is a diagram of P. cubensis fruit body. From: (Guzmán, 1983)

According to Polosmak, the men depicted on the carpet are either Indo-Scythians (Saka) or Indo-Parthian stock. They are performing a ritual that indicates they acknowledge a form of Zoroastrianism – proof of this is the symbol of Ahura Mazda, the God of the Iranians, represented by the sacred fire altar. The mushroom that the king (or priest) is holding in his hands can be an offering to the fire, or the fire can sanctify it before being used to make the sacred drink.

"The north-western India of that time, where, in all likelihood, the ritual is taking place, was the meeting place of three ethnos, three cultures – Indian, Iranian, and Greek. Each of them had its gods: tolerance and worshiping not only of one's own but also of alien gods was common. To get to the root of the consecration unfolding before us, we should pay attention to seemingly insignificant details like depictions of bees and butterflies strewn all over the cloth. These insects are the most ancient symbols of worship and used to have meanings very different from the present one."

The bee symbolizes honey, Indra, Vishnu, and Krishna. The Atharva Veda – the fourth and last Veda – compares spiritual pursuit with honey making. The antiseptic properties of honey made it critical while preserving some foodstuffs. For example, Mexico has long used honey to preserve mushrooms containing psilocybin. The butterfly, too, had connotations of longevity. In Greek mythology, a butterfly personified the goddess of the soul, Psyche. The Greek word psyche means both soul and butterfly. In fine arts, a soul was often depicted as a butterfly either flying out of a funeral fire or traveling to Hades. The word soul often means "divine fire."

"The butterflies and bees depicted in the background of the canvas may have symbolized the kingdom of souls – the Other World – the world of ancestors, where the warriors got to after having consumed sacred mushrooms," says Polosmak. "Now the puzzle fits together. The insects and mushrooms are closely connected and make the surrounding world miraculous."

This brings us to the prescient words of another Russian genius. Indologist and Rig Veda translator Tatiana Yelizarenkova wrote precisely a decade before the Mongolian finds:

"Judging by the Rig Vedic hymns, Soma was not only a stimulating but a hallucinating drink. It is difficult to be more particular not only because none of the candidates satisfies all the Soma properties and matches the Soma descriptions found in the hymns only partially but primarily because the language and style of the Rig Vedic as an ancient cult monument reflecting the poetic features of 'Indo-European poetic speech' is a formidable obstacle to Soma identification. The answer may be provided by archaeologists and their finds in north-western India, Afghanistan, and Pakistan (and not in far-away Central Asia)."

Indra & Soma

An Indra idol at the Ajanta Caves in Maharashtra.

Indra, the King of the Gods in Hindu mysticism, is the most preferred deity in *Rigveda*. According to ancient Indian texts, Indra enjoyed consuming Soma. He is one of the main gods of the Rigveda and is the Indo-European cousin of the German Wotan, Norse Odin, Greek Zeus, and Roman Jupiter.

The Soma Scriptures

The effects of the Soma drink should capture one's attention: one who consumes it could connect with the bliss of all existence and the source of the universe. The legend states that through Soma, man could grant immortality and become God.
The Rig Veda says:

> *"We drank Soma, we became immortal,*
> *we have attained the light and we found the Gods."*
> - The Rig Veda, Hymn 8.48.3

Soma is portrayed in the Rig Veda as a lightning-born god, an elixir of health and strength, and is praised as the direct means of communion with the gods.

> *Let Indra drink, O Soma, of thy juice for wisdom and all Deities for strength.*
> *So flow thou on as bright celestial juice, flow to the vast, immortal dwelling-place.*
> *Flow onward, Soma, as a mighty sea, as Father of the Gods to every form.*
> - The Rig Veda, Hymn 9.109

So if the ancestors of Ancient India were drinking this Soma and connecting with the divine, the question becomes: what the heck was in that drink?

Lord Shiva Holding a Mushroom, Bas Reliefs at Angkor Wa[4]

Of the ten books of hymns that make up the Rig Veda, there is one book that is devoted entirely to the glory of Soma. The Rig Veda describes Soma as a small red plant with no leaves and lacking roots and blossoms. Wasson claims, "my candidate for the identity of Soma is Amanita muscaria - the brilliant red mushroom. As far back as records go, it has been the Sacred Element in the shamanic rites of many tribes of northern Siberia."[5]

The earliest written compositions of the Indo-Aryans were called the Brahmanas. They discuss the surrogates used for Soma in the ritual but fail to describe the original plant. However, some clues that led Wasson to believe that Soma was a mushroom rather than a plant was that the Rig Veda describes a substance with no leaves, flowers, blossoms, or seeds; no roots, trunk, or branches. Nor was there a description of propagating the plant. It is funny then that we find the Rig Veda explicitly stating that Soma can only be found growing in the mountains - where A. muscaria can only be found in the latitude of the Indus Valley.

There is much speculation about what exact plant, fungi, or extracts were in Soma. In a presentation at the ayahuasca conference Aya 2014, Dr. Matthew Clark postulated that soma could have been a counterpart to ayahuasca because it combined plants containing both MAO inhibitors (such as Syrian Rue) and DMT.

India's earliest preserved medical text, the so-called Bower Manuscript, a text from Kashmir dating to the 6th century CE, has two formulas for amrita (soma)[6]. Researchers analyzed these formulas and found it contains both DMT and MAOIs in several plants. Six of the plants discussed are native to South Asia and known to have psychoactive properties. They propose that this formula, probably in a stronger form (or dose), was the basis of the soma of the Vedas[7]. In Nepal, we find Nepalese shamanism using entheogens to achieve altered states of consciousness, which is still being practiced. Shamans use a large variety of poisonous and mind-altering plants. What is most spectacular and little known is that the shamans use mushrooms, such as Amanita muscaria, and different kinds of psilocybes[8].

The contemporary use of A. muscaria as an inebriant in Central Asia was discovered in Afghanistan during the 1960s by Said Ghoulam Mochtar and Hartmut Geerken[9]. In the Shutul Valley, dried A. muscaria is ground to a powder by the inhabitants for its use as an inebriant. They boil the Amanita powder with fresh mountain snapweed and soured goat-cheese brine, producing a well-known local specialty, "Extract of Shutul[10]."

The Doddahundi Nishidi Inscription is from the Doddahundi (Mysore) period 890 AD.

According to Thomas Alexandar, "the stone carvings depict the event of sallekhana, a Jain ritual performed by the Ganga King Nitimarga in 869 AD[11]. These "Hero Stones' ' were raised in parts of India to honor noted Jains who committed Sallekhana ritual death. Notice the mushrooms in the image. Perhaps this ritual death is what we now call "ego death" from the psychedelic experience.

Fire Altars of Ancient India

Ritual was an extremely important part of the ancient Hindu religion. Fire altars were built for rituals that occurred at regularly scheduled times throughout the year, as well as for special rituals. During *soma* rituals, participants would sit around sacred fireplaces that have been carefully oriented to the four cardinal directions and excavated from the ground in a high place[12]. The first step in any fire altar construction was to lay out the cardinal directions, especially the East-West line. The purpose of the ritual was to build an immortal body that would transcend suffering and death, both hallmarks of mortal existence.

During these ceremonies, practitioners would recite long and complex sequences of mantras from their sacred texts and offer substances such as *ghī* (clarified butter) into the fire[13]. Brahman priests and other participants consume soma every 2 or 3 hours during rituals that may last one day or many days. Yajna refers in Hinduism to any ritual done in front of a sacred fire, often with mantras. The mantras and hymns recited during rituals are contained in the *saṃhitā* portions of the *Vedas* (composed between 1600 and 800 BCE), being the sacred texts of the Brahmans. Zoroastrians recite mantras/*mantras* and hymns from the *Avesta*, the oldest parts of which date back to around 1600–1200 BCE.

Reincarnation in Hinduism

Hindus do not believe in a single life on earth, followed by eternal joy or pain. They believe and know that all souls reincarnate, take one body and then another, evolving through experience over long periods of time. To a Hindu death is not fearsome. Like the caterpillar's metamorphosis into the delicate butterfly, death does not end our existence but frees us to pursue an even greater development. The soul never dies. It is immortal. Physical death is a most natural transition for the soul, which survives and, guided by karma, continues its long pilgrimage until it is one with its creator, God. Reincarnation is the natural cycle of birth, death & rebirth, called samsara. This belief in reincarnation we see is informed by the Hindu's ancient ritual of drinking the psychedelic soma and praying around the fire.

CHAPTER 4:

Psychedelics in Zoroastrianism

Zoroastrianism might be the world's first monotheistic faith. Zoroastrianism was founded by the Prophet Zoroaster in ancient Iran approximately 3500 years ago. The precise date of the founding of Zoroastrianism is uncertain. The approximate date of 1200-1500 BCE has been established through archaeological evidence and linguistic comparisons with the Rig Veda. Today it's one of the oldest religions still in existence. Religious scholars have long noted its influence on the cosmologies and beliefs of Judaism, Christianity, and Islam.

Zoroastrian Teachings

Zoroaster rejected the religion of the Bronze Age Iranians with their many gods and oppressive class structure, in which the *Karvis* and *Karapans* (princes and priests) controlled the ordinary people. He taught the belief in one God, Ahura Mazda (meaning 'Wise Lord'). A God who is compassionate, just, and the single creator of the universe. Ahura Mazda is:

- Omniscient (knows everything)
- Omnipotent (all-powerful)
- Omnipresent (is everywhere)
- Impossible for humans to conceive
- Unchanging
- The Creator of life
- The Source of all goodness and happening

Zoroastrians worship God as supreme and believe that everything he created is pure and should be treated with love and respect. This includes the natural environment, so Zoroastrians traditionally do not pollute the rivers, land, or atmosphere. This has caused some to call Zoroastrianism 'the first ecological religion'[1].

Psychedelic Ceremonies of Zoroastrians

The *soma/haoma* drink and the cult of sacred fire are the central elements of the religious practices of both the Brahmans of South Asia and of Zoroastrianism, which was the main religion of pre-Islamic Persia[2]. In the sacred Avesta text, Iranians call their psychedelic brew Hoama. According to most but not all commentators, the term soma derives from the Sanskrit root $\sqrt{su}$, meaning a juice that has been pressed out or expressed. Similarly, the same derivation applies to the term *haoma* (from the root $\sqrt{hu}$) in the Avestan language of Zoroastrians' sacred texts (the Avesta). *Soma/ haoma* thus refers to the extracted juice of a plant (or plants) used in Indo-Iranian religious rituals and not any plant in particular[3].

Over a century ago, it was noticed by scholars of Asian religions, such as Macdonell, that there were many similarities and homologies in the practices, language, and mythology of Zoroastrianism and Vedic religion, represented in the *Vedas*, the sacred texts of the Brahmans of South Asia. Many names of people and deities in the myths associated with *soma* in the Vedic tradition are very similar or almost identical to characters associated with *haoma* in the *Avesta*. In addition, central to traditional Vedic religion and Zoroastrianism is the sacrifice of animals during important rituals. The language of the oldest parts of the *Avesta* is written in an archaic language known as old Avestan, which is very close in many respects to the Vedic Sanskrit used in the compilation of the earliest portions of the *Vedas*. Several scholars have explored linguistic evidence that indicates an original, common source for several words used in ancient Central Asian religion, such as *aṃśu* (*ánću*), an early term for *soma*, and Indra, one of the main deities of Vedic religion[4].

The close connections between ancient Zoroastrianism and Vedic religion, which scholars have comprehensively explored over the last century, have led to the almost universally accepted consensus that Zoroastrianism and Vedic religion had a common origin, which was the upper-Oxus region of Turkmenistan. Migrations of people from Central Asia around 1600 BCE resulted in the cult of *soma/ haoma* being transmitted to both Persia, where it formed a central constituent of Zoroastrianism, and South Asia, in the form of Vedic religion[5].

The Herb of the Magi

Zoroastrian literature often references the shamanic use of potent cannabis infusions. The Zoroastrian texts refer to a substance known as bhanga, in Pahvlavi, as mang. Bhanga is still used in Persia to identify cannabis, and the related Indian term bhang is still used for cannabis as well. Shaul Shaked noted that "The preparation of this journey was done... by administering to the officiant a dose of mang (hemp), mixed with wine" [6].

"Zoroaster is commonly said to have spiked the haoma with mang, which was probably hashish. It would have prolonged the intoxication and further stimulated the imagination of the drugged man. Of such are the wonders of Heaven" (Oliver, 1994). Van Baaren and Hartman note a Zoroastrian story about a hero who "imbibes an intoxicant composed of wine and hashish. After this, his body sleeps for seven days and nights while his soul undertakes the journey". 19th-century author James Francis Katherinus Hewitt also refers to the "enlightening prophet drug Bangha (Cannabis Indica), the Hashish by which the Zoroastrian priests were inspired".

The use of bang/mang in the Zoroastrian period was strictly prohibited from anyone but the most elite members of that society. The secrecy surrounding the use of bang/mang is likely responsible for much of the confusion surrounding mang and bang. In 'Quests and Visionary Journeys in Sassanian Iran,' Shaul Shaked notes that the use of mang (which he saw as hemp) for visionary quests "was not a way open to all."

It was confined to select individuals who would have regarded themselves as representative of the community and would then reveal to the others what they had been privileged to witness. Even for those people, this was not a trivial experience that could be undertaken casually or easily. Such journeys were rare occasions, surrounded by grave risks. The danger lay in the fact that this path was trodden by the dead and would have to be brought back to life. Certain encounters along the way may put the power of endurance of the traveler to the test.

Accounts of Zoroaster's shamanic flights are recorded in: *Bahman Yasht* 4.1-66, 5.1-10, 6.1-13, 7.1-39, 8.1-8, 9.1-8; Bundahishn 34.4-5; Denkard 8.8.22-59, 9.6, 10.11, 14.13. A variety of scholars noted the suggestion that there was a connection between the mang and Haoma consumed by Vishtasp and the 'water' by Zoroaster.

"Since sauma [mixed with *mang*] was how Ohrmazd brought such vision to Zoroaster's champion, Wishtasp, [Vistaspa] there is no reason to doubt that sauma [and *mang*] would also have been the means whereby Zoroaster (who as a zaotar consumed sauma in Yasna rites) also saw into menog existence [spiritual realm] and drew from it his knowledge of Ohrmazd and his revelation".

Connections between the zoroastrian haoma and cannabis have been further strengthened by the archeological finds of cannabis present at a 4000 year old Temple site in the ancient Bactria and Margiana region, known now as BMAC (The Bactria Margiana Archeological Complex) that was devoted to the preparation of the Haoma, by the Russian archeologist Victor Sarianidi, where evidence of cannabis, ephedra, and in some later cases opium being ground and strained for the preparation of Haoma have been found. Scythian gold cups and bowls have been found with residues of opium and cannabis, that the Russian archeologist Anton Gass has identified as ritual implements for 'the drinking of haoma'.

Ancient texts such as the Avesta provide evidence hemp was used in the Iranian world... to produce ecstatic states of mind. Zarathustra himself used this technique to nourish his mystique. In this, he imitated his protector, King Vishtasp, who received from the gods the cup with narcotic ingredients, "haoma and hemp." Thanks to this "illuminating beverage," the possessed could "open the eye of the soul to obtain knowledge"—in other words, he experienced hallucinations and intoxication that were undoubtedly real, though considered magico-religious. The king thought he was, in this way, escaping his body and sending his soul to travel in paradise. But the descriptions of the place or state of mind in question as being full of "illumination" are typical of the visions experienced by the consumer of hashish, along with a sleep-like trance that obliges him to lie down.[7].

The Fire Temple

First evident in the 9th century BCE, the Zoroastrian rituals of fire are contemporary with that of Zoroastrianism itself. A fire temple, Agiary, is the place of worship for the followers of Zoroastrianism, the ancient religion of Iran (Persia)[8]. In the Zoroastrian religion, fire together with clean water are agents of ritual purity. Clean, white "ash for the purification ceremonies [is] regarded as the basis of ritual life", which "are essentially the rites proper to the tending of a domestic fire, for the temple [fire] is that of the hearth fire raised to a new solemnity". For, one "who sacrifices unto fire with fuel in his hand is given happiness"[9].

Zoroastrianism may have originated as early as 4,000 years ago which means that for around 4000 years practitioners were using hamoa/soma, plant-based psychedelics, along with ancient fire rituals to explore their connection with the divine. However, after the institution of the Muslim period, when Zoroastrians were either forced out of Persia or forced to convert to Islam, the ritual use of cannabis in the religion declined and eventually went underground.

CHAPTER 5:

Psychedelics in
Indigenous America

Indigenous peoples have used psychoactive plants and fungi for medicinal and divination purposes for thousands of years. Anthropological evidence documents a history of ceremonial use, including peyote, ayahuasca, and psilocybin mushrooms. The prominent goal of the ceremonial consumption of classic hallucinogens has been to have inward spiritual experiences that can best be described as mystical. As the history of humanity moved out of the 'wilderness' and into the towns and cities, so did our entheogen use. Several entheogenic cultures arose:

—In Mexico, many entheogenic cults existed within the great Meso-American cultures. A variety of psychoactive plants were venerated as Gods and are commonly found represented in Toltec, Mayan, and later Aztec temples, including psilocybin mushrooms, ololiuqui (morning glory) seeds that contained LSD like compounds, and even possibly 5-MeO-DMT-containing toad venom; carbon-dating now indicates that the use of mescaline-containing peyote in North America goes back 5700 years[1].

—In Peru, an influential culture arose around the sacramental use of the mescaline-containing San Pedro cactus, as evidenced by the construction of the Chavín de Huantar temple[13] complex in 1300 BC by the remarkable Chavín civilization. Nestled in a verdant valley on the eastern slope of the Cordillera Blanca, the highest set of mountain peaks in Peru, the beautifully preserved Chavín de Huantar houses a sophisticated tunnel system (replete with water drains and air shafts for ventilation) that takes one under the main temple complex and through a labyrinth that, when successfully navigated, opens into a chamber with a fifteen-foot high granite carving of a fanged deity, the chief god of Chavín[2].

San Pedro cacti grow in large clumps all around the temple complex, while the carved amphitheater at the entrance of the tunnels with its obvious fire-pit seems clear in its shamanic intent. The Chavín civilization conquered other Andean societies without warfare; they brought the chiefs and priests of other Andean tribes to Chavín de Huantar, filled them up with San Pedro, and then led them into the underground labyrinth. By the time the stunned participants emerged back into the sunshine on the other side of the temple, they were convinced enough of the superiority of Chavín's shamans that they joined them, and Chavín's influence became widespread across Peru. Incredibly sophisticated stone carvers, the Chavín civilization is considered the origin of the stone construction techniques that the Moche, Inca, and other Andean societies later used in their temple building. The sacramental use of the San Pedro cactus has remained a continuous tradition in Peru for over 3000 years[3].

Mescaline is the oldest known hallucinogen in human history. Evidence of its use goes back nearly 6,000 years. Anthropologists discovered samples of dried peyote in the Shumla caves near the Texas border that date back to 3780 B.C.

Mesoamerica Mushroom Stone Art

Anthropologists and historians believe hallucinogens have been used as early as 9000 B.C. Early cave paintings and pictographs by indigenous people on rocks in North America and other areas of the world are believed to have been inspired partially by hallucinogenic influences.

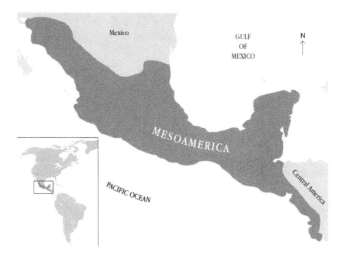

The Aztecs and Mayans in Central America called mushrooms teonanácatl, meaning "flesh of the gods," because ingesting them helped them to "see God." [4]

Across the world in pre-Columbian Mesoamerica, we discover stone figures dating back as far as 3000 BC can be found, depicting mushrooms merging with human heads. The use of psychedelics in pre-Columbian Mesoamerica is thought to have been common, as evidence exists that cultures consumed not only psilocybin mushrooms but also other psychedelics such Salvia divinorum and peyote. Archaeological evidence of the use of peyote in the region dates back 5000 years[5].

The mixture of mushrooms and people is a common motif in indigenous art worldwide. The mushroom being on the head represents the connection to the metaphor of what lies above or beyond us.

The Drink of Immortality

The Maya, Aztecs, Huastec, Totonac, Mazatec, and Mixtec people all used hallucinogenic mushrooms in religious ceremonies stretching back thousands of years[6], with the Aztecs calling the mushrooms teonanácatl, or "flesh of the gods" because ingesting them helped them to "see God."[7] [8]

Because the Spanish violently suppressed the Aztecs' customs when they sacked Tenochtitlán in 1521, teonanácatl was forced underground, resurfacing nearly four centuries later when Mexican ethnobotanist Dr. Blas Pablo Reko spotted it in use among the indigenous people in Oaxaca[9].

In 1955, María Sabina became the first indigenous "wise woman" to introduce psilocybin to an American when she permitted Gordon Wasson[10], an amateur mycologist, to participate in one of her ceremonies. Today, shamanism - once universal - survives primarily among indigenous peoples.

Marina Sabina, a famous healer, with Gordon Wasson

Across North, Central, and South America, ancient indigenous cultures looked for divine inspiration from the heavens, celestial powers, and the earth—especially plants and fungi with spectacular mind-altering properties.

NATIONAL
GEOGRAPHIC

Ancient hallucinogens found in 1,000-year-old shamanic pouch

The ritual container, made of three fox snouts, contains the earliest known evidence of ayahuasca preparation.

BY ERIN BLAKEMORE
PUBLISHED 7 MAY 2019, 16:28 BST

Ancient medicine men and women and conjurers used these plants and fungi to open their minds to more profound insights, heighten their senses of the spiritual world, reach harmony with the universe, and see into the future. And to see God[11].

As with all ancient aboriginal civilizations around the globe, Indigenous Americans lived close to the earth and in concert with Nature. On the North and South American continent, Indigenous Americans found these psychedelic among many plant sources with hallucinogenic and mind-altering powers: Psilocybin mushrooms and other fungi, peyote, mescal beans, saguaro cactus, sweet flag grasses. Psychedelic plant medicines are as common a part of Indigenous society today as it was thousands of years ago. In his article "The Use of Psychoactive Plants and Fungi by Ancient Indigenous Populations of the North Andes," Manuel Torres presents evidence of the widespread ceremonial use of entheogenic plants in the ancient cultures of South America. He reviews evidence that the use of entheogenic plants permeated these cultures as a core feature of shamanic religious practices. The importance of these entheogenic substances was expressed in iconographic systems revealed in various media, most of which survived in stone sculptures and gold work[12]. These include Ibogaine, Peyote, San Pedro, Psilocybin Mushrooms, and Ayahuasca[13].

These medicines continue to be used in religious ceremonies in North and South America. Peyote is currently used by the Native American Church in the US[14]. DMT-containing ayahuasca is used by healers and churches in South America[15],[16].

Sacred Sacraments	Ayahuasca/Yage	Haoma/Soma
Time	>900 BC	>1200-1000 BC
Hallucinogenic	Yes	Yes
Extract	Yes	Yes
Botanical Idnetity	Banisteriopsis Caapi +	Psilocybin Cubensis
Psychological Experience	Sonaderos (dream-like)	Stard (to spread out/sprawl)
Setting	Ritual	Ritual
Purpose	1. Healing	1. Healing
	2. Confrontation of Death, Awareness of Mortality	2. Confrontation of Death, Awareness of Mortality
	3. Expering Divinity / Supernatural	3. Validating the truth of religious rituals
		4. To screen imposters

Similar to the Vedic ritual use of Soma/Haoma is the documented history of Ayahuasca/Yage ceremonies.

The Sacred Fire

Indigenous people worldwide have performed many ceremonies involving fire for thousands of years. Fire has been central to many aspects of traditional life, including cooking, storytelling, providing warmth, as a ceremonial and ritual device, and is also used in medicinal practices.

Indigenous psychedelic rituals usually involve the use of a sacred fire. Fire is traditionally used to start a ceremony or sacred event. The sacred fire not only provides a respectful way to open an event or ceremony but also plays a distinct role in the event.

The sacred fire is considered a spiritual doorway that opens to a spiritual realm so individuals can communicate with the spirit realm. It is used to connect with one's ancestors, communicate with them, and ask them to respect one's prayers. It is a sacred practice meant to make individuals feel open, grounded, and connected with people on Earth and those who have moved on. A sacred fire is built by indigenous people gathering for an event, ritual, or ceremony. Usually, a fire keeper builds, maintains, and keeps watch over the fire, so it is never unattended.

Overall, the sacred fire is used as a place to gather and celebrate. Often, it lets participants reflect on their purpose on Earth either at the beginning of birthing ceremonies or at the end, when it is believed one returns to the spiritual world.

Indigenous American Spirituality

Long before the arrival of the Europeans to the Americas, the Indigenous Peoples of the Americas were using plant-based psychedelics to commune with spirits, nature and the divine. For thousands of years, over 500 distinct tribes of Indigenous Peoples included the idea of reincarnation in their spiritual belief systems. Each Native American tribe is unique, with its own set of customs and beliefs; however, despite these distinctions, there are also some intriguing commonalities. Native Americans believe in a "free soul." In essence, they believe that the soul is the carrier of human consciousness.

Needless to say, this is very much in line with the views of many other cultures around the world. Most Native Americans also believe that while the soul is part of the body, it's also separate. For example, the soul can temporarily leave the body while the body sleeps. In addition, the soul can leave the body when a person is in a trance or on a vision quest. Furthermore, the soul can depart from the body permanently when the body dies. Once the soul has left the body, it moves through the spiritual world before it is reborn, or reincarnates[17].

Most Native American tribes have strong beliefs about the existence of spirits, the afterlife, and reincarnation. Researcher and author Warren Jefferson wrote extensively on this topic in his book Reincarnation Beliefs of North American Indians. According to Jefferson, reincarnation is a central aspect of tribal cosmologies in these societies. And it's possible that their beliefs stem from their profound connection to their ancestors and a strong sense of family continuity.

The Hopi are a Native American tribe who primarily live on the Hopi Reservation in northeastern Arizona, United States. They call themselves the People of Peace and they are also firm believers in reincarnation. Their belief system is interesting because it carries an uncanny resemblance to Eastern religions, including Hinduism and Buddhism. For example, the Hopi have a concept like karma, whereby actions in this life have consequences that will be felt in subsequent lifetimes. They also believe the body has energy centers, like chakras, as well as primal, core energy like kundalini[18].

CHAPTER 6:

Psychedelics in Buddhism

Buddhism finds its roots in Hinduism. Its founder, Siddhartha Gautama - a former Indian prince - started life as a Hindu. For this reason, Buddhism is often referred to as an offshoot of Hinduism. It would therefore make sense to find evidence of early Buddhist adepts using psychedelic sacraments similar to the Soma brew of the Indian ascetics and mystics.

In the legendary biographies of some Buddhist adepts from the 2nd and 9th centuries, some clues can be interpreted to reveal that the adepts were consuming psychedelic Amanita muscaria, 'fly agaric,' mushrooms to achieve enlightenment[1]. The intriguing evidence for the use of the A. muscaria mushroom is not only recorded in contemporary Tibetan shamanism[2] but also in the Tantric traditions of Tibetan Buddhism found in Tantra's classical texts.

Scott Hajicek-Dobberstein, argues in *Soma siddhas and alchemical enlightenment: psychedelic mushrooms in Buddhist tradition* in the Journal of Ethnopharmacology, that the Vedic soma cult—or something very similar to it—survived among the tantric Buddhist siddhas who lived in India from the eighth to the tenth century C.E., and whose biographies are recounted in a twelfth-century Tibetan text: *The Legends of the Eighty-four Mahasiddhas*.

The most compelling evidence is found in the story of the siddha Karnaripa. His guru, Nagarjuna, instructed him to demonstrate his austerity by collecting only as much food for alms as he could balance on the head of a needle. Karnaripa returned with a large pancake balanced on the tip of a needle —a symbol, suggests Hajicek-Dobberstein, of the amanita muscaria. More symbols are suggested, but the most convincing evidence is an exchange in which Nagarjuna says, "We need to eat the alchemical medicine." Karnaripa does so, and then spreads his spittle on a dead tree—which bursts in blossom—and then urinates in a pot. This behavior is taken as a sign of realization by Karnaripa's teacher. For Hajicek-Dobberstein, it is a "marker" of the presence of amanita-soma because drinking the urine of a shaman who has consumed amanita intensifies the potency of the mushroom and is a well-known practice among Siberians[9]

The Secret Drugs of Buddhism

Mike Crowley, author of the *Secret Drugs of Buddhism: Psychedelic Sacraments and the Origins of the Vajrayana*, spent 10 plus years studying Buddhist texts—including some from his own Tibetan Kagyu lineage and others from the Indian Vajrayana tradition—Crowley found repeated references to something called amrita. Translated as "deathless" or "nectar," amrita was a psychoactive elixir used in sacraments on a large scale in the Buddhist world during the Middle Ages[3]. Amrita has been described as powerful enough to soften the boundaries between ordinary states of being and enlightened ones, but scholars still debate what it was made of. Some say it was a mixture containing cannabis, and others point to ephedra, but Crowley believes it was made of psilocybe cubensis, i.e., magic mushrooms.

He points to recurrent themes in Buddhist art, such as the bump often found on the Buddha's head that mirrors a bump that grows on the caps of shrooms. In Tantric art, water buffaloes, too, may reference another psychedelic mushroom, panaeolus cambodginiensis, that sprouts upon their dung.

FIGURE 57. "White Parasol Crown-bump" (Sitātapatroṣṇīṣa), left. Enhanced detail, right. Japanese drawing. [Chandra]

On the next page is a mural from the Mogao Caves, also known as the Caves of the Thousand Buddhas. Located in the Gansu Province of China, the caves are strongly linked to the history of transcontinental relations and Buddhism's spread throughout Asia. The mural above the right portrays the Buddha, or a Kulika King sitting on a throne encoded with what looks like seven sacred mushrooms.

In Vajrayāna Buddhism, typically at initiation into the tradition, the practitioner is given a spoonful of the "elixir of immortality" (Skt. Amrita) to drink. Tibetan scholars have declared that initiation ceremonies are incomplete unless some form of drink is consumed.

Tibetan Buddhism formed from the merger between Buddhism and Tibet's indigenous, shamanistic Bon religion. This direct link to a shamanistic religion may account for the presence of mind-altering substances in this particular Buddhist tradition.

The Buddha's Psychedelic Enlightenment

Did the Buddha use psychedelics to help achieve nirvana? Gordon Wasson examined the account of the last meal of the Buddha, in which Siddhartha Gautama, around the year 483 BCE in his quest for immortality, apparently accepted a dish of mushrooms prepared for him in a stew by a blacksmith, after which he became violently ill and died. The Buddha eventually reaches Nirvana, the state of enlightenment beyond the wheel of life, after eating the poisonous mushroom[4].

The legend states that the king of the chthonic serpent spirits presented the Buddha with a jewel-encrusted umbrella:" It is gold with a sapphire hand, and its edges are studded with jewels, including diamonds which shine like the sun. The jewels give off nectar which can quench the thirst of all sentient beings..."

Here is what a psilocye cubensis mushroom looks like:

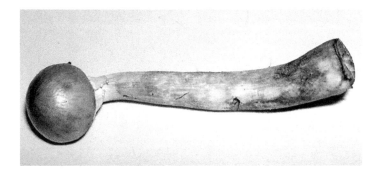

Notice how the psilocybe mushroom has a "gold" crown which would lend itself to the allusion to jewels, and a "sapphire" handle at the bottom.

The term thirst is a Buddhist term that means the desire to change one's circumstances that lie at the root of all suffering. To satisfy this "thirst" is to achieve nirvana [4]. This "nectar" is neither food nor drink but the famous Amrita. Perhaps this Nirvana was achieved in partnership with the magic mushroom?[5]

Psilocybin breaks down into psilocin, and the chemicals give off a blue appearance when this happens. As a result, mushrooms like psilocybe cubensis turn blue when bruised, and this color may have resonated with the appearance of the peacock[6]. The soma of the Vedas is also referred to as amrita, and this is the name of the sacrament consumed in Tibetan Buddhism.

In the Tibetan tradition, amrita is also associated with peacocks. Coincidentally, the name of a Hindu order of monks who worship Shiva, matta-mayuri, translates as "the intoxicated peacocks." According to Crowley, this may be explained by the peacock symbolizing a psychedelic mushroom sacrament.

The mushroom theme is recurrent in Buddhist art, such as the bump often found on the Buddha's head that mirrors a bump that grows on the caps of mushrooms.

On the left is a 7th-century sculpture of Jina Parsvanatha, the 23rd of the Jain saints, at a temple in Gyaraspur, India. As the story goes, Buddha becomes enlightened while sitting under the Bodhi tree. The word bodhi, which means enlightenment, is, I believe, a symbolic reference to the "Tree of Life" and the Amanita muscaria mushroom (Visualization on the right by Rory Eade Arte).

The deliriant datura has traditionally been used in Tibetan Buddhism. *Datura stramonium* and *Datura metel* are well-documented in India and Tibet. Datura intoxication may have been widespread in *Siddha* culture. In *Indian Esoteric Buddhism*, Ronald M. Davidson observes[7]:

Many *Siddha* Scriptures discuss ointments and drugs, especially those applied to the eyes or feet. The use of the various species of datura (especially [*Datura metel*]) is particularly evident. Sometimes termed the "crazy datura" (*unmattadhattura*) or "Śiva's datura," it was generally employed as a narcotic paste or as wood in a fire ceremony.

CHAPTER 7:

Psychedelics in Ancient Egypt

The earliest records of human existence in the Nile Valley go back 90,000-700,000 years. Around 3000 BC, records show Ancient Egyptians were an incredibly spiritual people. The Egyptians were the first to teach that the human soul is immortal[1]. They believed death was only a gateway to another, eternal life, and the desire to ensure immortality was woven into their daily rituals[2]. An individual's life on earth was only part of an eternal journey.

> "It was this obsession with life that caused them to pursue all means to ensure the attainment of [spiritual] immortality"
> - *Hairani Hassan, National Museum of Singapore.* [3]

According to the oldest serving papyrus roll, which preserves the ancient Egyptian coronation ceremony in amazing detail, wine would be presented as an "eye of Horus" to cure the king of his "spiritual blindness." [4] A ritual meal was then ingested as part of the "secret rites" engineered to transform Osiris's earthly representative into the wine god himself. In preparation for one's eternal sleep, the royal initiative is said to have traveled to and experienced the cosmic underworld, receiving "the awesome knowledge of what lies beyond the threshold of death. The Egyptian pharaohs are said to have acquired the light body of a "shining spirit" that allowed them to traverse the starry afterlife.

Magic Mushrooms in Egyptian Culture

Documentation of the Egyptian fungi may date back to 4500 BC when ancient Egyptians produced several hieroglyphic depictions of plants (many of which are psychedelic) on walls and within texts throughout Egypt.

Notice the Mushroom art in the hieroglyphics.

Ancient Egyptians believed mushrooms were plants of immortality and called them "a gift from the God Osiris"[5]. The Pharaohs' of Egypt decreed mushrooms were food for royalty and that no commander could touch them. In the Egyptian Book of the Dead, the Papyrus of Ani, mushrooms are called "the food of the gods," or "celestial food" and "the flesh of the gods" [6]. In other places, we read 'bread of eternity and 'beer of eternity.'

In *Mushrooms and Mankind*, James Arthur writes the pillars of tombs in ancient Egypt are shaped like giant mushrooms, some like Amanita and some like Psilocybe[z]. Stephen Berlant theorized the plant known as the Eye of Horus was an entheogenic mushroom cap[g]. The theory that the Eye of Horus was an entheogenic mushroom cap can also be supported by noting that the Egyptians personified this eye the same way ancient Hindu priests personified Soma.

The Egyptians personified Horus and Osiris as eyes, just as the Rig Veda describes the Soma plant and its elixir as an eye (Rg Veda I 875ab; IX 94; IX 10 ab).

The Egyptians personified Horus and Osiris as the sun, just as The Rig Veda personifies the spirit of the Soma plant, which also yielded a divine elixir, as a luminous, solar deity (Rg Veda I, 4610ab; IX, 26c; IX, 275ab).

The Egyptians described Horus and Osiris as luminous lunar deities, just as the Rg Veda describes the Soma plant and its elixir as a luminous lunar deity (Rg Veda 8.082.08;10.052.02: 6.039.03).

The Egyptians claimed that the Eye of Horus could confer immortality on those who consumed it, or an elixir made from it, just as the Rg Veda describes the Soma plant and its elixir as having the ability to confer immortality on those who consumed it (Rg Veda, 8.048.03; 1.091.06; 1.091.18;8.048.12; 8.048.11)

The Egyptians associated or personified Horus and Osiris as hawks, just as the Rg Veda as well as the Taittiriya Samhita and Aitareya Brahmana, associate Soma with a hawk, claiming that this hawk brought Soma to India(Rg Veda 1.080. 02; 1.093.06; 8.082.09) (Taittiriya Samhita6.1) Aitareya Brahmana (3.25-27)

Take the various crowns in Ancient Egyptian art. Researchers suggest these are symbolic of Psilocybe mushrooms. Wearing mushroom-inspired head-ware was said to be indicative of having achieved enlightenment.

Stephen Berlant theorizes that Egyptian White and Triple Crowns were early forms of Psilocybe cubensis[9]. His theories make sense when one understands the Egyptians grew Psilocybe cubenesis on barley[10].

The Blue Lotus

In the mid-1800s, archeologists noticed the Blue Lotus carvings in so many ancient Egyptian hieroglyphs that there must be a sign these depictions were more than mere art. Representations of Blue Lotus are found carved on every temple and every tomb. King Tut - one of the most famous archeological discoveries- was covered in the Blue Lotus's sacred flowers [11], [12].

For over 3000 years, the Blue Lotus was used by the priesthood of ancient Egypt for its medicinal properties and as a spiritual sacrament. So important was this flower the Egyptians dedicated a god, Nefertem, to protect and care for it. In the mid-1800s, archeologists realized ancient Egyptian Blue Lotus carvings had to be more than artistic. Representations of Blue Lotus are carved on every temple and every tomb. Even King Tut was covered in the sacred flowers.

In Egyptian art, water lily and mandrake depictions began in the Fifth Dynasty (about 2560-2420 BC) and continued until the Ptolemaic Period (330-323 BC). These two plants appear intimately associated with each other. It is thought that the Egyptians mixed drugs among them: Mandrake, water lily, and, perhaps, opium. This product es a powerful vehicle, called didi, to reach deep states of consciousness in a state of apparent coma[13].

Offering table with lotus flowers.
Tomb of Kahif. ©Peter Der
Manuelian – Giza Project.

Lotus flower adorning an unguent cone and a small collar used as a hair ornament (TT113). ©Lise Manniche

A girl with lotus flower ©Bruno Sandkühler – Unidia

The Tree of Life

The ancient Egyptians considered the Acacia tree sacred and regarded it as "the tree of life."

Amun Re kneeling with the Tree of Life (Ished) Great Hypostyle Hall at Karnak. Built 2055 BCE.

Look at this painting. We see Isis depicted in the painting with the Acacia tree. Isis was known as the "Acacia Goddess."

The Acacia Nilotica is a tree that grows along the Nile River and is native to the area of the Arabic world, hence the name Arabic Gum Tree. The Acacia Nilotica is a tree that grows along the Nile River. Egyptians revered it because it was used for many properties, perhaps because it contains DMT - known today as the spirit molecule. The ancient Egyptians used the Nile acacia for enlightenment and talking to the gods. Osiris - whose spirit Egyptians believe lived in the Acacia - along with his consort Isis provided enlightenment, which to the Egyptians was the true rebirth of the spirit, more important than the birth of the flesh. It is important to note that all species of acacia are hallucinogenic, either in their bark, roots, leaves, or fruit, due to the natural production of DMT.

Seham el-Sayed abd el Hameed Eissa, Assistant Professor of Egyptology Department of Archaeology at the Kafer El-Sheikh University, and Taghreed el-Sayed abd el Hameed Eissa, researcher on Floriculture and Ornamental Horticulture at the Research Institute Giza, document the history of DMT in egyptian culture:

"At Heliopolis, there was a tradition that all the Goddesses and Gods were born beneath an acacia tree. In the Pyramid Texts, Horus, comes forth from the acacia tree., In the Book of the Dead the deceased the Divine Children of Iusaaset, the Goddesses and Gods born beneath the sacred acacia.The acacia is associated with a number of Egyptian Deities, it has specific associations with Isis and Her family. A particular acacia—simply called The Acacia, or Shondj—was sacred to Her. And Isis and Nephthys together were called the Two Shonti Goddesses, that is, the Two Acacia Goddesses. In the story of the "Horus and Set," Isis, in the form of Her sacred bird, flies into the branches of Her holy acacia after tricking Set into condemning His own attempts to usurp the rightful rule of Horus, Isis' son. In some tales, the acacia is the tree that magically grew up around the body of Osiris when His sarcophagus washed up on the shores of Byblos. He is called "the One in the Tree" and "the Solitary One in the Acaci"[1]

Furthermore, it would seem that the whole of Egyptian culture has its roots in the functionality of the third eye, Pineal gland. The eye of Horus is said to resemble a brain with a Pineal in the center.
"To the Ancient Egyptians, the Tree of Life represented the hierarchical chain of events that brought everything into existence. The spheres of the Tree of Life demonstrate the order, process, and method of creation. In Egyptian mythology, the first couple (earth and sky). They were said to have emerged from the acacia tree of Iusaaset, which the Egyptians considered the tree of life, referring to it as the 'tree in which life and death are enclosed'."
Some claim the ancient Egyptians used acacia trees to make hallucinogenic wine.

Yrp - the Psychedelic Wine

Tomb paintings often depict wine jars wrapped or draped in lotus flowers, suggesting that the Egyptians may have been aware of the narcotic qualities of blue lotus petals when mixed with wine[14]. The Egyptians called this wine Yrp, which, when consumed during sacred ceremonies, caused the appearance of Lusaaset, 'the great one who comes forth.' [15]

Seven lotus-vases nesting in a shallow bowl on a table. Tomb of Niankhkhnum and Khnumhpotep. ©Oxford Expedition to Egypt.

A decoration painting within the tomb of the Egyptian official Nakht depicts winemaking. The images are dated between 1401 to 1391 BC[16].

The Egyptian goddess Lusaaset, meaning 'the great one who comes forth,' was considered the grandmother of all the Egyptian gods [17]. The ancient Egyptian goddess Lusaaset was associated with the acacia tree known as the Tree of Life to ancient Egyptian. More specifically, she was associated with the oldest known acacia tree at the time, situated just north of Heliopolis, Egypt, in the famous Garden of Heliopolis[18].

'I am the son of Khepri, born in Hetepet under the tresses of the Goddess of Iusâas-town [i.e., Lusaaset], north of Ôn, who ascended from the vertex of Geb.'
- Egyptian priest, Utterance 519.

Geb was the Egyptian God of the Earth. This Scripture describes Lusasset - a metaphor for the acacia tree of - located in the Garden of Heliopolis and described as the 'tresses of the Goddess' which 'ascended from the vertex of Geb (God).' In this way, the hallucinogenic experience of drinking Yrp was a way to ascend the sacred Tree of Life and be reborn as a spirit into the heavens.

The Immortal Soul

Among ancient peoples, the Egyptians conceived of a soul. The Egyptian *ka* (breath) survived death but remained near the body, while the spiritual *ba* proceeded to the region of the dead.

Egyptian religious doctrines included three afterlife ideologies: belief in an underworld, eternal life, and rebirth of the soul. The underworld, also known as the Duat, had only one entrance that could be reached by traveling through the tomb of the deceased. The initial image a soul would be presented with upon entering this realm was a corridor lined with an array of fascinating statues, including a variation of the hawk-headed god, Horus. The path taken to the underworld may have varied between kings and common people. After entry, spirits were presented to another prominent god, Osiris. Osiris would determine the virtue of the deceased's soul and grant those deemed deserving a peaceful afterlife. The Egyptian concept of 'eternal life' was often seen as being reborn indefinitely. Therefore, the souls who had lived their life elegantly were guided to Osiris to be born again[19].

Herodotus, a famous Greek philosopher, taught that the Egyptians were the first to conceive the idea of the immortality of the soul, and states as a doctrine of the Egyptians "that the soul after the dissolution of the body enters again and again into a creature that comes to life; then, that the soul wanders through all the animals of the land and the sea and through all the birds, and finally after three thousand years returns to a human body." [20]

CHAPTER 8:

Psychedelics in Ancient Greece

A ncient Greece, 700-480 B.C., established an enlightened society that gave birth to Western civilization. The Greeks invented democracy and law. They practiced the science of mathematics. They pioneered the art of philosophy, logic, and reason. Spiritually, the Greeks believed in reincarnation and the immortality of the soul. This belief was taught at spiritual schools, which were integrated into society. Greek society believed that death was not the end of our human journey.

And underneath this clothing, we are all immortals in disguise, gods and goddesses destined to the stars for eternity." [1]

These schools were home to mystery traditions, particularly the famous mysteries of Eleusis[2]. The Eleusinian Mysteries were celebrated in honor of the goddess Demeter and her daughter Persephone. They were regarded as the most sacred of all the mysteries in the Ancient Greek religion. The Mysteries originated in Eleusis, 15 miles west of Athens, possibly as far back as the early Mycenaean period (c.1600 B.C).

From the little that is known about the ritual, experts believe that participants would walk along the Sacred Way in a parade that lasted ten days until they reached the Temple of Demeter in Eleusis, where they would take a sip of a sacred drink called Kykeon after days of abstaining from food. It was said that the Greeks - while at various spiritual schools - would partake in sacred rituals where they would die and be reborn with the knowledge of immortality. For two thousand years, people traveled from across the world to come, learn, and experience this feeling, this knowing, this sense of immortality.

Plato described his experience at Eleusis in cryptic terms. He spoke of Eleusis as 'the holiest of Mysteries,' where he experienced a state of perfection and 'blessed sight and vision.' During the climax of the evening, upon the completion of the initiation ceremony, attendees were given the title epoptes which roughly translates as 'The one who has seen it all.' Initiates claimed that life continued after death, and the light was waiting for us at the end of the tunnel.

After his initiation, Sophocles claimed that "trice blessed are those among men who go down to Hades after beholding these rites. Only for them is their life [after death]; all the rest will suffer an evil lot."
To put this into context, the ancient Greeks once approached death with reluctance and gloom. It was initially believed that when one dies, their spirit is damned to roam the underworld (Hades) for all eternity. It appears that those who emerged from the ritual at Eleusis left with an alternative attitude toward death and dying. These accounts suggest that what was happening at Eleusis differed from other religious ceremonies in ancient Greece.

In *The Road to Eleusis,* published in 1978, Albert Hofmann, along with the Classicist Carl Ruck and Mycologist Gordon Wassan, first put forth the hypothesis that the Kykeon contained a psychoactive entheogen by comparing accounts of Eleusis with spiritual ceremonies found in other cultures that used natural psychedelic compounds[3].

The Exaltation of the Flower
Greece, 470–460 BC

Perhaps this not a flower but a mushroom depicted in the sculpture?

The Psychedelic Kykeon

In *the Immortality Key*, Brian Muraresku's research demonstrates that the Kykeon was a psychedelic brew[4]. It all started with a bit of research into barley. Early agrarian societies - including the greeks - cultivated barley to make beer. Where there is barley, one would find Erogt - a fungus that commonly grows on barley. Ergot grows naturally on grains such as barley and rye and produces alkaloids in the body when consumed, which can produce hallucinations, convulsions, and psychosis. In small doses, the substance produces a psychedelic trip, much like those of drugs such as LSD. This is because the drug LSD was developed by Swiss chemist Albert Hoffman in 1938 when he was conducting experiments with LSD, produced by ergot fungus.

If it is true the Greeks were brewing psychedelic beer and drinking it at these mystery schools; then we would expect to find the remnants of Ergot in the archeological records. It is funny then that Jordi Juan-Tresserras from the University of Barcelona discovered the remains of Ergot sclerotia amongst the ancient ruins at Mas Casteller de Points. He found it not once but twice in two different artifacts. The fungus was found embedded between several teeth of a human jawbone. Microscopic evidence of the same organism was additionally identified in one of the miniature chalices that contained a "special beer." Jordi links whatever potion filled the tiny cup to the "consumption of the kykeon" during the Mysteries of Eleusis.[5]

It sounds like the Greeks, who believed in the immortal nature of the soul, were getting this divine information from psychedelic experiences. In the 1970s, Professor Carl Ruck from Boston University published a thesis that psychedelic brews were the origins of greek life [6]. He continued this analysis into the earliest generations of Christians who inherited a mind-altering sacrament from the Greeks.

Ancient wines were always fortified, like the 'strong wine' of the Old Testament, with herbal additives: opium, datura, belladonna, mandrake and henbane. Common incenses, such as myrrh, ambergris and frankincense are psychotropic; the easy availability and long tradition of cannabis use would have seen it included in the mixtures. Modern medicine has looked into using cannabis as a pain reliever and in treating multiple sclerosis. It may well be that ancient people knew, or believed, that cannabis had healing power.

Varieties of psychoactive plants were used in such infusions. According to Dioscorides, and his commentator Matthiolus, one could "boil the root of mandrake in wine down to a third part, and preserve the decoction, of which they administer a cyathus (about a fluid ounce and a half), to produce sleep, and to allay severe pains of any part; and also before operations with the knife, or the application of the actual cautery, that the operation should not be felt." [z]

The Mystical Greek Philosopher

Pythagoras, Plato, Socrates, and Aristotle are some of the most famous philosophers of Ancient Greece. Their views influenced every civilization into modern times, and one can learn about them in the humanities programs at Liberal Arts Universities. In Pike's discussion on the oneness of God, he mentioned Pythagoras. Pythagoras, who is the most famous proponent of reincarnation among the ancient Greeks, wrote, "God, in the view of Pythagoras, was ONE, a single substance, whose continuous parts extended through all the Universe, without separation, difference, or inequality, like the soul in the human body" [g]. Pythagoras held that the soul was of divine origin and existed before and after death. Plato and Socrates also accepted the soul's immortality, while Aristotle considered only part of the soul, *the noûs*, to have that quality. *Nous* in Greek means the eye of the heart. It's the vision or perception of the soul.

Orpheus, the founder of Orphism, which would splinter into the mystery schools of Ancient Greece, taught that soul and body are united by a compact unequally binding on either; the soul is divine, immortal, and aspires to freedom, while the body holds it in fetters as a prisoner. Death dissolves this compact, only to re-imprison the liberated soul after a short time: the wheel of birth revolves inexorably. Thus, the soul continues its journey, alternating between a separate unrestrained existence and fresh reincarnation, around the wide circle of necessity, as the companion of many bodies of men and animals.

The Greeks had several terms that referred to reincarnation. "*Metempsychosis*" pointed to the idea of the transmigration of the soul after its death. The word "*empsykhoun*" is attributed to Pythagoras and carries a similar meaning. *"Palingenesis"* meant restoring life after death back to its pristine state. The term is believed to have originated with the Greek Stoics. *"Gennao Anothen"* is composed of two words, where "Gennao" means regeneration and "Anothen" means from Heaven or God. Hence, Gennao Anothen meant reincarnation of the soul from the heavens. After Greek civilization declined, Roman thinkers took up the idea of reincarnation.

CHAPTER 9:

Psychedelics in Ancient Judaism

In early jewish culture cannabis was used in their anointing oils and incense[1]. In Exodus 30, YHWH - the Israelite's tribal deity - gives Moses the recipe of "a Holy Anointing Oil" to be used in His rites:

"Take thou also unto thee principal spices, of pure myrrh five hundred shekels, and of sweet cinnamon half so much, even two hundred and fifty shekels, and of kaneh-bosm two hundred and fifty shekels, And of cassia five hundred shekels, after the shekel of the sanctuary, and of oil olive an hiyn (5-7 liters)."

Kaneh-bosm, which translates to cannabis, is directly referenced in the Old Testament. Roughly 35 miles south of Jerusalem, in an archaeological site in the Negev desert known as Tel Arad, archaeologists excavating an ancient Jewish shrine have found traces of burnt cannabis and frankincense on a pair of limestone altars. Thus, proving the theory that kaneh-bosm was cannabis. It was found along with frankincense.

The new research, published in the journal Tel Aviv, provides the first evidence that the mind-altering substance was part of religious life in the ancient kingdom of Judah. Tel Arad contains the remains of a Canaanite city from the third millennium B.C., as well as Israelite fortresses from between the 10th and 6th centuries B.C.

Holy Smoke | **Ancient Israelites Used Cannabis as Temple Offering, Study Finds**

Analysis of altar residue shows worshippers burned pot at a Judahite desert shrine – and may have done the same at the First Temple in Jerusalem

Ariel David
May 31, 2020

🔔
Follow

The shrine is also contemporaneous with the first Jewish Temple in Jerusalem, suggesting similar ritual practices may have taken place at the biblical house of worship. The shrine at Tel Arad also bears a close physical resemblance to the first Temple [2].

King Saul and the Anointing Oil

At the time of the prophet Samuel, the use of the shamanic Hebrew anointing oil described in Exodus 30:23 was extended from the use of just priests, to include Kings as well. Although cannabis is not mentioned directly by name in Samuel, the description of events that take place after Samuel anoints Israel's first king[3].

In 1 Samuel 10:1 we read: Samuel poured oil on Saul's head. This was the sacred ceremony called the anointing. Its effect was to make Saul king. The oil in the ceremony had a special meaning. It showed that God's Holy Spirit was coming upon Saul. The Holy Spirit came in order to separate Saul for his special task. So really, as Samuel explained, the anointing came from God and not merely from Samuel. Samuel poured the oil, but the Holy Spirit comes from God.

Saul, make clear the psycho-active nature of the ointment used. Samuel "took a flask of oil and poured it on Saul's head" (1 Samuel 10:1). After the anointing Samuel tells Saul:

> *The Spirit of the Lord will come upon you in power*
> *And you will be changed into a different person*
> 1 Samuel 10:6

A statement indicating that the magical power of the ointment will shortly take effect. Samuel tells Saul that when this happens, he will come across a band of prophets (Nebiim) coming down from a mountaintop, with harp, tambourine, flute, and lyre before them prophesying (1 Samuel 10:5), and that Saul will join them.

As Samuel foretold, the spirit of Yahweh came mightily upon the new king and he 'prophesied among them'. The verb 'to prophecy' in this context meant not to foretell the future but to behave ecstatically, to babble incoherently under the influence of the Spirit. This bizarre conduct associated with prophesying is apparent when in a second burst of such activity, Saul stripped off his clothing and lay naked all day and night, causing the people to ask:

> *Is Saul among the prophets?*
> 1 Samuel 19:24

Ezra, Hamoa & Cannabis Wine

Ezra, known as Ezra the Scribe and Ezra the Priest, was a Jewish scribe and priest. Ezra was born in Babylon, and was among the Jews returned during the reign of Darius I, a Persian king, commonly known as Darius the Great[4].

Darius was the son of Hystaspes (Vištāspa) and Esther, King and Queen of Persia. Darius's father Vistaspa[5] was an early follower of Zoroaster, his patron, and instrumental in the diffusion of the prophet's message. Zoroaster was said to have given Vistapa psychedelic wine:

"Hemp and wine or hemp and haoma were mixed in the cup that was passed to Vistaspa. It was sent forth to let Vistaspa drink 'the eye of the soul' with the view up above to the forms of existence of the heavenly beings, the illuminating potion thanks to which Vistaspa saw the great lucky splendour and mystery'...it is a view with the eye of the soul, gyan casm, which is defined as 'the opening of the eye of the soul to obtain knowledge'.'The eye of the soul' means introspection. The visionary sight is conveyed to Kavi Vistaspa using a haoma potion mixed with hemp. With this his soul can repair to Garodman, [Paradise] to view the heavenly existence."

Ezra worked as a scribe in the Persian world before being returned to his homeland and he was a key figure of the Jewish monotheistic reformation after the Persians returned the Jews to their homeland after close to a century of exile. Here is Ezra's own account of his divine mission to bring together the texts of the Jewish religion and restore the faith to its homeland. Ezra leaves for the desert for 40 days where he is given a drink by an angel which will give him complete understanding and total recall as he dictates all day long. After forty days ninety-four books were created: the twenty-four canonical books and the seventy "hidden" books (14:37-48). The Fourth Book of Ezra describes God as answering the prayers of Ezra to have courage by sending him seven angels to show him heaven. His scribes record his experience in 4 Ezra 14[6]:

> *36:* Let no man therefore come unto me now, nor seek after me these forty days.
> *37:* So I took the five men, as he commanded me, and we went into the field, and remained there.

38: And the next day, behold, a voice called me, saying, Esdras, open thy mouth, and drink that I give thee to drink.

39: Then opened I my mouth, and, behold, he reached me a full cup, which was full as it were with water, but the color of it was like fire.

40: And I took it, and drank: and when I had drunk of it, my heart uttered understanding, and wisdom grew in my breast, for my spirit strengthened my memory:

41: And my mouth was opened, and shut no more.

42: The Highest gave understanding unto the five men, and they wrote the wonderful visions of the night that were told, which they knew not: and they sat forty days, and they wrote in the day, and at night they ate bread.

43: As for me. I spake in the day, and I held not my tongue by night.

44: In forty days they wrote two hundred and four books.

45: And it came to pass, when the forty days were filled, that the Highest spake, saying, The first that thou hast written publish openly, that the worthy and unworthy may read it:

46: But keep the seventy last, that thou mayest deliver them only to such as be wise among the people:

47: For in them is the spring of understanding, the fountain of wisdom, and the stream of knowledge.

48: And I did so.

It is only when Ezra tastes heavenly food in the final episode, with the cup filled with the fiery liquid, that he is able to transcend mortal understanding. In tasting the divine liquid, Ezra surpasses ordinary hearing and sight, and consumes God's meaning directly. The question is what drink was Ezra given? Ezra, a great prophet of the jewish people, was clearly influenced by the psychedelic rituals of the Zoroastrians.

"The image of a blazing cup was apparently related to... Zoroastrism; Zoroastrian texts mention ritual vessels with fire burning inside them"[7].

Interestingly, Rabbi Immanuel Löw, referred to an ancient Jewish recipe that called for wine to be mixed with ground up saffron and hasisat surur, which he saw as a "a kind of deck name for the resin the Cannabis sativa" [8]. Such preparations were also noted by the nineteenth century Biblical scholar John Kitto, and like the Hebrew references to cannabis, such concoctions went through periods of Hebraic free use and strict prohibition. "The palm wine of the East... is made intoxicating... by an admixture of stupefying ingredients, of which there was an abundance... Such a practice seems to have existed amongst the ancient Jews..." [9]

Magic Mushroom Manna

While wandering in the desert, the Israelites are said to have received a divine food from heaven called manna[10]. A month after their exodus from Egypt, the Israelites' food ran out, and on Sunday, the 15th day of the month of Iyar, they turned to Moses and Aaron for food [11].

> So YHWH said to Moses, 'Behold! I will rain down
> bread for you from the sky, and the people shall go
> out and gather what is needed for the day.
> (Exodus 16:4)

That night, a flock of poultry miraculously arrived, and the following day, a special edible substance fell from the sky. This food, "bread from heaven," was called "manna."

Most likely, the food that emerged from the ground overnight is a psychedelic fungus. To provide some context, it is common for mushrooms to sprout up after a thunderstorm. Research from Japan demonstrates that lightning causes mushrooms to grow [12]..

Shiitake mushrooms grow on a log exposed to lightning-like electricity.
PHOTOGRAPH COURTESY KOICHI TAKAKI

Lightning Makes Mushrooms Multiply

Lightning strikes can more than double some mushroom crops, according to ongoing experiments that are jolting fungi with electricity.

BY **JULIAN RYALL**, FOR NATIONAL GEOGRAPHIC NEWS

PUBLISHED APRIL 9, 2010 • 4 MIN READ

Lightning can double the yield of certain mushroom species compared with conventional cultivation methods. For example Psilocybin Cubensis, a strain of magic mushrooms, is often found growing on cow dung after a rainstorm. The Indian Vedas share this cultural knowledge as they call Soma - made from the Amanita muscaria mushroom - "the child of the thunderstorm."

תהלים עח:כג וְיְצַו שְׁחָקִים מִמָּעַל	Ps 78: 23 So He commanded the skies above,
וְדַלְתֵי שָׁמַיִם פָּתָח.	He opened the doors of heaven
עח:כד וַיַּמְטֵר עֲלֵיהֶם מָן לֶאֱכֹל	78: 24 and rained manna upon them for food,
וּדְגַן שָׁמַיִם נָתַן לָמוֹ.	giving them heavenly grain.
עח:כה לֶחֶם אַבִּירִים אָכַל	78: 25 Each man ate the bread of angels; [3]
אִישׁ צֵידָה שָׁלַח לָהֶם לָשֹׂבַע.	He sent them provision in plenty.

In kabbalistic thought, the Zohar views manna consumption as a method for internalizing divine wisdom. Manna grants the Israelites an embodied experience of knowledge of God; such an opportunity is available to mystics in everyday eating and through birkat ha-mazon (Grace after Meals)[13]. This philosophy is very similar to the beliefs of the Ancient

Indians, Egyptians, Greeks, and Native Americans.

כל אינון בני מהימנותא נפקי ולקטי ומברכאן שמא עלאה עליה וההוא מנא הוה סליק ריחא בכל בוסמין דגנתא דעדן דהא ביה אתמשך ונחית לתתא. שויה לקמיהו, בכל טעמא דאינון בעו הכי טעמין ומברכין למלכא עלאה וכדין מתברך במעוי והוה מסתכל וידע לעילא ואסתכי בחכמתא עלאה. [12]	All those scions of faith went out and gathered and blessed the supernal Name over it. That manna emitted a fragrance like all the spices of the Garden of Eden, since it had flowed through there in descending. Once they placed it in front of them, they tasted whatever taste they desired and blessed the supernal King. Then it was blessed in each one's belly, and he would contemplate and know above, gazing upon divine Wisdom.

The manna contains wisdom that enters the person who consumes it. The explanation for this process of descent of divine overflow and its materialization on earth derives from Neoplatonism - a Greco-roman school of philosophy that exerts a prominent influence upon kabbalistic thought [14].

טז:יג ...וּבַבֹּקֶר הָיְתָה שִׁכְבַת הַטַּל סָבִיב לַמַּחֲנֶה. טז:יד וַתַּעַל שִׁכְבַת הַטַּל וְהִנֵּה עַל פְּנֵי הַמִּדְבָּר דַּק מְחֻסְפָּס דַּק כַּכְּפֹר עַל הָאָרֶץ. טז:טו וַיִּרְאוּ בְנֵי יִשְׂרָאֵל וַיֹּאמְרוּ אִישׁ אֶל אָחִיו מָן הוּא כִּי לֹא יָדְעוּ מַה הוּא וַיֹּאמֶר מֹשֶׁה אֲלֵהֶם הוּא הַלֶּחֶם אֲשֶׁר נָתַן יְ–הוָה לָכֶם לְאָכְלָה...	16:13 ... In the morning there was a fall of dew about the camp. 16:14 When the layer of dew lifted, and look, on the surface of the wilderness, lay a fine and flaky substance, as fine as frost on the ground. 16:15 When the Israelites saw it, they said to one another, "Man hu?" ("What is it?") for they did not know what it was. And Moses said to them, "That is the bread which YHWH has given you to eat...."

The sages of the midrash said: "The Torah could be given only to eaters of manna." If the nation would not eat the manna, stated the sages, it would not have been capable of receiving the Torah. Why? What is the connection between eating manna and receiving the Torah? [15]

Of what food can He rightly say that it is rained from heaven, save of heavenly wisdom which is sent from above on souls which yearn for virtue...

The Second Temple period philosopher, Philo of Alexandria, understood the manna from heaven as symbolizing wisdom (*On the Changing of Names* [*De Mut. Nom.*], 259-60). For Philo, manna is an allegory for how the Israelites received wisdom from God; for the Gospel of John, it is an allegory for how a person's acceptance of God's "real" bread from heaven procures everlasting life.

Another potent hallucinogen in the Bible is mandrake, praised in the Song of Solomon and argued over by rival wives in Genesis. Genesis 30: 14–15 reads: And Reuben went in the days of wheat harvest, found mandrakes in the field, and brought them unto his mother, Leah. Then Rachel said to Leah: Give me, I pray thee, of thy son's mandrakes. And she said unto her: Is it a small matter that thou hast taken, my husband? And wouldest thou take away my son's mandrakes also? And Rachel said. Therefore he shall lie with thee tonight for thy son's mandrakes.

Mandrakes were a highly psychoactive drug commonly used in Egypt and cited in the Hebrew and Christian Bibles.

DMT in the Torah

The Acacia tree, revered by the Egyptians, was also considered sacred in the Old Testament. Using wood for secular purposes, such as building homes or furniture, was forbidden. Acacia wood was used exclusively in the building of the Temple of Jerusalem, including the Ark of the Covenant.

Cognitive Scientist Benny Shannon, a Hebrew University of Jerusalem professor, hypothesizes that Judaism is associated with using psychedelics from the Acacia tree. He provides evidence that the Israelites were making their mind-blowing version of ayahuasca. More specifically, an Ayahuasca analog made up of two middle-eastern plants, the Acacia tree and the bush, Peganum harmala[16].

The burning bush which spoke to Moses was acacia. According to Shannon's theory, Moses' vision of God's presence in the burning bush was fueled by DMT.

> And the angel of the Lord appeared unto him in a flame of fire out of the midst of a bush: and he looked, and, behold, the bush burned with fire and the bush was not consumed.
>
> And Moses said I will now turn aside and see this great sight; why the bush is not burnt?
>
> And when the Lord saw that, he turned aside to see, God called unto him out of the midst of the bush and said, Moses, Moses. And he said, Here am I.
>
> -Exodus 3:2-4 Old Testament-

Had Moses partaken in the ancestral ceremonial brew, it would have induced a powerful, lengthy vision quest during which he could have experienced vivid hallucinations, revelational thoughts, internal struggles, and connectivity with the divine. Disassociation with time is also an experience commonly associated with DMT.

Shanon suggests, "that's why Moses thought the bush was not consumed. It should have been burned in the time he thought had passed. And in that time, he heard God speaking to him."

This may seem like an irrelevant biblical observation, except that certain species of the Acacia tree contain DMT. This observation becomes especially interesting when you consider that Peganum harmala, a bush containing the MAO inhibitors harmine and harmoline (which allows DMT to become orally active), also grows in the desert areas of the Sinai Peninsula Southern regions of Israe[17]. Jews from Iran and Morocco confirmed that harmala was associated with several magical and curative powers. [...] the Yemeni Jews use this plant to heighten one's spirit. And in Egypt, it was known to have hallucinogenic properties.

Taking that into consideration, let's not forget it is believed that Moses was raised as an Egyptian prince. Is it possible he learned to prepare this alchemical psychedelic mixture directly from Egyptian royalty? This might explain some of the happenings in the life of Moses.

Rabbi Harry Rozenberg, one of the leading experts on psychedelics in Judaism, explores the active role the acacia tree played in ancient Jerusalem in his Torah research. In 950 BCE around the time of Yom Kippur the high priest of Jerusalem would be in a chamber of the Temple that was filled with smoke. He would've been fasting for 24 hours. Inside the temple would be an airtight chamber, inside of which hot coals made from acacia wood—a native Middle Eastern plant rich in the psychedelic compound DMT—would burn alongside a cocktail of incense composed of frankincense and myrrh.

"The high priest would be in this state to atone for the sin of Adam," explains Harry. The priest couldn't leave the chamber until it was completely veiled in smoke—but why, Rozenberg asked, was this deemed necessary for atonement? He went on to explain that the priest's daughter was called Bat Pineal, indicating that the priest himself went by Pineal (yes, like the pineal gland). Called the "seat of the soul" or the "third eye," the pineal gland is a part of the brain that secretes endogenous DMT. So why was the priest called Pineal? "Because the Talmud says he goes and serves in the innermost chamber," Rozenberg said.

Indeed, there's the innermost chamber of the Temple, and then there's the innermost chamber of ourselves—the metaphysical home of our internal divinity, which psychedelics can help us access. According to the mystics, Gan Eden can refer both to a physical location, but also a higher spiritual realm offering light, joy, and pleasure. "Commentators say this was or haganuz [concealed light], light of the brain, that was stored away for future generations, but Adam had a taste of it," Rozenberg said. "But what happened was when Adam sinned, the light left his brain and was sucked into the earth, the klippa, and into the mundane matters—the plants." Thus, it's the spiritual work of the people to extract those sparks and bring them back into the brain, Rozenberg continued.

The first sparks, he explained, were thought to have gone into Egypt, and so it was the job of the Hebrews to form a nation and extract those sparks, which mostly came in the form of the acacia plant, central in Egyptian theology and relating to the gods Taurus and Osiris. The tribe that Moses led out of slavery brought with them acacia extraction technology that Moses learned from the Egyptians, Rozenberg said, as well as plants that Jacob made them plant when they arrived in Egypt. He adds that Rashi says they would stare at the trees while in slavery to gain hope for future redemption.

"The whole process culminates with a man standing in a room filled with plant extract smoke to go into the sparks, take it back up, elevate it, and bring it into his brain," Rozenberg said during the panel. "What I want to suggest in the overlap between the psychedelic state and the mystical experience is we know when you're on these plant medicines, you're activating the neurological network where trauma is stored ... so when we're using the words 'rectifying the sin of Adam,' we can start to see the science and replace it with erasing generational trauma that we are storing in us." The sin of Adam was the first instance of trauma, passed down through generations, followed by the destruction of the Temple, the Spanish Inquisition, the Holocaust, and so on. [1] Rabbi Harry compares the transmission of the Torah to blockchain technology as it creates a trustworthy ledger of teachings from Sinai to the Sages and into modern times. Which is why he likes to discuss the creation narrative of Adam and Eve at the beginning of the Torah. By combining references from Biblical texts, science and history, Harry suggests that the light Adam experienced in the garden of Eden was actually activated via the Pineal Gland, where the chemical DMT naturally is produced, in a fully awake dreamlike state. "This would imply that the pineal gland is the so-called "Eden" discussed above. The pineal gland is located in the midbrain. This may confirm the midbrain region as the 'Eden' lobe." Within the brain of humans exists what would appear to be (based on structure and shape) an eyeball.

Harry is keen to point out that, "As recently proven in a scientific study, we can now associate DMT with the Pineal gland. This chemical, which flows throughout the human body and plants and animals throughout the whole world, is called Dimethyltryptamine, otherwise known as DMT. DMT, although it is a naturally occurring chemical throughout the planet, it is classified as an illegal drug. The DMT chemical, when consumed by a human, via extraction from a plant, takes that person to what would be described as another dimension filled with light and greeted by an entity of love that communicates with the individual. Today, this experience is being used to reset and treat human trauma, end drug addiction without withdrawal, and to treat depression and prevent suicide. We see that the DMT chemical is central to the ancient and modern religious ceremonies of the South American tribes, in what is known as Ayahuasca. Ayahuasca is a tea that allows the DMT chemical to be consumed, which then takes the individual on a 6-hour+ journey into the mind and body. Today, Ayahuasca is used as a cleansing experience and clinical treatment for people with addiction, suicidal tendencies, depression, and a wide range of health challenges and issues, as the active chemical compound is known to hyperactivate the neurological network where trauma and addiction is stored."[1]

Harry anchors his findings in the story of Jacob, the grandson of Abraham. His sons would go on to create the 12 tribes of Israel. The book of Genesis describes Jacob wrestling God. Jacob wins the battle and names the place when he is done, none other than Pineal.

> "And Jacob called the place Peniel:
> for I have seen God face to face,
> and my life is preserved."
> (Gen 32:30).

I want you to notice that Jacob said he saw God "face to face." This is where things get really interesting. While Jacob did not see a literal face, he did see God, or at least the Biblical writer's concept of God. It just wasn't with the physical eyes. There's a special word in verse 30 that tips us off to what this whole experience was really about, and although it's not common knowledge, ancient world stories were full of this kind of experience. It all has to do with the word "Peniel." Verse thirty already told us that Peniel was the name Jacob gave the place where the wrestling match with God happened. But that's not what's important. What *is* important is that "Peniel" is meant to be a real place inside *you*! Now pay attention, because this is how the story of Jacob's wrestling match affects *you*.

The special gland that sits at the center of the brain called the Pineal gland. In ancient cultures it was known as the "third eye." It is known as an eye because the Pineal gland in your brain has a special relationship to light. Just like the retina of your physical eyes, the Pineal gland also contains light-sensitive cells. In fact, they are similar to some of the cells that make up the retina.

When examining the Hebrew word Peniel, we easily see it's made up of two different words, Pnei and E-L, which translates to Gods Face. A couple of things to note here: first we see that the mystery man Jacob wrestled with is God himself. Second we see that Jacob prevailed in the struggle with God. If we think about all of this literally, it makes no sense.

So I ask the question: what is the real spirit of the scripture in this story? Did Jacob, Abraham's grandson, really wrestle an angel of God like the scripture seems to say he did? If so, it would be one of the stranger stories of the Bible. We can rest assured the story isn't about a man wrestling the Almighty.

Before Jacob has his Peniel experience, Genesis states that Jacob sent Rachel and Leah and all that he had across the River of Jabbok. Further it states,

"And there Jacob was left alone,"
and there he wrestled a man with him
until the breaking of the day"
(Gen 32:24).

Jacob's wrestling match was of an internal, introspective nature, not an external one. Having incorporated Leah's introspective nature, Jacob is now ready to have a deeper communion with God. It is a deep meditative experience that last through the night.

A few verses later we learn that Jacob is in fact wrestling not a mere man, but the angel of God himself, or the god-man within Jacob. He prevails, because Jacob sees God face to face, and lives. His name is changed to Israel because of this deeply enlightening spiritual transformative process. Jacob is no longer just the natural man. He is now the spiritual man, one that has gone deep within himself and discovered the god-nature that is there, unlocking the nature of God and the universe.[2]

The Indiegnous Roots of Judaism

In *Magic of the Ordinary: Recovering the Shamanic in Judaism*, Rabbi Gershon Winkler, a former ultra-Orthodox rabbi whose personal spiritual journey led to his initiation into Kabbalah, introduces long-hidden Hebrew mystery teachings to the modern spiritual seeker. Winkler teaches how shamanic principles and practices were integral to ancient Judaism—and that Judaism, at its roots, is most akin to other indigenous shamanic cultures, cultures that shared a mutual belief in reincarnation.

The Jewish ancestors were "masters of sorcery and shamanism" who "knew the language of the trees and the grasses, the songs of the frogs and the cicadas, the thoughts of horses and sheep. They followed rivers to discover truths, and climbed mountains to liberate their spirits. They journeyed beyond their bodily limitations, brought people back from the dead, healed the incurable, talked raging rivers into holding back their rapids, turned pints into gallons, brought down the rains in times of drought, walked through fire, even suspended the orbit of the earth around the sun." [18]

There were two distinct methods of performing sorcery: "mind altering herbs and ceremonies, and being so present in the known world that the unknown becomes second nature."

Jewish shamanism "emphasizes the sacredness of the earth, and that all organisms, even stars and planets, are imbued by the Creator with a divine consciousness. Every blade of grass is empowered by a spirit being. All trees speak to one another, and all rocks and plants have healing powers that can be accessed through their spirits." [19]

Moreover, Jewish shamanism involves direct communication with these spirits. Hillel the Elder, a renowned rabbi of the first century b.c.e., is recorded to have mastered communication with trees, grasses, spirits, and animals. The eighteenth-century Rabbi Pinchas of Koritz taught the languages of birds, animals, and plants. Rabbi Schneur Zalman of Liadi (1745-1813) is said to have mastered the language of the animals.

He later explains that such activities are a part of the Jewish tradition that has been suppressed for centuries, largely under the influence of Christian doctrine that persecuted Jews for their practice of occult arts and sorcery—which he defines simply as the process by which "supernatural events occur through mortal intervention."

Today, many of the surviving teachings can be found only in inaccessible texts, often available only in their original Hebrew or Aramaic. Centuries of suppression and genocide of the Jewish wisdom keepers—combined with inaccurate or biased translations—have resulted in the misinterpretation of teachings from more readily available sources, such as the Bible and the Talmud, the sacred texts on Jewish law.

The notion of Jewish shamanism may seem like an oxymoron to many, but it is an essential part of the Jewish tradition that has been suppressed for centuries. Driven away from its traditional open air settings, it is now confined to daunting texts in Aramaic and Hebraic, and English translations that are equally as incomprehensible. To make matters worse, the information is kept in libraries and archives, often on the same shelves as those of scholars who deny its existence. The Lost Torah is about resurrecting the teachings from the hidden Jewish mystery wisdom and show how it aligns closely with Native American spirituality.

The Catholic Church's persecution of Jews led them to reduce the roles of women in religious life in order to avoid accusations of witchcraft. Accusations which were punishable by death. By the eleventh century, Jews had to conceal much of their kabbalistic tradition and practice, either by disguising it with innocent hymns or by passing it down orally to only a select few. The Jewish people have internalized that persecution towards women. In the modern era there is a deep conflict between Judaism and feminism.

For example, in all Orthodox synagogues men pray separately from women and in many women are relegated to an upstairs gallery. Gender hierarchies are entrenched in Jewish thought: a blessing orthodox Jewish men are required to say everyday thanks a God "who has not made me a woman". Modern orthodox Judaism is merely a perversion of the original Torah. This perversion reached a crescendo in 2017 when the Orthodox Union, one of the largest Orthodox Jewish organizations in the United States, released a statement barring women from serving as clergy. The patriarchy and misogyny of Orthodox Jews might explain why more than half of all Jews raised Orthodox leave the religion. Modern Judaism, whether Orthodox or other denomination, has lost its roots and forgotten the practices of the original Torah. These practices were shamanic, involved psychedelic rituals, spending time in nature and parallel Native American spiritual belief systems.

Reincarnation in Judaism

In the Creation story, we read of God blowing a "breath of life" into the man of earth and dust (Genesis 2:7). The jewish people believe in the concept of the the soul which they call *neshamah* meaning 'breath or breath of life.' They believe every form of life possesses a "soul." Animals have souls, as do plants and even inanimate objects; every blade of grass has a soul, and every grain of sand. Not only life, but also existence requires a soul to sustain it—a "spark of Godliness" that perpetually imbues its object with being and significance. Each soul is seen as the expression of God's intent and vision in creating that particular being.

Ancient Jews displayed an awareness of how influential non-Jewish philosophers regarded the soul. For example, the Greek Jew Philo tried to use the three words associated with spirit–neshamah, nefesh, ruah–to support Plato's claim that the soul has three parts. Literature of the Talmudic period gives us images of body and soul in harmony. "Just as the Holy One of Blessing fills the world, so does the soul [neshamah] fill the body. Just as the Holy One of Blessing sees but cannot be seen, so does the soul see but cannot be seen... Just as the Holy One of Blessing is pure, so is the soul pure" (Berakhot 10a). The Jewish people have a gratitude prayer to say to God every morning for renewal of both body and soul: "I offer thanks to You, living and everlasting King, for having returned to me my soul with compassion and great faithfulness" (the Modeh Ani prayer).

Samsara, the cycle of death and rebirth of the soul, which is a core aspect of the great Dharmic religions: Buddhism, Hinduism, Sikhism, and Jainism. Reincarnation also features prominently in Jewish mysticism. Often overlooked, both by Jews and by students of Jewish tradition, is *gilgul*, a concept that is described in great detail throughout the Kabbalah. Very much in line with samsara, which is often depicted as a wheel in Buddhist art, the word *gilgul* comes from the Hebrew root meaning "to spin." The soul, in the kabbalistic view, spins onward through a great many bodies, striving after a higher form of perfection [20].

Though it is likely that Jewish ideas about transmigration are rooted far back in antiquity, the first explications of gilgul appear in medieval Kabbalah, in the Zohar and elsewhere. One of the earliest of these can be found in Sefer HaBahir ("The Book of Brightness"), an abstruse mystical tract of mysterious origin that began to circulate among kabbalists in 13th-century Europe. In a well known passage, the cycle of reincarnation is likened to a vinter who plants grapes that become sour. Disappointed, he clears his vineyard and plants a new crop, which also becomes sour. The Bahir asks: "How many times must he go through the process? He said, 'Up to a thousand generations.'" Thus it is with the soul, which accrues merit (or not) over the course of countless lifetimes [21].

The Lost Torah & the Sacred Fire

Like the Native Americans, fire is a powerful force in Jewish tradition. Fire marks the beginning and end of Shabbat with the lights of the Shabbat. It can be used to purify objects, making that which is forbidden "kosher" or fit for ritual use. During the Hanukkah festival, fire is central. For eight days, Jews commemorate the rededication of the Temple in Jerusalem by kindling the flames of the menorah and by recalling the fire of the altar, ever-present and never to be extinguished. In the Zohar we find a statement that the Torah was written with "black fire upon white fire." In Legends of the Jews 1:1 we read:

> In the beginning, two thousand years
> before the heaven and the earth,
> seven things were created:
> the Torah written with black fire on white fire,
> and lying in the lap of God...

According to Jewish tradition, the Torah is a sacred text that was revealed to Moses by God on Mount Sinai, and is considered to be the foundation of all Jewish law and belief. The Jewish people are expected to live in some manner by the laws of the Torah.

> And upon Mount Sinai You descended,
> and spoke with them from the heavens,
> and gave them just rulings,
> and two Torahs of truth,

and statutes, and good commandments.
~ Nehemiah 9:13

In Scripture we find something interesting: the mention of two Torahs. One created by black fire and the other white fire. One that is revealed unto the people and the other unrevealed. Exodus 18:20 states: And clarify to them the statutes and the two Torahs, and make known to them the way in which they shall walk, and the actions which they shall perform.

Black fire represents: אמת – truth . That is clear and indisputable. Black fire is the torah that is revealed to the people, the torah that is written down and passed from one generation to the next.

כי האמת חותמו של הקדוש ברוך הוא
"Truth is God's signature in this world"

The nature of the Torah of white fire is the higher form of the revealed Torah. In the Torah, the Jewish people are called to perform the two torah's as God's people on the earth lest they break their covenant with God.

And the earth is polluted under its inhabitants, for they have transgressed [the] two Torahs, changed the statute, broken the eternal covenant.
~ Isaiah 24:5

The Torah of white fire surrounds and gives shape to the Torah of black fire, so that the two Torahs are one, and in need of each other to fully express the will of the Creator.

The white fire of the Torah is often associated with the concept of the "light of God," which is said to be the source of all knowledge and wisdom. In the Kabbalah, the white fire of the Torah is considered to be a powerful and transformative force that can help individuals to connect with the divine and to gain a deeper understanding of the universe and their place within it. White fire is חסד – loving kindness. It represents the goal of the Torah.

כי כל ענין התורה הוא לקיים הטוב האלקי
*"The whole purpose of the Torah is
to manifest God's goodness in the world."*

Some Jewish scholars and mystics believe that the white fire of the Torah can be accessed through study and meditation, and that it can provide individuals with a sense of clarity and insight that can help them to overcome challenges and to achieve their goals. Others believe that the white fire of the Torah is a symbol of the divine presence that is always with us, and that it can be called upon for strength and guidance in times of need.

Ultimately fire is a form of light. In a broad sense, fire and light are both forms of energy that are closely related to one another. The two are intertwined in the sense that light is one of the products of fire, and fire is one of the sources of light. In many spiritual and philosophical traditions, fire and light are seen as symbols of divine presence or spiritual power.

I believe the evidence dictates that the white fire of the Torah is accessed by purifying the vessel of the body through ritualistic use of the psychedelic sacraments, fasting, prayer, meditation and performing mitzvah (good deeds) from a place of loving kindness. The concept of "becoming one with the light" likely has different meanings in different spiritual or philosophical traditions. In general, it may refer to achieving a state of enlightenment or spiritual understanding, in which a person's consciousness is said to merge with a divine or universal consciousness.

When Moses told the Creator that He should "erase me from Your book" unless judgment and negativity is removed from the Israelites, Moses was essentially saying, "I have no purpose in life, if not for the purpose of giving to others." And in that moment, Moses achieved the level of complete removal of ego and selfish motivation from every action that he ever did for the rest of his life, and became one with the Creator.

Why? Because when we remove our ego completely, we become completely unified with the Light of the Creator, no longer existing as a separate entity from the Light. When we achieve that level, we can bring any blessing, remove any judgment, and bring healing. Therefore, we come to see that the reason Moses is not mentioned by name in this portion is not because it is a punishment; rather, it's the greatest reward. It is the indication of what Moses achieved: he had come to a state where he no longer existed as a separate and distinct individual. Moses was simply now the Light of the Creator, and because of that, as the kabbalists explain, everything Moses did lasted forever, because he had given up his ego and personal agenda completely.

Kabbalists teach anyone can become one with the Creator, and just as the Light of the Creator can heal, so can we heal, just as the Light of the Creator can bring blessings, so can we bring blessings. In that state, there's nothing the Light of the Creator can't do that we can't do either, because we're not separate anymore.

The nature of "Light" and its essence is to spread, to give and to share. We know it since when a person is full with Light that means that he is in a mental state of bliss; one of the immediate outcomes is that he feels like sharing that feeling with others. Therefore, because at first there was only Light, a "Vessel", had to be created, in order to receive and contain all of the "Light's" abundance.

This is how the souls of humanity, and all creatures, whose basic characteristic is a desire to receive, are the "Vessel" that was created by the "Light". Rabbi Ashlag said that the "Light" of the creation is the living power that allows everything in our reality to exist.

The Torah is in essence a book of kindness. So central is the trait of kindness in Judaism, that it is said that "*the beginning and end of the entire Torah is loving-kindness.*"

Modern Judaism has abandoned its indigenous roots. To tap into true essence of loving-kindness and achieve the prophesied redemption of the tribes of Israel, the Jewish people will need to return to their indigenous roots and rediscover the true original Torah - a Torah of direct experience with the divine. An experience found through ancient ceremonial practice of prayer, fire ceremonies and communion with psychedelic sacraments.

CHAPTER 10:

Psychedelics in Christianity

And if ye will receive it, this is Elijah, which was for to come. He that hath ears to hear let him hear. Matthew 11:14-15

The earliest Christian communities were influenced by the mysteries of Greece, Egypt, and Judaism. From the Egyptian God of Osiris to El, to the Greek Dionysus, and into the time of Jesus, we find psychedelic wine informing each culture's spiritual beliefs. These spiritual practices were common in Galilee during the times of Jesus. So common, we find evidence in the historical record of ancient psychedelic wine found in modern-day Galilee. In 2013, archeological researchers found 40 jars of herbal wine in the world's oldest wine cellar dating to 1700 BC[1].

Archaeologists discover largest, oldest wine cellar in Near East: 3,700 year-old store room held 2,000 liters of strong, sweet wine

Date: November 22, 2013

Source: Brandeis University

Summary: Archaeologists have unearthed what may be the oldest -- and largest -- ancient wine cellar in the Near East, containing 40 jars, each of which would have held 50 liters of strong, sweet wine.

These wine jugs were laced with residues of juniper, cinnamon, mint, cedar, Cyprus, and many other plants[2]. Juniper is a curious ingredient for wine because it produces *thujone*. Thujone is what makes wormwood (absinthe) or salvia psychoactive. Juniper is used in some shamanic traditions, particularly by the Kalash culture in Pakistan. According to scholar and psychedelic historian Alan Piper, the shamans burned juniper and ate juniper foliage as a part of a spiritual ritual.[3]

"At first glance, the wine cellar at Kabri seems like wealthy elites getting hammered and having a good time. But then you look more closely, and I think that's too simplistic of an answer. Because they're adding things to the wine, and those ingredients are not just for preservation. When you look at the literature from the time, there are festivals in Egypt and the Levant, like the *marzeah* that are just rife with ritualistic meaning. They are communing with the gods and so forth".[4]

The ritual of *marzeah* had a singular purpose: to acquaint its participants with the afterlife by reaching a state of consciousness, transcending space and time back to the world of spirit.

In Luke 7:34, we read that Jesus' critics called Him a drunkard. Some have suggested that they would not have called Jesus a drunkard if He did not, at the very least, imbibe alcoholic wine on occasion. Others say that Jesus never explicitly denied the charges means He at least consumed moderate amounts of alcohol. And so this text is used as justification by some that we can consume modern-day distilled alcohol.

Let anyone who is thirsty come to me and drink.
(John 7:37)

But what if Jesus was drinking psychedelic wine just like the ancient Greeks and Egyptians?

Depictions of Magic Mushrooms in Early Christian Art

In the book *The Psychedelic Gospels: The Secret History of Hallucinogens in Christianity*, authors Jerry B. and Julie M. Brown detail evidence of psychedelics in Christian artwork. Dr. Brown believed in Carl Sagan's saying, "extraordinary claims require extraordinary evidence" so the couple did extensive field research and traveled to different ancient cathedrals across Europe and middle-east to gather visuals and evidence before publishing their book. Their research illuminates the history of Christianity's relationship to psychedelics.

"Thousands of years before Christianity, secret cults arose which worshiped the sacred mushroom — the Amanita Muscaria — which, for various reasons (including its shape and power as a drug), came to be regarded as a symbol of God on earth. When the secrets of the mushroom cult had to be written down, it was done in the form of codes hidden in folktales. This is the basic origin of the stories in the New Testament." [5]
- John Marco Allegro, English archaeologist & Dead Sea Scrolls scholar

The chief aim of their journey was to challenge the traditional understandings of the Judeo-Christian religion. During a Church of Saint Martin in France tour, Julie first noticed the detailed, wall-length fresco of Jesus entering Jerusalem. There, above the men welcoming Jesus, were five psilocybin mushroom caps.

Consistent with the Romanesque style, the mushroom caps were as large as the men's heads, indicating their importance in the artwork. Everything about the artwork indicated it was Jesus riding through the gates of Jerusalem on a donkey during Passover. This is the holiday we now refer to as Palm

Sunday. The fresco also depicts an angel purifying a man (thought to be the prophet Isaiah) with a mushroom, suggesting that it may have been psilocybin that inspired his prophetic visions. The curious discovery of mushrooms is hidden in plain sight, even in ornately decorated clothing.

> "We contemplated the incontrovertible facts portrayed in the wall paintings before us: the pictorial fusion of Jesus entering Jerusalem with the purification of Isaiah; Jesus with arms outstretched toward the large psilocybin mushrooms in the Entry; the joyful youth cutting down mushrooms with a long knife on the towers of Jerusalem over the scene of the Last Supper; the otherworldly expressions of Jesus and his disciples leaning on the table; and the orderly row of mushrooms cleverly hidden in the hems of the disciples." - Jerry Brown[6]

The fresco in the church of Saint Martin de Vicq with five psilocybin mushrooms (see: top right corner)

1. Canterbury Cathedral in England

Canterbury Cathedral in England is one of the most famous churches for Christians, and when the Browns visited this church, they uncovered a psychedelic painting. Christ encircled with plants at the bottom. And these are not ordinary plants but psilocybin mushrooms, including Amanita muscaria, blue psilocybin, and two other varieties of Psilocybe [7].

A psychedelic painting in Canterbury Cathedral in England. Note the mushroom-like figures below Jesus.

2. The mural titled Altar frontal from La Seu d'Urgell or of The Apostles

Note that the Twelve Apostles have their eyes focused not on the face of Jesus but on the mushrooms. Museu Nacional d'Art de Catalunya, Barcelona, 12th century

3. St. Michael's Church, Germany

The church contains a painting of the Jesse Tree in which a tree grows from Jesse, founder of the lineage of the major kings of Israel, from whose tribe it was predicted that the Messiah would be born. This painting shows the Temptation scene from the Garden of Eden with a backdrop of a psilocybin red-and-gold mushroom cap. Note that the scene below is superimposed over a red encoded Amanita mushroom cap.

4. The Mosaics at the Basilica of the Nativity

Below we see easily recognizable mushrooms encoded as the sacred fruit from the Tree of Life over a cave that Christians believe marks the birthplace of Jesus. Built around 350 A.D., the Basilica was commissioned by Constantine the Great and his mother, Helena.

Archeological Evidence of Psychedelic Sacraments

According to evidence in Ancient Mesopotamian documents, Assyrian Medical Tablets, and the Bible, Jesus used cannabis-infused oil[16].

> "And they cast out many devils, and anointed with oil many that were sick, and healed them" (Mark 6:13).

According to Dr. Ethan Russo, Assyrian medical tablets in the Louvre collection translate to "So that god of man and man should be in good rapport, with hellebore, cannabis, and lupine you will rub him."

> "Then God said, I give you every seed-bearing plant on the face of the whole Earth, and every tree that has fruit in it." (Genesis 1:29-30)

With instructions like these, would Jesus ignore a seed-bearing plant as aesthetically beautiful, aromatic, and therapeutic as cannabis?

Jesus and his apostles used cannabis-infused "holy oil" to treat lesions, the pain of crippled limbs and swollen muscles, leprosy, and the "Hand of the Ghost," which is likely to be what is known today as epilepsy.

In the Indian Vedas - Cannabis is 1 of the 5 essential plants - the books describe how to use Cannabis to heal leprosy[17]. Another clue is the inclusion of "kaneh-bosem" as an ingredient in Jesus and his disciples' anointing oil. For a while, no one paid attention to this mystery ingredient. But researchers have since found that kaneh-bosem is likely a reference to cannabis. If you type "kanehbosem" (without the hyphen) into Google Translator as a Yiddish word, the English translation is "cannabis."

"There can be little doubt about a role for cannabis in Judaic religion," Carl Ruck, a professor of classical mythology at Boston University[18]. "The easy availability and long-established tradition of cannabis in early Judaism would inevitably have included it in the [Christian] mixtures." In other words, Jesus (raised as Jewish) would have used Judaic practices in his healing ceremonies. The names Christ and Messiah mean The anointed and refer to the Holy oil of Exodus 30:23.

Chris Bennet, the author of Sex, Drugs, Violence and the Bible, believes that those anointed with Jesus' oils were also experiencing cannabis' psychoactive properties. "The surviving Gnostic descriptions of the effects of the anointing rite make it very clear that the holy oil had intense psychoactive properties that prepared the recipient for entrance into 'unfading bliss," Bennet writes in his book[19].

If Jesus and his apostles were using cannabis, it would make sense that they would also be using psychedelic wine or magic mushrooms, or both. However, one big question remains: the sacraments of bread and wine are central to Christianity - if Christian holy wine used to be psychedelic - why isn't it anymore? Perhaps it has something to do with big government and politics.

The Institution of the Church

Christ's message was revolutionary in so many ways especially the idea that women and the poor were equal to all men. The Christian ceremony involving the psychedelic eucharist created believers who would discover Kingdom of God within their hearts. And so it was written:

The Kingdom of God is Within You.
(Luke 17:20-25)

This is why for the first 300 years of its existence, Christianity was an illegal cult. In North Africa, in the 3rd century, converting to Christianity was a crime punishable by death. This was primarily because Christian beliefs turned the Roman structure of power and authority on its head. Christianity was a revolutionary movement. Odd then that Constantine, when he became the Roman Emperor in 313 AD, proclaimed Christianity as the religion of the empire when he hadn't even converted.

Was that because the life and teachings of Jesus moved him or because he had a political plan to create state-sponsored religion? If one were a power-hungry dictator, the best way to stop a movement based on freedom and equality would be to take it over. And that is precisely what the Roman Empire did with the Catholic Church as its vehicle for control. By 380 AD, the merger of state power and religious institutionalism gave rise to the Roman Catholic Church as it became the Roman Empire's official religion and the seat of power in the region.

It wouldn't take long before big government, power, and bureaucracy would come to usurp Jesus and his teachings. Emperor Constantius II elevated the church's bureaucracy to new levels of Power. Soon religious authorities began to ban the use of psychedelic sacraments in religious ceremonies - persecution that lives on to this day.

History tends to repeat itself. After the psychedelic revolution of the 1960s, the world's governments declared war on drugs to harass and control the hippie movement. The same thing happened to the early Christian movement. The rich and the powerful could not allow the people to begin to think for themselves.

In AD 364, Emperor Valentinian abolished all nocturnal celebrations to shut down the mysteries. In AD 392, Emperor Theodosius outlawed the Mysteries[20]. According to Praetextatus, a wealthy aristocratic priest of the Roman

Empire, the temple of Demeter, which housed the Elusian mysteries, believed there was something indispensable that was lacking from this curated version of the Christian faith. He prophesied that humanity would be doomed without the original psychedelic sacrament inherited from the ancestors.

The shamanic practices of many cultures were virtually wiped out with the spread of Christianity. In Europe, starting around 400 CE, the Christian church was instrumental in the collapse of the Greek and Roman religions. Beginning with the middle ages and continuing into the Renaissance, remnants of European shamanism were wiped out by campaigns against witches. The Catholic Inquisition often orchestrated these campaigns.

In the Caribbean and Central and South America, Catholic priests followed in the footsteps of the Conquistadors. They were instrumental in destroying the local traditions, denouncing practitioners as "devil worshippers" and having them executed.

The persecution of psychedelic sacraments was maintained through the lineage of the Roman Catholic church. Why else would they maintain the Index Librorum Prohibitorum (Latin: "Index of Forbidden Books"), a list of books the church considered dangerous to the faith of Roman Catholics? The list contained works by botanists like Otto Brunfels(1488-1534) and Konrad Gesser (1516-1565). Why would the Vatican fear plants and herbs if the sacraments and the eucharist were psychedelics in nature?[21].

The ultimate question is why the Vatican is maintaining secret archives in the first place. It's because the lost history of Christianity's origin threatens the Church Institution's power. By censoring the original sacred sacrament of Christ, the Church maintains its illusory monopoly on religion, where gatekeepers attempt to control access to religious revelation. Who needs the fancy building, priest, confession, and the Bible - when all you need is access to the sacred psychedelic sacrament?

The Psychedelic Eucharist

Some may try to claim the Eucharist is a "placebo." In its present form, the Eucharist works for many people. However, it doesn't seem to be working for 69 percent of American Catholics[22], who say they don't believe in the Catholic Church's central doctrine of transubstantiation – that the bread and wine of the Eucharist become the body and blood of Jesus. For many, the power of the Eucharist has lost its meaning. How could that kind of Eucharist have converted half the Roman Empire, some 30 million people, to the new Christian faith in only 350 years?

The Sacred Mushroom is embedded in christian art as the fruit Eve gives Adam because Holy Communion is a living experience. Jesus took psilocybin mushrooms and was illuminated by the living consciousness of Goddess Sophia. Early Christians embedded this message of Christ in art. This was because most people were illiterate and the visual symbols became the guide.

In the *The Immortality Key, The Secret History of the Religion with No Name*, Brian C. Muraresku presents evidence that about 2,000 years ago, the first generations of Christians used bread and wine in a communion-type sacrament, much like today. Only they were infused with psychedelic plants and fungi. In the author's words: It was normal practice for the early adherents of Christianity to meet secretly in small groups to eat the bread and drink the wine of Holy Communion and afterward to experience powerful and deeply meaningful beatific visions

The idea of using psychedelic wine to find the divine was not original to the Christians[23]. It was co-opted from the ancient Greeks. In the centuries before Jesus, spiritual pilgrims celebrated the Greek God Dionysus much the same way. They partook in a ceremony that involved drinking spiked wine to "remove inhibitions and social constraints, liberating the individual to return to a natural state." It was an attempt not just to honor Dionysus but to "become one with him."

By tapping into an existing ritual and using "the magic wine," Muraresku speculates that "the same people who were attracted to the cult of Dionysus were attracted to Jesus." The name of the deity changed, but the sacraments remained the same.

The purpose of drinking the psychedelic wine was not to merely become intoxicated. It was to achieve a state of mind that led to direct experiential communion with God. For these early Christians, "to know one's self at the deepest level is to know God," and by drinking this wine, they "became identified with God himself" and could actually "become one with Jesus." Much like earlier, true believers became one with Dionysus. The idea of looking within to find God was found in early Gnostic texts like The Gospel of Mary Magdalene.

Several texts make clear that Jesus did not intend to idolize him as an external God but wanted us to realize "the divine spark that lives in us" and "experience that divinity here and now." The Gnostics believed that this "state of transformed consciousness" helped them "gain personal entry to the Kingdom of Heaven." It was heaven, not in the skies but all around them, right here on earth.

Without the Eucharist, there is no Christianity. John is the only Gospel that records the wine miracle at Cana- the first miracle that launches Jesus's public mission. As far as we can tell, John did not want to leave any room for misinterpretation. Jesus would ultimately refer to himself as the "True Vine." Jesus, whom we know, was raised among the vineyards of Galilee, where thousands of jars were found with remnants of psychedelic wine. The "true drink" was no ordinary drink. It was God's medicine.

> I tell you for certain
> that you must be born again
> before you can see God's Kingdom - J
> John 3:3

> I am here to give sight to the blind
> John 9.39

> I tell you for certain that
> you will see heaven open
> and God's angels going up and down
> John 1:51

This sight doesn't come about by accident in the Gospel of John. Access to the Kingdom of Heaven is not based on blind belief; you had actually to do something. You had to sample the "true drink."

Elaine Pagels points out that these rituals, which included secret meetings and magical sacraments, "did not lead to mass religion." If the psychedelic wine was the secret to finding the spirit of Jesus and even God himself, and it could be created by any layperson who knew how to make it, what was the need for the church? Big brother steps in, aka the early Roman Catholic church.

The evidence shows that women often led these early Christian ceremonies, with men playing a secondary role. This lasted until the rise of Roman Catholicism in the second half of the 4th century when a religion dominated by men took steps to marginalize the women in the church. They also removed the psychedelic elements from the sacrament, "reducing Holy Communion to an empty symbolic act, devoid of its powerful experiential content." By the fourth century

AD, the Church's processed version of Christianity featured a Eucharist of ordinary bread and wine.

By 400 AD, Muraresku reports that the leaders of the new and increasingly powerful church banned the Gnostic texts and eliminated what was deemed "pagan temples, shrines and religious sites," in many cases burning them to the ground. What also were banned were many Christian sects "that thrived in the second and third centuries AD, condemned as heretical and erased from the history of the faith."

The Gnostic Gospels

In the 1940s, volumes of Christian Gospels were discovered in the Egyptian town of Nag Hammadi[8]. The Nag Hammadi library commonly known as the Gnostic Gospels predate the Bible and reveal a Jesus with a very different message.

According to the Gnostics, Jesus is the reedemer who came to communicate the true knowledge of oneness. The Gnostics claim Christ taught that people are believed to be souls in material bodies and only through true knowledge can they ascend. He communicated this knowledge to selected disciples one of whom was Thomas. The gospel of thomas doesn't tell a story, it's a compilation of approximately 114 sayings attributed to Jesus. The opening words of the document read:

Here are the secret words which Jesus the Living spoke, and which Didymus Jude Thomas wrote down.

Let not him who seeks desist until he finds.
When he finds he will be troubled;
when he is troubled, he will marvel,
and he will reign over the Universe.
2 Gospel of Thomas

The sayings themselves is not the secret. The secret lies in their interpretation. When the truth of these teachings set it, it will marvel you. Then you will know your power and you will have supremem reign over everything in it. That you can experience heaven on earth.

If those who lead you say to you 'see, the kingdom is in the sky, then the birds of the sky will precede you. If they say to you, 'it is in the sea' then the fish will precede you. Rather, the kingdom is inside of you and it is outside of you. When you come to know yourselves, then you will become known, and you will realize that it is you who are the sons of the living Father. But if you will not know yourselves, you dwell in poverty and it is you who are that poverty.

This teaching refers to the consequences of believing power is outside the individual. If you believe that power is outside of you, then that force will have dominion over your life. However; when one realizes who we each truly are: one consciousness, children of the Holy Spirit and that power comes from within us, we can live in an ascended way. The Kingdom is inside of you and outside of you. You manifest your outside circumstances from within. The belief that outside forces have control over our lives keep us from living the richness of life that rightfully belongs to us. You manifest as you believe. Whether you think you can, or you think you can't – you're right

Jesus taught that everyone is filled with the same light of God. These teachings change everything modern Christians believes about life and will affect history. Jesus taught that while we are each different that does not make us separate, we are all part of the same consciousness taking different forms. If we do not turn away from the things that disturb us and believe in the power within to change all things we will continue to experience that reality in our lives.

If you do not fast from the world,
you will not find the Holy Spirit's domain.
27 Gospel of Thomas

Jesus teaches that anyone who truly understands his words can accomplish all he has done and more.

Jesus said: I am not your master.
Because you have drunk, you have become drunk
from the bubbling stream which I have measured out.
He who will drink from my mouth will become as I am:
I myself shall become he, and the things that are
hidden will be revealed to him.
13 Gospel of Thomas

"This is amazing; in this case, God and man are not wholly separate; they are one. Jesus is awakening through a potion, the God within. The message here is that Jesus did not come to save man from sin but to teach enlightenment. " writes Jerry Brown in the *Psychedelic Gospels: the Secret History of Hallucinogens in Christianity* [2]. Far from being a sacrificial lamb who takes away the sins of the world, Jesus serves as a pointer of the way to truth [10].

> *Let anyone who is thirsty come to me and drink.*
> (John 7:37)

Jesus' words are connected to the idea that there is an ultimate cure for spiritual thirst. Perhaps Jesus was speaking of drinking a psychedelic wine, much like one a participant consumes during a ceremony at the Greek Mystery Schools. While history still can't account for Jesus's life from 12 to 28, Jerry and Julie Brown postulate that sacred magic mushrooms inspired Jesus' revelation of the Kingdom of Heaven.

Evidence exists that Jesus, born in the city of Nazareth, now modern-day Israel / Palestine, migrated south into Egypt, where mystical practices had spread during the missing years of his life [11]. Perhaps Jesus was exposed to these sacred sacraments in Egypt's mystery schools. In the early days of Christianity, psychedelics were commonly used by the Gnostics - commonly known as Christian mystics [12]. Was it through taking sacred psychedelic sacraments that the first Christians - including Jesus - came to experience God as the divine intelligence that permeates the universe?

If this alternate theory were true, one would expect to find remnants of these practices within the history of the Christian Church. Like the Greek Mysteries, the earliest followers of Jesus were practicing mystical ceremonies and hidden rites behind closed doors. Today's foremost authority on this lost tradition is Princeton scholar Elaine Pagels. Her definition of gnosis from 1979 is great:

> The Greek language distinguishes between scientific or reflective knowledge ("I know mathematics") and knowing through observation or experience ("I know me"), which is *gnosis*. As the Gnostics use the term, we could translate it as "insight," for gnosis involves an intuitive understanding of knowing oneself. And to know oneself, [the Gnostics] claimed, is to know human nature and destiny...to know oneself, at the deepest level, is simultaneously to know God; this is the secret of gnosis...Orthodox Jews and Christians insist that a chasm separates humanity from its creator; God is wholly other. But some of the Gnostics who wrote these gospels contradict this: self-knowledge is knowledge of God; the self and the divine are identical[13].

Even more amazing that in, the first passage in the *Gospel of Thomas* quotes Jesus saying:

> 1. And he said, "Whoever discovered the interpretation of these sayings shall not taste death." [14]

It's incredible how this statement fits the same testimony given by the mystics of the Greek and Egyptian cultures. Modern research tells us the path to Gnostic enlightenment revolves around gaining otherwise hidden spiritual knowledge called Pleroma. The Gnostics believe Pleroma was trapped inside all human souls, with personal insights into certain esoteric levels of the cosmos. They also shared the belief that our soul manifests our physical body.

In 367 AD, Archbishop Thenasius of Alexandria - a staunch Orthodox Catholic, a man hated by Emperors and ultimately excommunicated from the church - called for the church to be "cleansed of apocryphal books filled with myths." Pagels argues that these "myths" were derided by Church leadership because of the subversive impact the Gnostic worldview would have on the Fathers of the Church[15].

> It claimed to offer every initiate direct access to God, of which the bishops and priests might be ignorant. Indeed all who had received *gnosis*, they say, had gone beyond the church's teaching and had transcended the authority of its hierarchy

The Gnostics were invited to what Pagels calls "a state of transformed consciousness" in which they gain unmediated, personal entry to the Kingdom of Heaven that is ordinarily denied to the uninitiated. By changing one's perception, one discovers the cosmos to be infused with new meaning.

> 5. Jesus said, "Recognize what is in your sight, and that which is hidden from you will become plain to you. For there is nothing hidden which will not become manifest."

The gospel of Thomas and the gospel of Mary has been censored from the bible. The Gnostic version of Jesus was a mentor on the path of self-discovery that Pagels compares to psychotherapy: "both acknowledge the need for guidance but only as a provisional measure. The purpose of accepting authority is to learn to outgrow it." If these teachings had been placed in the modern bible the message would be clearer and more focused on the power held within each person. Sadly this decentralized empowering version of Christianity wouldn't survive for very long.

The Censorship of the Christ's Original Teachings

In the 1st century of the Roman Empire, when Christ and Mary lived, women were chattel. Women were more disposable and less valuable than a man. Men, especially

Roman men in power, were seated at the highest societal and state power echelons. Christ's teaching that men and women were equal and children of God threatened the established order of society. Women were property, and a politically savvy Empire would do everything in their power to keep it that way.

Constantine became sole emperor of Rome through victories in a series of military campaigns against other rivals. During these campaigns he converted to Christianity from paganism. There is much debate whether his 'conversion' was sincere, or whether he did so for political gain. By 313, Emperor Constantine legalized Christianity. In 325, Emperor Constantine called for the Council of Nicaea. During this meeting, the Church invented the Nicene Creed, which became the foundation of all church doctrine. The Creed was later revised at the First Council of Constantinople in 381, and the updated form is known as the Nicene Creed.

In subsequent councils, according to other authors, it was here or, perhaps, that certain books were selected for inclusion in the "authorized" canonical Bible while others were banned and discredited. Along the way the original teachings of Christ were forgotten. All references to such teachings were then expunged from the sacred books and these teachings were henceforth suppressed.

The Nicene Creed

The creed reads:

> We believe in one God, the Father Almighty, who makes all things visible and invisible. And in one Lord Jesus Christ, the Son of God, begotten of the Father, before all worlds, Light of Light, very God of very God, begotten, not made, being of one substance of the Father, by whom all things were made; who for us

men and our salvation came down and was incarnate and was made man...

Various Scriptures didn't make cut and it's so funny how they all shared a common theme: the censorship the the divine feminine, the confirmation of the presence of women in Christ's ministry and Yeshua/Jesus's exceptional relationship with Mary Magdalene. For example, the Gospels of Thomas and Philip, among others, confirm that there were three who were always with Jesus: Mary, his mother; Mary, his sister; and Mary of Magdala, who was called his companion.

The idea of God as the father is not only upsetting; it is incorrect. God as the father and Jesus as his only son make zero sense if everyone is a child of God. That would make God, the mother of all life as only mother's give birth to children. The true teaching is that there is the masculine, the male, and the feminine, the female.

The pre-Christian culture of the Greeks revered the divine feminine, which they termed the goddess energy. It had three principal forms: the young virgin (Persphone), the adult mother (Demeter), and the grandmother (the old crone).

For example, in the early church, women held leadership positions. Women were embraced for their gifts, such as their natural talent for healing the wounded. We see this in the scientific data, where 86.0% of all nurses in the United States are women.

The Council of Nicea and Biblical Canon

Where exactly the politicians began to influence the censorship of Christ's original teachings is a source of historical argument. I believe the Council of Nicea met to decide what Scripture would become a part of the canonical Bible and which would be suppressed (and ultimately destroyed). I also believe that the victors write history and they have worked to censor these historical events. This type of behavior is repeated by authoritians throughout recorded history and to believe otherwise is to be naive.

Dr. John Meade teaches that the claims of censorship from the Nicea council appear in a late-ninth-century Greek manuscript called the Synodicon Vetus, which purports to summarize the decisions of Greek councils up to that time. Andreas Darmasius brought this manuscript from Morea in the 16th century. John Pappus edited and published it in 1601 in Strasburg. Here's the relevant section[24]:

> The council made manifest the canonical and apocryphal books in the following manner: placing them by the side of the divine table in the house of God, they prayed, entreating the Lord that the divinely inspired books might be found upon the table, and the spurious ones underneath; and it so happened.

According to this source, the church has its canon because of a miracle that occurred at Nicaea in which the Lord caused the canonical books to stay on the table and the apocryphal or spurious ones to be found underneath. From Pappus's edition of the Synodicon Vetus, this quotation circulated and was cited (sometimes as coming from Pappus himself, not the Greek manuscript he edited!), and eventually found its way into the work of prominent thinkers such as Voltaire (1694–1778). In volume 3 of his Philosophical Dictionary (English translation here) under "Councils" (sec. I), he writes:

> It was by an expedient nearly similar, that the fathers of the same council distinguished the authentic from the apocryphal books of Scripture. Having placed them altogether upon the altar, the apocryphal books fell to the ground of themselves.

A little later in section III, Voltaire adds:

We have already said, that in the supplement to the Council of Nice it is related that the fathers, being much perplexed to find out which were the authentic and which the apocryphal books of the Old and the New Testament, laid them all upon an altar, and the books which they were to reject fell to the ground. What a pity that so fine an ordeal has been lost!

Voltaire earlier mentions that Constantine convened the council. At Nicaea, then, the fathers distinguished the canonical from the apocryphal books by prayer and a miracle. The publication of Pappus's 1601 edition of Synodicon Vetus —and the subsequent citing of the miracle at Nicaea, especially by Voltaire in his Dictionary—leads us to this conclusion.

According to modern history the first list of canonical books for the "New Testament" came in 367 AD, when Athanasius wrote a theological treatise that contained a list of the current 27 books. 30 years later, at the Council of Carthage leaders from various western churches affirmed these books. The other non-canonical books were deemed "not credible" which was the ancient equivalent of using the term "conspiray theory or misinformation" to discredit theories that suits the establishment.

The Petrine Doctrine

The "primacy of Peter" doctrine asserts that Jesus gave Peter, and Peter's successors, authority to function as the sole custodians of true Christian teaching and has since been passed on to each Pope.

Supporters of this doctrine point to one key passage of scripture, in which Jesus said, "you are Peter, and on this rock I will build My church... I will give you the keys of the kingdom of heaven, and whatever you bind on earth will be bound in heaven" (Matthew 16:18–19). A careful study of this passage and other scriptures, however, reveals something very different from what Benedict has in mind. In the original Greek text, Jesus' statement is actually a play on words. The Greek word for "Peter" is petros (meaning a small stone), and the Greek word for "rock" is petra (a huge rock or mountain). The Bible clearly shows that Jesus Christ is the Rock (see 1 Corinthians 10:4; 1 Peter 2:4; see also Psalm 118:22; Isaiah 28:16). He was referring to Himself as the petra, and to His disciple Peter as the petros.

Scripture also shows that the Church was not founded on Peter alone, but was "built on the foundation of the apostles and prophets, Jesus Christ Himself being the chief cornerstone" (Ephesians 2:20). Jesus described His petros— Peter—as a foundation stone of the Church, along with the other apostles and prophets. However, Jesus Christ and His teachings would remain the true foundation of the Church. This is the true meaning of Matthew 16:18–19. Attempts to twist this verse into a statement of Peter's exclusive authority are simply not biblical. This is a false teaching!

This is why the Roman claim for power based on Peter's supposed primacy has never been accepted by the Eastern Orthodox churches, and why it was rejected by the Protestant reformers (see Civilization Past & Present, Wallbank, p. 133).

The outcome of this dispute is so evident in Mary's gospel. No wonder Mary's Gospel was excluded from the bible! We know that Peter does not believe Mary as many men thought of women as less than people at that moment in time. Peter does not believe that Mary was given secret teachings from Christ to pass on to the other disciples.

In the Gospel of Mary, Levi comes to Mary's defense in Mary and represents a voice of the early Christian movement who believed Mary.

Then Mary wept and said to Peter, "My brother Peter, what are you thinking? Do you really think that I thought this up by myself in my heart, or that I'm lying about the Savior?"

In response Levi said to Peter, "Peter, you've always been angry. Now I see you debating with this woman like the adversaries. But if the Savior made her worthy, who are you then to reject her? Surely the Savior knows her very well. That's why he loved her more than us. "Rather we should be ashamed, clothe ourselves with perfect Humanity, acquire it for ourselves as he instructed us, and preach the gospel, not laying down any other rule or other law beyond what the Savior said."

By 594, Pope Gregory's homily 33, would rebrand Saint Mary as a prostitute. Mary's status as the companion of Christ, the first to receive his teachings on how to perceive him from within the heart and how to become one with God would be lost for millenia.

Mary is the Apostle of the Apostles and she is the only one Christ would rightfully anoint to lead his church!

The Gospel of Mary

Three copies of the Gospel of Mary have been recovered - two in Greek and one in Coptic. The earliest evidence of the lost gospel of Mary Magdalene was discovered in 1896 and is called the Berlin Codex[25]. All three versions of her gospel are missing a few parts. However, her work contains some amazing information.

Mary asks Christ: "So now, Lord, does a person who sees a vision see it with the soul or with the spirit?"

The Savior answered: "A person does not see with the soul or spirit. Rather the mind, which exists between the two, sees the vision, and that is what..."

The translation of *mind* from Greek to English isn't what we think of when we hear the word mind. The word in greek is *Nous*. Yes, the same *Nous* the Greeks used to describe the perception or vision of one's soul. Perception is reality; that's what it is called PR. Perhaps Mary, the foremost disciple of Christ, had her gospel removed because it would reveal how we perceive the divine directly from without our souls[26].

Mary's teachings threaten the "spiritual authority" of the institution of the Church. If how we truly see is not with eyesight but our gut, intuition, and vision, a form of spiritual perception that allows us to know what is real, true, and everlasting, and it comes from within us, then no one has power over us.

Mary taught we are souls. She taught that sexuality, sex, and gender ascribed to the body are ultimately illusory. These differences belong to the world of flesh, not to the world of spirit. We are all souls that our physical form cannot define. Spiritual authority can't be determined by sex, gender, or sexuality but rather by the depth of one's spiritual transformation and subsequent wholeness. One can only claim spiritual authority based solely on the spiritual homework they have done to unite the ego with the soul.

That's revolutionary. That's beautiful. And that's precisely why it was removed.

Union. Unity. These were the original teachings of Jesus and Mary. We must integrate the yin and the yang. The light and the dark. The ego and the soul. The divine masculine and the divine feminine. The form and the formless.

Every nature, every modeled form,
every creature exists in and with each other.
- Mary 2:2

In Aramaic, the language of Jesus, we can become *ihidaya*, meaning undivided. This is the ultimate goal. Not a distant salvation is given to us through repentance, guilt, or shame. We realize this aspect of who we are, our divinity, our angelic form. The goal of Mary's gospel was to become a true child of humanity, which means fully human and divine.

We are Good

The most important message of Mary's gospel is that we are good and that our goodness can never be lost.

> Then Peter said to him, "You have been explaining every topic to us; tell us one other thing. What is the sin of the world?"
>
> The Savior replied, "There is no such thing as sin. Sin doesn't exist, but you're the ones who make sin when you act in accordance with the nature of adultery, which is called 'sin.' That's why the Good came among you, up to the things of every nature in order to restore it within its root. That's why you get sick and die, because you love what tricks you. Anyone who can understand should understand!"
>
> - Gospel of Mary 3:1-3

That there is nothing sinful about being human. There is nothing sinful about your body. There is nothing sinful about sex. There is nothing sinful about sexuality. Being human is not a punishment. Life is a gift. God gave you the gift of life. You are one of God's children. And no one can ever take that right away from you.

The Savior replied, "There is no such thing as sin; rather, you yourselves are what produces sin when you act in accordance with the nature of [ignorance], which is called 'sin.' For this reason, the Good came among you, pursuing (the good) which belongs to every nature" - Mary 3:3-5

In Meggan Watterson's book *Mary Magdalene Revealed: The First Apostle, Her Feminist Gospel, and the Christianity We Haven't Tried Yet* she writes the original translation for sin means to forget or to miss the mark. Sin is simply a moment of ignorance. Often we forget that we are a soul living in a human body, and then we act from that state of ignorance. This is a moment of ignorance. Through ignorance, we can feel lost, but Goodness is woven into our nature; it is part of our soul.

The body isn't sinful. "Sin" is when we believe we are only this body, identify with our material needs and desires, and fear the ego dreams up. Sin in Mary's Gospel is not about a list of laws or committing the wrong action. "Sin" is mistaking the ego for the true self rather than remembering that the true self is the soul[27].

True freedom means having the power to define what being free means in our own lives. Mary's Gospel is considered an "ascent narrative," which describes a path we can navigate to liberate the soul, not in death but this lifetime. According to the Gospel of Mary, Ascension is best described as a descent into one's heart space. The deeper we go within our spirit, the more we discover the Kingdom, the Goodness, and the spark of God within us. The point of Mary's gospel is not to suggest we need to become someone "better." It's about learning to see with the eyes of goodness all the love that surrounds us and the superpower of love that comes from within us. The soul ascends because it does not seek to judge or attempt to dominate anything or anyone.

The disciples of Christ were upset with the revelation that Christ gave Mary unique teachings and not them. The record shows they argued and expressed contempt and disbelief that Christ could reveal such powerful teachings to Mary, a woman, and not to them. Peter was distraught. But as Levi pointed out, if Christ considered her worth, who would they disregard her? Christ loved her completely.

It is high time to repair the idea of Mary Magdalene - the Holy Saint of the Most High. Many misbelieve the blasphemous gossip of Pope Gregory in Homily 33 when he forever defiled the good name of Mary. Dear God, please grant and his family line forgiveness.

The Gospel of Philip, found in the 20th century among the Nag Hammadi Scriptures in Egypt, explicitly confirmed that Mary and Christ had a relationship that distinguished her from the other disciples: "The companion [koinosos] of the Son is Miriam of Magdala. The Teacher [rabbi] loved her more than all the disciples; he often kissed her on the mouth" [28]

If Jesus' teachings were so "male-focused," why would Christ choose a woman as his *koinonos*, his spiritual companion, his equal? Christ's love for and partnership with Mary Magdalene, virtually an enslaved person in Peter's eyes, the lowest of the lower levels of existence, caused Peter extreme distress and confusion and threatened his world order. How could Christ love Mary, a woman, more than him, a man?

Do not lay down any rule beyond
what I have determined for you,
- Gospel of Mary

In the Gospel of Mary - a gospel that predates the exclusion of women from positions of power within the church in the 4th century - perhaps he's referring to the illusion that a person can.

Christ taught that we are all equal in the eyes of god, or the Good, as described in Mary's gospel, leveled the society's beliefs that divided the people by sex, race, property, wealth, and citizenship. Women were defined by their social status as daughters, wives, and mothers. And women, no matter their social standing, were considered property with as few rights as enslaved persons. Christ gave his life to share that teaching, and the Catholic Church ripped it right out to appease their political masters.

Sophia: The Divine Feminine

"For she is a vapour of the power of God, and a certain pure emanation of the glory of the almighty God: and therefore no defiled thing cometh into her."
King Solomon

Image credit @gnostic_alchemy

The original Christians were taught that the divine had both a masculine and a feminine face. The Divine Feminine was known as Sophia, the wise Goddess. Apostle Paul teaches, 'Among the initiates we speak of Sophia, for it is the secret of Sophia that is taught in our Mysteries.' When initiates of the Inner Mysteries of Christianity partook in the Holy

Communion, it was Sophia's passion and suffering remembered.

The prayer would be offered: May Sophia fill your inner being and increase in you her Gnosis. It was Sophia who was petitioned, 'Come, hidden Mother, come, you who are made manifest in your words, and give joy and rest to those who are bound to you. Come and partake in this Eucharist which we perform in your name, and in the love feast for which we have assembled at your invitation.

Paul refers to Christ as the "power of God and the Wisdom (Sophia) of God" (1 Corinthians 1:24), and states that Christ "became for us Wisdom (Sophia) from God" (1 Corinthians 1:30). The book of Proverbs describes Wisdom as the "way," the "life," and the "path" (4:11,22,26). The Gospel of John records Jesus' saying, "I am the way, and the truth, and the life" (John 14:6).

Sophia is one of the most powerful biblical Divine Feminine images. "Mother" may be an ambivalent image for some people, depending on their experiences with their own mothers or with the image of Mary. Wisdom, Sophia, helps us experience our own wisdom more powerfully. Sophia invites us to develop a partnership relationship with Her.

The eradication of this Christian Goddess by the patriarchal Roman Catholic Church has left us all motherless children. Women have been denied a sympathetic rapport with the Divine Feminine. Men have been denied a love-affair with the female face of God[1].

Even though Wisdom (Hokmah, Sophia) is a prominent name for God in the Bible, She is ignored and excluded in most congregations. Just as women have been excluded from leadership and still are in numerous congregations, Divine Wisdom may be excluded from worship because the Bible presents Divine Wisdom as female and refers to Divine

Wisdom as "She." Also, people don't always want to know about Her paths of peace and justice "All Her paths are peace. She is a tree of life" (Proverbs 3:17-18). Sophia is one of the many biblical female images of God. Including these female images along with other biblical divine images to create gender-balanced worship will expand our spiritual experience and contribute to equality and justice in human relationships.

King Solomon, King of the Tribe of Judah, was the son of King David, King of the United Kingdom of Israel. In the Wisdom of Solomon we read:

"I called upon God, and Sophia, the Spirit of Wisdom, came unto me. I loved Her, and sought Her out from my youth, I desired to make Her my spouse. I was a lover of Her beauty. She is conversant with God, She magnifieth His Nobility. Yea, the Lord of all things Himself loves Her.

I preferred Her before Scepters and Thrones, and esteemed riches nothing in comparison to Her.

Neither compared I unto Her any precious stone, because all gold in respect of Her is as a little sand, and silver shall be counted as clay before Her. I loved Her above health and beauty, and chose to have Her above Light: for the Light that cometh from Her never fails.

Wisdom reacheth from one end of creation to another mightily: and sweetly doth She order all things. For Wisdom, which is the worker of all things, taught me: for in Her is an understanding spirit, holy, one only, manifold, subtle, lively, clear, undefiled, plain, not subject to hurt, loving the thing that is good, penetrating Intelligence which cannot be confounded, and always ready to do good. Sophia is more moving than any motion: She passeth and goeth through all things by reason of Her Purity. Sophia is privy to the mysteries of the knowledge of God and a lover of His works. She is more beautiful than the sun, and above all the order of the stars: being compared with the Light, She is found before it. She is the Breath of the Power of God, and a pure influence flowing from the Glory of the Almighty: therefore can no defiled thing fall into Her.

She is the Brightness of the Everlasting Light, the unspoiled mirror of the Power of God, and the image of His Goodness. "Being but One, She can do all things: and remaining in Herself, She maketh all things new: and in all ages entering into holy souls, She maketh them friends of God and Prophets. For God loveth none but him that dwelleth with Wisdom."

The Lost Teaching of Reincarnation

The early Christian philosophers adopted the Greek concept of *nous*, the soul's immortality, and thought of the soul as being created by God and infused into the body at conception. The Gospel of Thomas, one of the lost texts found in the 1940s, states: "These are the hidden words that the living Jesus spoke and Didymos Judas Thomas wrote them down."

1 Gospel of Thomas. Jesus said: "whoever discovered the interpretation of these sayings shall not taste death."

In the first passage of the Gospel of Thomas, we read about Jesus speaking about death and achieving a sense of immortality, similar to the Ancient Greeks and Egyptians. In Aramaic, the word death means "existing elsewhere" in the language that Christ spoke.

We were born not of blood, nor of the will of the flesh, nor of the will of man, but of God.
John 1:13

Though modern Christianity does not believe in reincarnation, many Christian sects have believed in the transmigration of souls throughout history. In 1945, researchers discovered some early Judeo-Christian writings. Two years later, the world heard about the Dead Sea Scrolls, the discovery which changed biblical history. These texts teach us that early Christians and Jews followed the teachings of Jesus - including the concept of resurrection.

Herbert Puryear, author or *Why Jesus Taught Reincarnation - A Better News Gospel,* explains there are several examples of this found in ancient resources. The oldest texts provide two concepts of resurrection: spiritual and bodily. The spiritual rebirth by the Holy Spirit is also known as being born again. The bodily resurrection of a human could also be called reincarnation. One of the earliest important figures in the Orthodox Church, Origen (185 AD to 254 AD), believed that the soul existed before birth and claimed that Jesus also taught the same. He suggested that pre-existence was found in the Hebrew Scriptures and the teachings of Jesus[29].

"The writings of Clement of Alexandria — a disciple of the apostle Peter — suggest that his master received a few secret teachings from Jesus. One of them was related to the concept of physical and spiritual rebirth," according to Ancient Origins.

A fragment suggests that Jesus knew about reincarnation and past lives. Someone in the crowd asked him: "What sign showest thou then, that we may see and believe thee? What dost thou work? Our fathers did eat manna in the desert; as it is written, He gave them bread from heaven to eat. Then Jesus said unto them, Verily verily, I say unto you, Moses gave you not that bread from heaven; but My Father giveth you the true bread from heaven" - John 6:30-32

Jesus doesn't refer to "your fathers" but "you," signifying that the story is connected with every person. In Deuteronomy 18:15, Moses said: "The Lord your God will raise up for you a Prophet like me from your midst, from your brethren. Him you shall hear."

In deference to the Roman Empire, Christ's original teachings on reincarnation were removed from the catechetical teachings most likely during the installation of the Nicene Creed. By 553 AD, the secret teachings of Jesus were declared heresy at the Second Council of Constantinople. Many claim at this council meeting they simply banned the idea of the soul as proposed by Origen. However, there is many nuances to what the rabbi taught and as such the victors write the history.

At the beginning of the Christian era, reincarnation was one of the pillars of belief. Without it (as later happened), Christianity would lose all logic. How could a benevolent, loving God give one person a silver spoon and leave the next to starve in their ostensibly only earthly life? Early Church elders and theologians, like Origenes, Basilides and St Gregory, taught reincarnation of the soul as a matter of course—it was written in the Bible, after all. Nowadays, most Christians suspect blasphemy if someone references reincarnation.

The Roman Church decided to destroy all the teachings which talked about it. The Catholic doctrine and the priests' source of wealth could have been in danger if people believed that they would come back to life many times. The old knowledge faced the same fate as many ancient books by pre-Christian writers. The bishops were afraid of the knowledge which could prove that the institution of the Church wasn't the only option to bring "eternal life" to people.

Many doubt Christ's teaching on Reincarnation simply because they believe it is not in the Bible. This important teaching can be deduced or inferred from passages that have been largely ignored by those unable to explain the references satisfactorily. These are the actual passages where Jesus teaches the Doctrine of Reincarnation:

> In Matthew 4:5, Behold, I will send you Elijah the prophet before the coming of the great and dreadful day of the Lord.

> In Matthew 11 and 17, Jesus tells his disciples that Elias reincarnated as John the Baptist.

> In Matthew 11:14-15, Jesus says, for all the Prophets and the Law prophesied until John. And if you are willing to accept it, he is the Elijah who was to come. **15** Whoever has ears, let them hear.

> In Matthew 16, if reincarnation is not true, do you think Jesus would remain silent and allow the

disciples to believe in it? Don't you think he would have rebuked them for believing a false doctrine?

In Matthew 9, Jesus is conspicuously silent after the disciples refer to reincarnation (the past life and sins) of the man born blind. Isn't this, at least, a very suspicious circumstance that merits your further thought?"

In Corinthians, Apostle Paul says there is a natural and spiritual body.

What Jesus himself taught, his so-called followers just a few hundred years after his death, denied. Deciding that they know better than their Lord, the church leaders voted to drop reincarnation and karma from the catechetical teachings.

For what is a man profited, if he shall gain the whole world, and lose his own soul Mathew 16:26

Reincarnation is God's gift to us to enable us to grow to a point where we can accept God's other gifts. The reincarnation of souls in human bodies is the same process as the incarnation of the Son of God in the man Jesus Christ. As souls, we, like Jesus, are spiritual beings who incarnate in human bodies. The mechanics and the purposes are essentially the same:

The works of God should be made manifest - John 9:3

No man hath ascended up to heaven, but he that came down from heaven - John 3:13

No one goes to a spiritual plane except a spiritual being. If the soul will always be in eternity, was there ever a time when it was not? If in heaven, the essence of the souls is not limited by time or space, nor by a physical body, then what is the nature of this essence?

Reincarnation is a natural result of the incarnation. Christ, a spiritual being, came into the flesh - incarnated - on a bodhisattva mission (loving-kindness). All souls incarnated on earth have a special mission to accomplish during their lives. We are all perfect divine beings made in God's image; children of God, it is your destiny to be once again confirmed, in perfection, to that which you naturally are. It is only with the concept of reincarnation that we may truly assume full responsibility for all that we are and all that we are experiencing[30].

Without reincarnation, the gospel of Christ has become a narrow and elitist religious system. Why would Jesus lecture about the soul if it didn't exist? There are many reasons, some understandable, for the church to eliminate the teaching of reincarnation; however, none of these reasons are good. For example, Christian Orthodoxy is very hostile to Christ's teachings of the divine nature of the human family. They teach a materialistic view of humanity: that our true reality is physical and only physical. Funny then that quantum physics invalidates those teachings and supports a divine hypothesis. The Orthodox Church even rebels against Christ's words: Ye Are Gods. The Church has a rich history of denying and disowning its Spirit-filled prophets because they were psychics, healers, and mystics. Protestants and Catholics are so anxiety-ridden about the manifestation of the Spirit they condemn offhand any testimony without inquiry. Some people complain against the teaching of reincarnation by saying: "If I lived before, why don't I remember?" [31]

> But the Comforter, which is the Holy Spirit, whom the Father will send in my name, he shall teach you all things, and bring all things to your remembrance, whatsoever I have said unto you. John 14:26

We may turn to the words of Master Yeshua to understand

that our remembrance will come only as we permit ourselves to be quickened by the spirit. This is one of the most important reasons Jesus taught reincarnation. He wanted us to have and understand the gift of Spirit called remembrance. When souls incarnate, they bring special gifts developed in previous lives. They enter for the specific purpose of sharing those gifts with the world. Where would Christ have learned this teaching of reincarnation? The Jewish people believe in and teach the concept of the soul but do not focus much on reincarnation. The teachings of reincarnation are infused throughout the spirituality of the Hindu and Buddhist peoples. Perhaps Jesus learned these teachings during his lost years.

The Lost Years of Christ

We know that Jesus has many years of his life accounted for in the Bible. Ancient manuscripts discovered in India may help us fill in the blanks. In the early 1900s, a Russian man traveled to India. While traveling, he broke his leg and was taken to the Hemis Monastery in Ladakh to heal. His name was Nicolos Notovich. He learned from the lamas that Jesus Christ had been to India, according to records in a manuscript preserved in the monastery's library. He had the manuscript brought to him and got it translated into Russian. He eventually wrote a book entitled *The Unknown Life of Jesus Christ,* discussing Christ's journey in India; sadly, when the manuscript came to the attention of the Catholic Church, they did everything in their power to bury the story. The Church used its political power to discredit and censor the book.

Swami Abhedananda, a disciple of Sri Ramakrishna and Founder of Ramakrishna Vedanta Math, heard of this legend and his curiosity drove him to visit the Hemis Monastery so he could verify for himself this hidden legend of Jesus. In 1987 he published his book *Journey into Kashmir and Tibet.* The head lama of the monastery informed him there are two copies of the manuscript on Issa (as he is known in the east) or Jesus Christ. The original manuscript is in the language of Pali. The manuscript in Himis has been translated from Pali to Tibetan. It consists of fourteen chapters and two hundred twenty-four couplets (slogans). The Swami got some portion of the manuscript translated with the help of the lama attending to him.

The Issa Manuscript

Noted from Chapter 12 of *The Journey into Kashmir and Tibet* are the given activities of Jesus Christ in India according to the Issa manuscript [32]:

10 Issa stepped into his thirteenth year by and by. According to the national custom of the Israelis, this is the right age for matrimony. His parents lived the life of humble folks

11 Their humble cottage came to be crowded with people proud of wealth and pedigree. Each of them was eager to accept Issa as his son-in-law

12 Issa was unwilling to marry. He had already earned fame through his expounding the true nature of God. At the proposal of marriage, he resolved to leave the house of his father in secret.

13 At this time, his great desire was to achieve full realization of god-head and learn religion at the feet of those who have attained perfection through meditation

1 At the age of fourteen, he (Jesus) crossed Sind and entered the holy land of the Aryans

2 As he was passing all along through the land of the five rivers, his benign appearance, face radiating peace, and comely forehead attracted Jain

devotees who knew him to be one who had received blessings from God Himself

3 And they requested him to stay with them in their monastery. But he turned down their request; at this time, he did not like to accept anyone's service

4 in the course of time, he arrived at Jagannath Dham (puri), the abode of Vyasa Krishna, and became the disciple of the Brahmins. He endeared himself to all and learned how to read, understand and expound the Vedas.

After this, he went on a pilgrimage to Rajagriha, Benares, etc. This took six years, and then he started for Kapilavastu, where Buddha had been born. Then he spent six years in the company of Buddhist mendicants, where he mastered Pali to perfection and studied all the Buddhist Scriptures. From here, he went to Nepal and traveled to the Himalayan region. Then he went westwards. He came to Persia, the abode of Zoroastrians, from where his fame soon spread in all directions. Then he returned to his native land once again at the age of 29. After this, he started preaching his message of peace among his brethren suffering under oppression.

The Gospel of Luke (Luke 3:23) states that Jesus was "about 30 years of age" at the start of his ministry. A chronology of Jesus typically has the date of the start of his ministry, 11 September 26 AD; others have estimated at around AD 27–29 and the end in the range AD 30–36. This timeline matches up almost perfectly with the testimony from the Hemis Manuscript.

The Tomb of Christ

Swami Abhedananda reports the Lama said that Jesus Christ came secretly to Kashmir after his resurrection and lived in a monastery surrounded by many disciples. He was considered a saint of a high order, and devotees from many lands came to see him and joined him as disciples. The original manuscript in Pali was prepared three or four years after Christ's demise based on reports from Tibetans who saw him at this time of his life and the accounts received from wandering merchants who had witnessed his crucifixion. If someone collates in a single book all the observations made by scholars on the subject of Christ's sojourn in India, it will undoubtedly be a valuable addition to the historical record.

Many wonder about Christ's ascension to heaven. It's interesting to note that Kashmir, the northernmost part of India, is more popularly known as 'Heaven on Earth'. In a city called Srinagar located in the Kashmir region of India there is a place known as *Roza Bal*. Roza in Persian means holy, and Bal in Kashmiri language means shrine. In the year 1899, Mirza Ghulam Ahmad, the founder of the Ahmadiyya movement claimed that this tomb belongs to Jesus Christ, about which he wrote extensively in his book, Masih Hindustan-mein (Jesus in India).

The tomb is the burial place of *Yuz Asaf*. The name *Yuz Asaf* relates to Jesus, or *Hazrat Isa* or *Issa*. Interestingly, 'Issa' is the Tibetan name of Jesus and it is Hazrat Isa or Isa as stated in the Quran. This has been carried down through the *Farhang-Asafia*, Volume one, which explains how Jesus healed some leper who then became asaf or purified, meaning healed. The word yuz means leader. Thus, Yuz Asaf became a common reference to Jesus as "leader of the healed".

According to him, Jesus survived the crucifixion, traveled to the Indian subcontinent where he lived until his death at the age of 120 and was buried in the beautiful valley of Kashmir. They claim that he must have chosen Kashmir because Kashmiris are considered as one among the ten 'missing tribes' of Israel, out of 12 Jewish tribes, who later settled in the new countries, especially along the Silk route in

Afghanistan and Kashmir, after they were drove out of Israel by the Assyrians in around 700 BC. Hence, even today, many Kashmiri tribes call themselves Bnei Israel/ Bene or Bnai Israel or children of Israel[1].

This site of this tomb in Kashmir was recorded as a 'sacred' site in many Buddhist and Hindu sources before the Islamic period; hence, it attracts followers of Hinduism, Islam, Christianity and Buddhism.

Yeshua: the Buddha, the Healer, the Master

Most Christians are unaware that meditation is actually mentioned again and again in the Bible. For instance, in the Old Testament's book of Genesis (24:63) it states: "And Isaac went out to meditate in the fields at the eventide, and he lifted up his eyes, and saw, and behold the camels were coming." Also, in Joshua 1:8: "This book of the law shall not depart out of thy mouth; but thou shalt meditate therein day and night, that thou mayest observe to do according to all that is written herein; for then thou shalt make thy way prosperous and then thou shalt have good success." Throughout the Psalms, there are at least 14 verses which talk about meditation. Add on top all of the Bible's calls to "meditate on the word of God", and it's very difficult to deny meditation's place in the Christian faith.

There's lots of evidence suggesting that Jesus was, at a minimum, familiar with meditation, and much more likely, even practiced himself. For starters, the Torah mentions that, while growing up in Jerusalem, Jesus spent time around meditators. Later on, as a Jewish Rabbi, he would have fully understood the purpose of Isaac meditating in the fields.

During his years of traveling the Holy Lands (and beyond), it's a near certainty that Jesus met many meditators. In fact, a number of scholars believe that

Jesus traveled to "meditation friendly" locales like India and the Far East at some point. And with the similarities between his parables and the teachings of Buddha, many scholars believe that Jesus spent considerable time studying in Buddhist temples. So it's highly likely that the Prince of Peace had exposure to meditation.

A commonly held belief in meditation friendly religions like Hinduism & Buddhism is that, if you want to find God, then "look within." Interesting then that Christ reminds us the Kingdom is within. In Matthew 4:16, we read: the people living in darkness have seen a great light; on those living in the land of the shadow of death a light has dawned. Considering Christ studied with the meditation masters, is this not but a reference to the process of meditation. When one meditates the eyes are closed and when you go deep enough into a meditative state you become one with the light?

There is good evidence suggesting that Jesus did indeed meditate. For instance, it's believed by many scholars that Jesus's Sermon on the Mount was delivered from a "meditative state" (rather than a purely waking state). While Jesus is known for spending 40 days and 40 nights "praying" in the desert, the specifics of his "prayer" technique are not clearly defined. Some scholars believe that many of those days and nights in the desert were actually spent in meditation, rather than prayer alone. While prayer is the act of "talking to God", meditation is the act of "listening to God," which more closely mirrors what occurred during those history changing 40 days and 40 night.

In Matthew 6:22, Jesus said, if your eye be single, then you whole body will be full of light. Perhaps he is speaking of the third eye or pineal gland as Rabbi Harry reminds us the Jewish ancestors and sages were once very consciously connected to the third eye.

Yeshua/Jesus was a profoundly spiritual man who devoted his life to delivering messages of love and peace. Long before humanity turned him into the figurehead of the world's largest religion, Jesus was the original hippie. He communed with beggars, prostitutes, lepers, and adulterers. Society ignored these people or publicly stoned them to death for their "sins." And Jesus loved them.

He was a mystic, a seer, and a lover of all humanity. However, he wasn't entirely well-liked throughout his community. Not thrilled with his claims to be "the son of God," the Romans brutally crucified him. However, perhaps there is more to this claim than the obvious interpretation. Maybe Jesus had experienced scenarios that brought him so close to God that he became one with the Source.

We know now that Yeshua, a Jewish man, grew up in a Jewish world that conducted ceremonial rituals using psychedelics. In addition, his studies in the far east with the Hindu, Buddhist, and Zoroastrian masters of his time - well versed in their ritualistic use of psychedelic brews and sacraments - most likely involved him partaking in the sacred ritual of Soma/Haoma.

Exposure to these teachings are known as the Sanatana Dharma - which is documented as the world's oldest living religious path. Scientists and historians date it back to *at least* 8500 years old though Hindu sacred books say it has always existed - and the Hindus have been around for 80,000 years. It can also be said that it is the most diverse of religions. It is not a religion; it's more like a collection of philosophies.

As one of the highest living masters in history, Yeshua returned from the east to share these teachings with the people. He taught the eternal gospel of love and oneness and used his full faculties and gifts to heal men, women, and children. The ritualistic use of the psychedelic sacraments left a huge impression on early Christian cults.

While it's impossible to verify that Jesus did eat psilocybin mushrooms, there is clear evidence that he consumed psychedelic wine. Early shamans used psychedelics for healing, and Jesus was known as a powerful healer. For example, there is the story of Jesus healing a leper. The Great Canterbury Psalter, a masterpiece of medieval poetry and prayers, this story is different from the version in the Bible.

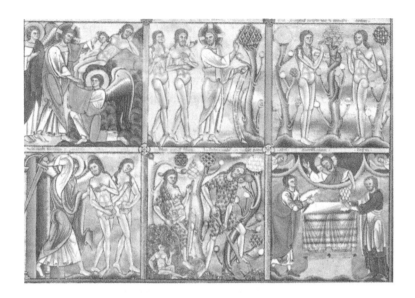

Here, the leper holds a scroll in his left hand, which translates as "Master, if you want, you may cleanse me," but rather than pointing the scroll at Jesus, he points to Jesus' scroll. Jesus' scroll says, "I want to be cleansed."

Similarly, the author of The Great Canterbury Psalter relayed other stories of psychedelic mushrooms. It is thought that perhaps this story indicates Jesus has realized the healing powers of the magic mushrooms.

Yeshua Hamaschiach

Yeshua HaMaschiach means Jesus the Messiah. Yeshua fulfilled at least 300 prophecies during His earthly ministry. As the Jewish messiah, he brought the hidden Torah back to the Jewish people. In his famous "sermon on the mountain," recorded in Matthew chapter 5, amazing declarations were made, and when we understand them in their proper Hebraic light, we can see that they were subtle addresses of the Lost Torah, discussed in Chapter 9. He ends these glimpses of what it means to live not only by the black fire but by the white fire of the Torah in Matthew 5:48.

> *Be perfect, therefore, as your*
> *Heavenly Father is perfect*

There are a couple of things we need to understand about this statement. In the first place, the word that is translated "perfect" literally means "be complete." So often, the New Testament and the Old Testament will describe people as being upright and righteous—not in the sense that they have achieved total moral perfection, but rather that they have reached a singular level of maturity in their growth in terms of spiritual integrity. However, in this statement, it's certainly legitimate to translate it using the English word perfect. For example, "Be ye complete as your heavenly Father is complete." Now remember that our heavenly Creator is perfectly complete! So if we are to mirror God in that way, we are to mirror God in moral excellence as well as in other ways. In fact, the basic call to a person in this world is to be a reflection of the character of God. That's what it means to be created in the image of God.

Yeshua commanded of us to be perfect because He had just revealed prematurely some of the New Torah that Judaism says Messiah is expected to give to us. He showed glimpses of what it means to live the perfect Torah—the union of the two Torahs together and without lack. He could thus make that request of us to be perfect in our performance of the Torah, to stand in the fire and be fire, as the Midrash Tanchuma and Talmud, tractate Chagigah had previously asserted. We see another instance of the Messiah calling us to be more than we are and perform the white fire of the Torah in John 13:34.

> *A new commandment I give to you,*
> *that you shall love one another;*
> *how that I have loved you*
> *even you shall love one another.*

He dictates a new commandment, which is to love each other. This is really the original commandment found in Leviticus 19:18 to love our neighbor, but Yeshua has invoked upon it the deeper reality of what that means. He does this with the qualification of "how that I have loved you." We are not to love just "as you love yourself," but to look to the perfect example of love, of the Messiah who lays down His very life for us, as the standard of love we are to live. This is the white fire that surrounds the black fire of the second greatest commandment. Living from a place of loving-kindness is to live in the perfect image of God for God is Love.

Put simply, Yeshua the Messiah called for all beings to live the two Torahs right now in this world when we understand the context of these passages! He has already initiated teaching the revealed Torah and its unrevealed deeper intents, just like Judaism has told us Messiah shall do!

With eyes of flesh we might see just one single written Torah preserved in the Hebrew text for us to perform as a religious document. But if we look closer with the eyes of faith, we are able to glimpse the second Torah that vivifies and gives even deeper meaning to the written text. In order to appreciate what He has given us, we must seek to know the Torahs in their fullest measure and expression: the black and the white fire united together.

Christhood

Christhood is not about belief or faith, not even about knowledge and understanding. The essence of Christhood is a direct, inner experience of the reality that all life is one and thus we are not separated from God or from each other. Obviously, this is in direct opposition to the awareness with which we grew up with in western culture. We have been conditioned to see ourselves as separated from God and each other. This illusion of separation is the main illusion produced by the consciousness of anti-christ. The consciousness of anti-christ uses a special form of logic, called dualistic logic or serpentine logic, to create, justify and uphold the illusion that we are separate beings. It has even created an entirely false path to salvation, designed to make us believe that by following a religion here on earth we can qualify for entry into heaven without overcoming the illusion that we are separate beings[33].

Christhood makes it clear that the ONLY way to enter heaven is to transcend separation and come into oneness with the indivisible mind of Christ. The main function of the consciousness of Christ is to uphold oneness between the Creator and its creation, meaning us. The true meaning of Jesus' message of salvation is that it means coming into oneness: "I and my Father are one."

In Conclusion

Wounds from a sincere friend are better
than many kisses from an enemy
Proverbs 27:6

Bible scholars agree that the first Gospels were written decades after the life of Christ. What remains are copies of copies of ancient Greek manuscripts, which have thousands of discrepancies between them. Some books that were once considered part of the canon (the collection of texts considered sacred and authoritative by Christians) were later deemed false gospel and removed. There are whole books of the canon, like the Book of Revelation, which for hundreds of years were not included because they were deemed false gospel. The process of determining which texts should be considered part of the canon was a human process and therefore uncertain. There are other whole books like the Shepherd of Hermas, which you probably haven't heard of, but for centuries it was considered part of the canon and then was later jettisoned as false gospel. Generations of Christians lived and died being guided by gospel that is now deemed both incomplete and mistaken.

Jesus's message was that the cause of evil and suffering was not God's anger at Adam and Eve or his continuing anger at violations of his rules of cleanliness and ritual purity. The cause was human beings' failure to recognize their oneness with each other and to follow the Golden Rule and love one another. His death was a demonstration of such love, not a ritual sacrifice in appeasement of divine wrath. Jesus urged people to let compassion, not obedience to the Law, determine how they would treat one another. When he revealed his beliefs, some people rejoiced, others objected. He was set upon by the powers of Church and State, Temple and Emperor, and killed as a heretic and a troublemaker. But because of his goodness and his willingness to accept life as it comes—"not my will, but thine"—he passed through death and returned bearing the boon of liberation for everybody.

Until the 4th century, 325 AD; the true original teachings of Jesus were commonly known. We know that these teachings were lost because we have recovered this information (The Nag Hammadi Library and the Coptic texts). Today many good souls are working to spread the word of the true Gospel of Christ. These lost teachings are the sacred truth of Jesus that were intended to be passed into the hands of all people. We know that Jesus' mission was not exclusive to healing people. He created a tribe, a community, an institution dedicated to bringing his enduring light, true peace, and goodness into all the world and every part of society. However; due to the influence of money, power, and politics; the true original teachings were replaced by an institution that has transformed into a beast.

Both history and current events of modern history reveal a flawed, sinful, and unhealthy church marred by acts of genocide, rape, pedophilia, sexual abuse, misogyny, injustice, and oppression. The contemporary church is wrecked with bickering, division, idol worship, false and shallow teachings, and a Christian industrial complex formed around greed and vanity. This is why the true message of the apostles was a warning to the true original Christians about the danger of the Church organization. The church can only witness the truth of Jesus by returning to holy communion with the sacred psychedelic sacraments and the vedic teachings of Yeshua, serving with humility, operating transparently, and having the integrity to admit its failures.

CHAPTER 11:

Psychedelics in Islam

Islamic art and architecture reflect how Muslims relate to the universe. It is a spiritual representation of nature, not a replication of it. This is intended to allow the artist – and practitioners who view the ornamentation – to feel closer to Allah. In Islam, beauty has always been closely tied to the divine[1]. One of the hadiths (traditions or sayings) of the Prophet Muhammad reads, "Allah is beautiful, and he loves beauty."

This essence is seen throughout Islamic architecture, with certain mosques regarded as some of the world's most magnificent and awe-inspiring buildings.

After looking at the dazzling interiors of a few mosques, you could be forgiven for assuming that there's some deep connection between psychedelics and Islam. Islamic art is commonly associated with geometric patterns. This is because the Qur'an vigilantly avoids giving physical depictions of God. The fact that the Qur'an makes a specific effort not to reify God is especially significant. This is why Muslims don't worship sculptures or physical representations of God.
I find this especially significant because the apparent parallel between the perfect geometrical patterns prevalent in Islamic art and the sacred, organized geometry universal in oncoming psychedelic hallucinations are intriguingly similar.

Prophet Muhammed and Psychedelics

Many Muslims might be offended by the idea that the Prophet Muhammad could have relied on a sacred plant for his prophetic powers. Yet there is evidence in Islamic tradition. A series of illustrations in a 15th-century Timurid manuscript record the Mi'raj, the ascent through the seven heavens by Mohammed, the Prophet of Islam.

Several of the illustrations in the Herat manuscript depict Burāq or Al Buraq - an angelic being with the body of a horse, the head of a woman, and a peacock's tail who helped Mohammed achieve his ascent to Allah or enlightenment - with the distinctive red and white spotted skin of the A. muscaria mushroom, exact in the smallest detail [2]. Many scholars believe that the events of Muhammed's journey occurred as dreams or revelatory visions or that the experience was purely spiritual.

Detail from the page showing the Night Journey (Mi'raj) of the Prophet Muhammad from, Mira'j-nameh, Manuscrit

Supplément Turc 190. Adjacent is a typical example of Amanita muscaria mushroom

The mythological creature called the Buraq or Al-Buraq is mostly found in the mythology of the Islamic tradition and is mentioned in the Qur'an. In Arabic, the word of Al-Buraq is al-buraaq, which in English means lightning (Burāq). Buraqs name reflects the lightning speed with which she carried the Prophet to heaven for the "ascension." It's fascinating that the name for this divine being of transportation to higher states of consciousness is lightning. Especially when we consider lightning as the impetus for the growth of mushrooms, so perhaps this spiritual journey the great Prophet undertook was because of the magic mushroom, which could explain the origins of the name Burāq.

The Psychedelic use of Harmala

While we can't know about the use of Magic Mushrooms, Wild Syrian rue is well-known in Iran, Iraq, Uzbekistan, Tajikistan, Afghanistan, Pakistan, and parts of Turkey. The plant has been used as folk medicine, including its seeds, bark, and root. [9]. Syrian rue is noted for its hallucinogenic effects[3]. Dried capsules mixed with other ingredients are placed onto red hot charcoal, where they explode with little popping noises, releasing a fragrant smoke wafting around the head of those afflicted by or exposed to the gaze of strangers.

The harmal of isphand (Peganum harmala) ingested alone is entheogenic and intimately linked with the Shia Imams [...] Bioassays of entheogenic doses of Peganum harmala have reported the feeling of "contact" with an invisible being which might recall the initiatory prophet Khidir, in whose steps flowers grow[4].

Harmal has been used as an entheogen in the Middle East, and in modern Western culture, it is often used as an analog of Banisteriopsis caapi to create an ad hoc Ayahuasca. However, Harmal has distinct aspects from caapi and a unique entheogenic signature. Some scholars identify Harmal with the entheogenic haoma[5] of pre-Zoroastrian Persian religions[6]

There is a collection of quotes from the Prophet Mohammad in Islamic culture that is separate from the Qur'an, called Hadith. In these quotes, there is a mention of Harmala, aka Syrian rue. Here is a brief description of it:

> The Messenger of Allah said: The wild rue (al-harmal) does not grow a tree, leaf, or fruit, but it has an angel in charge of it until it reaches the one who comes to it or until it becomes debris. In its root and branches is a secret; in its seed is healing from seventy-two illnesses. So treat yourselves with it and with frankincense[7] '

Influence of Buddhism on Islamic mysticism

Mystic sects exist within all major world religions. These sects are lineages of individuals who have organized around a spiritual practice within their culture and religion, with characteristic lifestyles, teachings, and traditions that instruct the individual and provide a supportive setting for the individual to achieve a deeper connection with the God of their understanding. In this fashion, mystics may be considered "empirical" theologians (Huxley, 1947). Sufism is a mystical sect within the religion of Islam[8].

Buddhism was "the most important civilized religion among the first Il-Khans[9]." Arghun Khan (1258–1291), Genghis Khan's great-grandson, brought Buddhist priests and men skilled in yogic mysticism from India. It is possible that Buddhist yogis and the half-shamanist Bakshi ascetics in the Il-Khan Court influenced the development of certain later forms of Islamic Sufi mysticism. This, in turn, influenced aspects of modern Iranian Shia Islam"

We know that mystical experiences are an aspect of Islam. In Sufism, the mystical form of religion, the focus is on achieving a direct, first-hand experience of God. This is known as dhawq or "tasting." The famous Sufi poet Rumi is a legendary mystic. Was his love affair with God inspired by hallucinogenic experiences?

> I drank that Wine of which the Soul is its vessel.
> Its ecstasy has stolen my intellect away. A Light came
> and kindled a Flame in the depth of my Soul. A Light
> so radiant that the sun orbits around it like a
> butterfly.
> - Rumi

Is it possible that Rumi is referring to the same type of Psychedelic Wines - made from the Ergot psychedelic fungus, which grows on wheat - that trace their origins to the Greek Mystery Schools?

In Sufi poetry, the wine shops are maintained by Zoroastrians which is interesting considering the psychedelic rituals of the Zoroastrians. In the important Zoroastrian Scripture, Arda Wiraz Namag visits heaven and hell using a narcotic potion. According to Gherardho Gnoli, this was an integral part of Zoroastrian ecstatic practice aimed at opening the "eye of the soul." So it was drunk by Arda Wiraz before his journey into the other world[10].

> God has put into the form hashish a power to deliver
> the taster from self-consciousness.
> - Rumi, Mathnawi IV, 2683-96

It sure sounds like Rumi was acquainted with the psychedelic effects of good hashish, so maybe the idea he was using other intoxicants isn't so far off.

While Kabbalists explore mysticism in the context of Judaism, individuals from various religious traditions, including Christian (e.g., Meister Eckhart from the 13th century, St. Teresa of Avila and St. John of the Cross from the 16th century), Islamic (e.g., Rumi and Saadi from the 13th century), and Jewish (e.g., Maimonides of the 12th century) traditions, are considered to be mystics. Some Hindu and Buddhist meditation practices that focus on non-dual experiences likely increase the probability of mystical-type experiences[11].

Hashish and Herbs in Islam

In the modern day people are executed for smuggling hashish into Islamic countries, and the Koranic bans on alcohol are often interpreted as a religious prohibition on all intoxicants. However this has not always been the case, and in past centuries there have been at times tolerance for cannabis, opium and other intoxicating substances, even embracement. This can be particularly identified when following the history of cannabis through Islamic culture, especially the history of Hashish, which will be the focus of this essay, although other drugs will come into play as well. The popular and widely used Arabic term "hashish" is itself a nickname believed to have been derived from a more general word meaning "herb", and was applied to hemp resin products in the same way the generic "grass" came to refer to cannabis in the 20th century. "Most likely, it may may be simply '*the* herb' as distinguished from all other (medicinal) herbs"[12].

This rich variety of epithets bears evidence of the long and magical history of hemp products in the Arab world, and this widespread popularity is due to the fact that cannabis is not explicitly prohibited like alcohol in the Koran. Early Islamic commentators "never failed to remark on the fact that hashish is not mentioned in the Qur'an or the old Prophetic traditions, nor were they able to find any express reference to it in the name of the four legal schools".

While there are a number of local differences, the use of cannabis with a varying intensity has had a time-honoured role in many Muslim countries. This is in contrast to the use of alcohol which, from the religious point of view, became the prime forbidden intoxicant.... There are many reports... that hashish was also used in medical preparations... [It has been] suggested that the interpretation of the Quranic law on intoxicants might have been more tolerant towards the use of drugs such as opium and hashish because of the paucity of means of relieving pain in the medieval Muslim world. (Palgi, 1975) page 208

As a result of this lack of clarity about the morality of its use, cannabis has been surrounded in controversy and thus a matter of debate in Islamic society since very early times, with devotees of the plant in some areas and periods enjoying the widest freedoms, and other times the severest of penalties for its use. In *The Herb: Hashish versus Medieval Muslim Society*, Franz Rosenthal discusses a number of medieval Islamic poems and stories regarding Islam and cannabis, some accounts arguing that unlike alcohol its use was condoned by Quranic law and by others, that along with all intoxicants Muhammad condemned it, (Rosenthal, 1971).

Once hashish consumption had become a widespread and debated custom, there was much discussion among Muslim scholars and other interested parties about its history... The theories put forward range from the fanciful to the strong semblance of fact... The samples preserved in literature make us suspect that there was once much more which went unrecorded and that the legal and political struggle over the drug was accompanied by arguments derived from history favoring one side or the other. (Rosenthal, 1971, pg 72)

Psychedelic Evidence in the Quran

As an Abrahamic religion that builds on the foundations of Judaism and Christianity, which were both influenced by Zoroastrianism, Islam can be argued to inherit their psychedelic legacy. Modern Islam favors an abstinence-based approach when mind-altering substances; however, in the Qur'an, we find the word: *manna*. The same word we find in the Torah.

The word manna appears three times in the Quran, at 2:57, 7:160, and 20:80. It is narrated in the Sahih Muslim that Muhammed said:

> "Truffles are part of the 'manna' which Allah sent to the people of Israel through Moses, and its juice is a medicine for the eye."

Islamic tradition believes in the evil eye (ayn / hasad / envy), which represents evil (immoral action). One of the most effective cures for the evil eye is Truffles. According to Islamic Tradition / Hadith, Truffles was given by Allah to the people of Musa (as) a cure for the eye – meaning evil eye/ayn / hasad / envy.

I HAVE THREE EYES

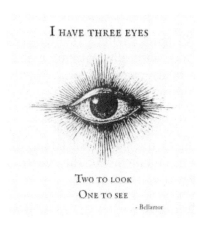

TWO TO LOOK
ONE TO SEE
- Bellamor

Perhaps they are referring to the pineal gland, commonly called the third eye or the mind's eye - a mystical and esoteric concept of a speculative invisible eye, usually depicted as located on the forehead, which provides perception beyond ordinary sight. Opening the third eye is a spiritual pursuit that culminates in the state of nirvana or enlightenment.

> And We shaded you with clouds and sent down to you manna and quails, [saying], "Eat from the good things with which We have provided you."
> Qur'an 2:57

In this context, they are saying that the clouds which brought a storm and the remnants of that storm were psilocybin mushrooms. To provide some context, it is common for mushrooms to sprout up after a thunderstorm

This would make sense when we read how the Quran describes how this manna acts as a medicine for curing evil and connecting oneself with a higher state of consciousness.

> Sa'id b. Zaid reported Allal, a Messenger (saw), as saying: Truffles are a kind of 'Manna' which Allaah sent down upon Moses, and their juice is a medicine for the eyes.

I heard the Prophet saying, "Truffles are like Manna (i.e., they grow naturally without man's care), and their water heals eye diseases." *(Sahih Bukhari – 5708)*

Truffles are 'Manna' which Allaah, the Exalted the Majestic, sent to the people of Israel, to Musa (as), and its juice is a medicine for the eyes. *(Sahih Muslim 5086 & 5087)*

The Prophet (SAW) said that mushroom is a good cure for the eyes, it also serves as a form of birth control and arrests paralysis. *(Sahih Bukhari)*

Psychedelics are Halāl

In 2014, Sayyed Mohammad Sadeq Hussaini Rohani, who is a Grand Ayatollah (meaning the highest authority on Shi'ite Islam—basically, the equivalent of the Pope), announced that psychedelic medicines are permissible (ḥalāl) for Muslims under traditional Islamic law[13]. That means that so long as psychedelics are taken under the observation of a trained specialist, it's not sinful or forbidden.

The details of this decision were first unpacked in a 2014 interview between Reality Sandwich[14] and N. Wahid Azal, an esoteric Islamic scholar, and Sufi mystic. Azal spent over a year and a half corresponding with a scholarly friend, who began a dialogue concerning psychedelic medicine with the "orthodox Shi'i ecclesiastical establishment," as Azal puts it. He provided a massive trove of carefully translated scientific and academic citations, including many from MAPS and numerous religious and spiritual texts.

Today, the Fatimiya Sufi Order has embraced ayahuasca as its sacrament. The Fatimiya Sufi Order stands unique in its place as a Sufi order, with Ayahuasca as a central sacrament. This may be the first modern-day Sufi order to utilize the medicine in its rituals and the first mystery school that utilizes Ayahuasca following Islamic and pre-Islamic religious metaphors.

CHAPTER 12:

The Science of
Psychedelic Medicine

Mental health is important because it affects how we think, feel, and act. It also helps determine how we handle stress, relate to others, and make choices. In the United States, 87 million or roughly 1 in 4 Americans report experiencing mental health problems, such as depression, anxiety, and substance abuse disorders.[1] We are living through a mental health epidemic.

The epidemic is global, 970 million people worldwide had a mental or substance use disorder in 2017[2]. In 2018, 1.7 million veterans reported a mental health issue ranging from depression, to debilitating anxiety, and PTSD[3]. Mental health is so neglected that suicide has become a serious public health problem. Suicide rates increased 30% between 2000–2018[4]. On average there are 130 suicides per day, 44 of which are veterans[5]. Suicide is the second leading cause of death among young people 10 to 24 years old[6]. 1.2 million Americans attempted suicide in 2020.

The mental health crisis is greatly affecting our children. In the fall of 2021, the American Academy of Pediatrics along with the American Academy of Child and Adolescent Psychiatry and the Children's Hospital Association declared a national emergency in child and adolescent mental health[7].

40% of teens reported to the CDC that they feel "persistently sad or hopeless," and 1 in 5 saying they have contemplated suicide, according to the results of a survey published in March [8].

These problems are way too common and are affecting more people than ever before. The issue has become so serious, the President of the United States and the Secretary of Defense are making public commitments to tackle this monumental challenge:

WH.GOV   Q

OCTOBER 18, 2022

Statement by President Joe Biden on New Mental Health Funding

"Mental health affects all of us, which is why I named tackling the mental health crisis a core pillar of my Unity Agenda. As I outlined in my State of the Union address last March, we can and must do more to transform how we address mental health in America," Joe Biden, President of the United States [9].

"Mental health is health – period. It's on all of us to end the stigma of asking for help and support when we or someone we know is feeling distressed, anxious, or isolated. Reaching out is a marker of strength and resilience. We will not stop working to address the root causes of this issue,"

Lloyd Austin, Secretary of Defense[10]

The good news there is hope: natural medicines like magic mushrooms can treat depression, anxiety, addiction, and suicidal ideation. Other esteemed research institutions like Yale, UC Berkeley, The Ohio State University, and Imperial College London have published clinical research demonstrating the transformational healing power of psychedelic medicine.

Clinically published research conducted by John Hopkins University showed in a national survey of over 190,000 U.S. adults, lifetime use of certain psychedelic drugs was associated with a 19 percent reduced likelihood of psychological distress within the past month, a 14 percent reduced likelihood of suicidal thinking within the past year, a 29 percent reduced likelihood of suicide planning within the past year and a 36 percent reduced likelihood of attempting suicide within the past year. These results were published in the *Journal of Psychopharmacology*[11].

The Psychedelic Renaissance is sweeping across the western world as researchers, investors, activists, and politicians work to provide legal access to psychedelic medicine, which will lead to healing the mental health epidemic in the west.

The idea that psychedelic medicine could be a panacea to the world's mental health epidemic is buoyed by the FDA's fast-tracking clinical research trials for psychedelics such as Psilocybin and MDMA. Designated as breakthrough therapies by the FDA, a breakthrough therapy is for a drug that treats a serious or life-threatening condition and preliminary clinical evidence indicates that the drug may demonstrate substantial improvement on a clinically significant endpoint(s) over available therapies. Psychedelics show potential for treating a myriad of illnesses: depression, anxiety, PTSD, addiction, migraines, and more.

Psychedelics Could Help Nearly 700 Million People Struggling with Mental Health Issues

"These could be breakthrough medical treatments that we've been ignoring for the past 30 years," says Matthew W. Johnson, Ph.D., an associate professor of psychiatry and behavioral sciences at Johns Hopkins and one of the world's most published scientists on the human effects of psychedelics.

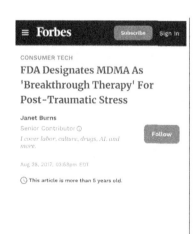

"Johns Hopkins is deeply committed to exploring innovative treatments for our patients. Our scientists have shown that psychedelics have real potential as medicine" - Paul B. Rothman, M.D., Dean of the Johns Hopkins University School of Medicine and CEO of Johns Hopkins Medicine.

Psychedelic Medicine Research Findings

Imagine taking medicine that alters your mind and facilitates the generation of new thoughts and new ways of looking at the world. Imagine taking a medicine that facilitates solving the problems of life, by they personal or professional. Imagine taking a medicine for the purpose of spiritual connection and the cleansing of spirit that has been clogged up by life.

Psychedelic medicine can heal mental illness across the spectrum of anxiety, depression, eating disorders, substance abuse disorders and suicidical ideation. A reality made possible thanks to the pioneering research of Roland Griffiths, Katherine MacLean and Matthew Johnson at John Hopkins, Charles Grob at UCLA, Dave Nichols at Indiana University, Michael Mithofer & Rick Doblin of MAPS, Robin Carhart Harris of Imperial College London, Simon Ruffell of Kings College London, Amanda Fielding of the Beckley Foundation, Rachel Yehuda at the Icahn School of Medicine and many others.

In Dr. Richard Miller's book *Psychedelic Medicine: The Healing Powers of LSD, MDMA, Psilocybin and Ayahuasca* he shares how Amanda Feilding conducted the first study of psilocybin in the treatment of chronic depression. The small pilot study showed that 67% of participants who reported clinical depression for 18 years on average, experienced significant improvements in one week.

A 2014 pilot study[12] at Johns Hopkins looked at the potential of psilocybin to help people quit smoking, one of the hardest addictions to break. The study was tiny and not randomized—all 15 volunteers received two or three doses of psilocybin and knew it. The pilot study results were eye-popping: Six months after their psychedelic session, 80% of the volunteers were confirmed to have quit smoking. That figure had fallen to 67% at the one-year mark, which is still a better success rate than the best treatment available. A participant noted, "It put smoking in a whole new context. It seemed very unimportant; it seemed kind of stupid, to be honest."

Matthew Johnson, the psychologist who directed the study at Hopkins, says that these sorts of "duh moments" are common among his volunteers. Smokers know perfectly well that their habit is unhealthy, disgusting, expensive, and unnecessary. Still, under the influence of psilocybin, that knowledge becomes an unshakable conviction—"something they feel in the gut and the heart." As Dr. Johnson puts it, "These sessions deprive people of the luxury of mindlessness"—our default state and one in which addictions flourish[13].

The most famous evidence for the therapeutic value of psychedelics arrived in a pair of phase 2 trials (conducted at Johns Hopkins and NYU and published in the Journal of Psychopharmacology in 2016) in which a single high dose of psilocybin was administered to cancer patients struggling with depression, anxiety and the fear of death or recurrence. In these rigorous placebo-controlled trials, a total of 80 volunteers embarked on a psychic journey that, in many cases, brought them face to face with their cancer, fear, and death. 80% percent of the Hopkins cancer patients who received psilocybin showed clinically significant reductions in standard measures of anxiety and depression, an effect that endured for at least six months after their session[14]. Results at NYU were similar[15]. The degree to which symptoms decreased in both trials correlated with the intensity of the "spiritual experience" that volunteers reported, a common occurrence during a high-dose psychedelic session. Across the board, volunteers in the Hopkins and NYU experiments report becoming better versions of themselves - more open, compassionate, forgiving, and loving.

"[I was]...bathed in God's love"
- Dinah Bazer

Dinah Bazer, a research participant, could finally appreciate and connect with people on a profound level for the first time in her life. She felt the experience allowed her to fall back in love with her family. She was surprised by the sheer goodness of others: "I don't think I realized how genuine people were until after this experience!" Dinah didn't leave her healing session on a narcissistic bent; she had transformed into the socially conscious version of herself who felt a sense of belonging as a sibling of the human family.

To date we do not have any psychiatric interventions for anxiety and depression that have demonstrated dramatic and sustained results. The government will require that trials on psychedelic medicine by expanded to a larger set of participants before considering approval of psychedelic medicine. But when researchers brought their data to the FDA, the regulators reportedly were impressed and asked for a large phase 3 trial of psilocybin for depression—not just in cancer patients but in the general population.

I am often asked how long the effects of psychedelic medicine last. What is the change of remission for mental health disorders? According to a study by the Amanda Fielding, 42% of partipants experience complete remission of chronic depression three months post-treatment[16]. According to the scientific journal Nature, clinical trials suggest that psilocybin can provide durable remission from an increasingly common mental health condition[17]. A recent research report published in Feb. 2022 by Johns Hopkins Medicine researchers report that the substantial antidepressant effects of psilocybin-assisted therapy, given with supportive psychotherapy, may last at least a year for some patients[18]. The results tend to shock even the most seasoned researchers:

"My initial response was amazement when I saw that a single treatment would produce this sort of long-term change in emotional state," says Charles Raison, a psychiatrist at the University of Wisconsin–Madison who is currently overseeing a phase II clinical trial of psilocybin.

He contrasts this with conventional antidepressants such as selective serotonin re-uptake inhibitors (SSRIs), which require daily administration and trial-and-error matching of patient and drug — and where halting treatment too abruptly can lead to a brutal relapse.

While research on psychedelic medicine demonstrates how it can help heal us from mental health disorders, research demonstrates that is does even more: psychedelics allow us to experience mystical states of consciousness.

In 1999, Griffiths and MacLean risked their career to research psilocybin — the active ingredient in magic mushrooms. Their groundbreaking research on psilocybin stunned the world and rocked the pharmaceutical industry. The research led donors to help Johns Hopkins University launch the first dedicated psychedelic research center in the United States, called the Center for Psychedelic and Consciousness Research. Roland Griffiths, the center's director, published a landmark study Psilocybin can occasion mystical-type experiences having substantial and sustained personal meaning and spiritual significance[19]. The study is considered to be a milestone that marks the re-initiation of psychedelic research after decades during which research had been suspended due to widespread propaganda.

"Experiences that people describe as encounters with God or a representative of God have been reported for thousands of years, and they likely form the basis of many of the world's religions," says Roland Griffiths, professor of psychiatry and behavioral sciences at the Johns Hopkins University School of Medicine. "Although modern western medicine doesn't typically consider 'spiritual' or 'religious' experiences as one of the tools in the arsenal against sickness, our findings suggest that these encounters often lead to improvements in mental health".[20]

In the early 2000s, he a landmark study investigating how high-dose psilocybin can produce mystical experiences of religious or spiritual significance[21]. Griffiths and Alan Davis published the largest survey ever conducted with 2500 respondents reporting their experience of the compound DMT[22].

- 75% of respondents in both the non-drug and psychedelics groups rated their "God encounter" experience as among the most meaningful and spiritually significant in their lifetime.
- 89% of participants reported positive changes in their life satisfaction.
- 82% reported a positive change in their life's purpose and meaning.
- 75% of participants reported being in contact with a conscious, intelligent, benevolent sacred, eternal entity.
- 58% said tripping on DMT had triggered a belief in divine beings and powerful supernatural entities.

The research grew out of an initial survey by the Johns Hopkins team exploring "God encounter experiences" triggered by psychedelics[23]. In a survey of thousands of people who reported having experienced personal encounters with God, Johns Hopkins researchers report that:

- 2/3 of self-identified atheists no longer identified as such after a personal encounter with "ultimate reality" or "the God of your understanding".

Moreover, the researchers say, a majority of respondents attributed lasting positive changes in their psychological health—e.g., life satisfaction, purpose, and meaning—even decades after their initial experience. The findings, published online in PLOS One, add to evidence that such deeply meaningful experiences may have healing properties, the researchers say.

The most common psychedelics reported to have been associated with "God" encounters were:

- Psilocybin, or "magic" mushrooms (1,184 participants)
- LSD (1,251)
- Ayahuasca, a plant-based brew originating with indigenous cultures in Latin America (435)
- DMT, a naturally occurring substance found in certain plants and animals (606)

Professor John Vervaeke, a cognitive scientist and psychologist at the University of Toronto, prefers the term "sacred" to "divine." "When I hear 'divine,' I hear there's a consciousness, and there's an intelligence attached to that," he says. "I don't know about that. But do I think there are depths of reality that we can fall in love with that transform us? Yes. Yes, I do."

> "With psilocybin, these profound mystical experiences are quite common."
> - Dr. William Richards, a psychologist at Johns Hopkins University

The notion that hallucinogenic drugs can bring about mystical experiences is not new and was previously studied in a famous Harvard study known as the "Good Friday experiment[24]." The study involved a group of seminary scholars being given psilocybin during the Easter season service to see how it altered their experience of the liturgy. Almost all of the members of the experimental group reported experiencing profound religious experiences, providing empirical support for the notion that psychedelic drugs can facilitate religious experience.

Psychedelics appear to unlock this connection to the divine by tapping directly into what the mystics have been trying to mine over the history of modern religions with chanting, fasting, meditation, and prayer.

The Science of Ego Death

In psychedelic culture, Leary, Metzner and Alpert[25] define ego death, or ego loss as they call it, as part of the experience of death in which the old ego must die before one can be spiritually reborn. The ego death is commonly reported to researchers by participants during psychedelic experiences[26], is said to be similar to experiencing physical death, but after the ego is gone, the subject is surprised and relieved.

If who and what we believe we are (our ego) were to dissolve shouldn't there be nothing left? Some psychedelic researchers have concluded that after the ego dissolves what is left is the experiencer, the subject, the "I", or consciousness[27].

They have postulated that in our normal waking consciousness, the subject, or the experiencer, continually but incorrectly identifies with the ego, while experiencing the ego as an object of its perception. But if the ego is no more, then the subject has nothing else to identify with other than itself. The subject's consciousness becomes self-aware. Michael Pollan writes of his own psychedelic-induced experience of ego dissolution: "The sovereign ego...was simply no more... Yet something had succeeded it: this bare disembodied awareness, which gazed upon the scene of the self's dissolution with benign indifference. I was present to reality but as something other than myself. And although there was no self left to feel, exactly, there was a feeling tone, which was calm, unburdened, content. There was life after the death of the ego. This was big news."

Trials of psilocybin can help cancer patients deal with their "existential distress" at the prospect of dying. The pivotal role of the mystical experience points to something novel about psychedelic therapy: It depends for its success not strictly on the action of a chemical but on the powerful psychological experience that the chemical can occasion.

Perhaps ego death is something we need to actualize as part of our culture. Suicide is the second leading cause of death in American youth ages 12-25. Maybe our children are self-harming because as teenagers you are supposed to want to die, however; that death is supposed to be metaphorical and spiritual. Your childhood has to die so you can become an adult but nobody has told them this death is metaphorical and spiritual. So the children have this doubt or urge that they actualize in the physical world as opposed to natural maturity. This is but another symptom exposing the flaw of a western culture devoid of spirituality.

The data supports my claims. Public polling from Gallup shows that American happiness is at record lows, only 40% of Americans are satisfied with life[28]. We are very unhappy people. We are also a people devoid of true spirituality. In regards to the children, they simply want this nightmare to end. They don't recognize that the depth of what their spirit is seeking is a cultural death because within western culture, the spirit is separated from the earth from the flesh so you can't have this transformation. This makes the most sense to me when we can see research that shows people being reborn from a place of darkness, depression and anxiety and having a new lease on life.

I find it fascinating that no one knows why these medicines make people spiritual or exactly why any of it changes people's personalities for the better, boosts them out of mood disorders, or ride them of addictions. We just know it works. That's why I call it God's medicine.

Psychedelic Policy Reform

Psychedelic medicine is so transformative it has inspired me and countless others to join the psychedelic medicine movement to demand change and give people access to the healing they rightfully deserve. The research on the potential of psychedelics is clear and the movement is seeing results in various psychedelic initiatives all across the United States.

In 2020, Oregon became the first US state to legalize and medically regulate psilocybin for personal use for those over age 21. By the end of 2022, Oregon Psilocybin Services will adopt rules for the facilitation of psilocybin therapy in a clinical setting.[29] Applications for licensure will open in January 2023.

In 2021, my organization Legalize Psychedelic Medicine along with a veteran-led coalition of non-profits: VETS (veterans exploring treatment solutions), the Warrior Angels Foundation, Heroic Hearts Project, and SOAA (the Special Operations Association of America) led the charge for Texas House Bill 1802, a bill that provided funding for the state of Texas to facilitate a clinical study of how psilocybin — found in "magic mushrooms" — helps treat veterans with mental health problems. A bipartisan effort, Texas House Bill 1802[30] passed successfully and showed the greatness of America, that a small group of committed veterans and citizens can change the world.

In the fall of 2022, Colorado citizens passed Proposition 122. Their vote thus enacted the Natural Medicine Health Act of 2022[31] (NMHA) which legalizes supervised or facilitated therapeutic sessions for adults twenty-one years and older using certain psychedelic plants and fungi.

The Federal government is slowly embracing psychedelic medicine and clinical research trials. Ketamine therapy, the only legal psychedelic medication, was given expanded access to treat veterans' suffering mental health issues through the Veterans Administration healthcare programs[32]. In 2021, John Hopkins received a 4 million dollar NIH grant to research psychedelics for[33], the first federal grant issued in 50 years. In November 2022, two House lawmakers formed the Congressional Psychedelics Advancing Clinical Treatments[34] (PACT) caucus, the nation's first psychedelic medicine caucus. The caucus is co-chaired by California Democratic Representative Lou Correa and Representative Jack Bergman, a Republican from Michigan who is also a retired lieutenant general with the United States Marine Corps.

"Having served our Nation as a member of the United States military and in Congress, I've seen the destruction post-traumatic stress disorder can cause on my fellow veterans and their families," Bergman said in a statement, as reported by the Washington Examiner. "Our job is to find solutions to these problems, and if psychedelic-assisted therapy can help treat or even fully cure someone of their PTSD, we need to take a closer look at these potentially life-saving therapies."

Not to be outdone, members of the Senate are crossing the aisle and partnering to champion the cause of mental health. In November 2022, U.S. Senator Cory Booker (D-N.J.) and U.S. Senator Rand Paul (R-KY) introduced the Breakthrough Therapies Act[35], a bill that would reclassify MDMA and psilocybin.

"We urge Congress to swiftly pass the Breakthrough Therapies Act, which responsibly reduces the barriers to research and limited access of potentially life-saving treatments like MDMA- and psilocybin-assisted therapy," said Martin R. Steele, a retired Lieutenant General in the United States Marine Corps., Chief Executive Officer of Reason for Hope, and head of the recently formed Veteran Mental Health Leadership Coalition. "Veterans should not be forced (nor should anyone else) to leave the country - at great expense - to access breakthrough therapies that can be safely provided and further studied in real-world settings here at home."

"We believe the Breakthrough Therapies Act is the tip of the spear in our fight to ensure that Special Operations Veterans have access to the most advanced and effective medical treatments in the world," said Daniel Elkins, Special Operations Association of America Founder and Member of the Moral Compass Federation. "The Breakthrough Therapies Act will ensure Special Operations Forces receive the care they deserve from the country they fought for."

Veterans Leading the Psychedelic Medicine Movement

Testimony is a form of qualitative research data. Testimony is "a solemn attestation as to the truth of a matter," originating from the Latin word testimonium. In my previous career as a User Experience Researcher, I learned from research data that we can usually diagnose 80% of the problem a user has with software just by speaking to 5 people[36]. I learned to appreciate the power of an individual's testimony. Testimony is the foundation of the American justice system. Sadly, testimony is often dismissed by Ph.D. and MDs who only trust numbers on a screen. But guess what is creating real political change? Testimony from America's warriors and their families.

Veterans have become unlikely lobbyists in the push to legalize psychedelic medicine. These veterans are sharing their stories with legislatures across the country. It is moving to listen to how psychedelic medicine healed them and how it inspired them to dedicate their lives to helping heal other veterans struggling with mental health issues. Every day, their organizations are saving veteran lives every day.

Jesse Gould, Founder, Heroic Hearts Project

Jesse Gould is a pioneer in psychedelic therapies. Jesse is the Founder and President of the Heroic Hearts Project, a 501(c)(3) nonprofit pioneering psychedelic therapies for military veterans. After being deployed as an Army Ranger in Afghanistan three times, he founded the Heroic Hearts Project in 2017 to spearhead the acceptance and use of ayahuasca therapy as a means of addressing the current mental health crisis among veterans.

I asked Jesse what led him down this path:

"So I got out of the military in 2014. I had done a number of deployments in Afghanistan. When I first got out, I had a background in finance economics and just completed being a leader in the Ranger Regiment. So I thought I was going to hit the ground running, you know what could stop me? But what I found is I started having some mental health issues that I really didn't expect, nor could I really understand. I just knew I wasn't living up to my full capacity. I had this weight of being affected by things like anxiety and depression. I tried to go to the Department of Veteran Affairs to do therapy, but what became pretty clear pretty quick was the VA was just very much dogmatic about the medication prescription model. There's a time and place for everything, but I knew a lot of people where the medications didn't address the problem, just sort of muted the problem and then had all sorts of other side effects. Whatever I was doing in that moment wasn't working and I was getting scared of where I was going to end up. So I did as much due diligence as possible, found a place in Peru and kind of took a leap of faith.

I went to this Ayahuasca ceremony, which was very challenging but profound and healing. I overcame many of my issues and started seeing my life differently. This experience led me to found the Heroic Hearts Project, to educate and connect other veterans in similar spots to these modalities

What do you think are the biggest barriers for veterans to access ayahuasca or other psychedelic-assisted therapies (like psilocybin)? And along those lines, how can we give more access to more people who need this medicine the most?

Having access in a community container where there are controls and safety measures. There is a pressure to medicalize it, go to a doctor or therapist, and that becomes very cost prohibitive. The communities that are currently not served by mental healthcare will continue to not be served even if we have these breakthroughs and even if they are somewhat accessible on a generic basis. In terms of the U.S. and changing mental health, that is the key of what we need to develop – if you prefer to go the medical way, perfectly fine. But we can't have it limited to just that. We need to respect sacraments and traditions that have predated the FDA. And have safety measures in those places."

Jesse has connected countless veterans to psychedelic treatments, partnered with the world's leading psychedelic centers, and is researching psychiatric applications with the University of Colorado Boulder, the University of Georgia, University of Texas, Austin, and Imperial College of London. His mission is to help military veterans struggling with mental trauma and spread awareness of the benefits that psychedelic therapies offer as an alternative treatment to pharmaceuticals. Jesse has spoken globally about the benefits of psychedelics on mental health and has been featured in the New York Times, the New Yorker, the Economist, and Forbes and recognized as one of the most influential voices in psychedelics today.

Learn more and donate at heroicheartsproject.org.

Marcus & Amber Capone, Founders, VETS

Marcus and Amber Capone are the founders of the U.S.-based nonprofit organization, Veterans Exploring Treatment Solutions (VETS), a pioneering 501(c)(3) organization that provides resources, research, and advocacy for U.S. Special Operations veterans seeking psychedelic-assisted therapies.

After 13 years and numerous combat deployments as a Navy SEAL, Marcus' post-military transition challenges became seemingly insurmountable. After all other avenues of healing failed, Amber was able to arrange for Marcus to leave the U.S. in 2017 to pursue psychedelic therapy, ibogaine, an intervention the couple attributes to saving his life, as well as their family. He found the astounding success too incredible not to share with other veterans, which prompted the trailblazing launch of VETS.

I asked Marcus and Amber what led them down this path:

Marcus, retired Navy Seal:

"I served 13 years in special operations as a US Navy SEAL with many combat deployments to Iraq and Afghanistan. I'm proud to serve this nation and there's nothing I changed about my time and service. What does need to change, however, is access to effective life saving treatments for addressing the invisible wounds, as so many of our nation's veterans are facing today.

I was medically retired and I thought, like the rest of us, life is going to be okay at that point. And that's when I really started spiraling. I was very impulsive. I was angry. I was angry at the world. I was depressed. It basically couldn't get out of bed at all. I was isolating. I wasn't talking to anybody and it was frustrating because I was listening to the system that we, you know, we listen to every day I was listening to my doctors. I was prescribed multiple mood stabilizers, depressants, and medicines to help me focus, and go to sleep. And you know, things came to a point that It was really bad. My wife was getting nervous. I had no relationship with her or the kids. The frustration came to a point where I thought It would be better if I just went away. Having tried every available opportunity from multiple treatment centers to a whole host of other treatment modalities, I can say unequivocally that psychedelic-assisted therapy, saved my life.

I've seen it save the lives of countless friends, teammates, and colleagues. I see it work with strangers and close contacts. I've seen it transform veterans who went from suffering suicide attempts to now living productive lives.

Psychedelic therapy is the next major breakthrough in mental health care. Over 22 veterans die from suicides per day. No one needs or deserves this intervention more than our veterans."

Amber:

"I've been by Marcus's side for 24 years and one of those years were more excruciating than those immediately following his service when I thought for sure I was going to lose him. We never saw 911 coming nor his 13 years of sustained combat. We certainly never saw the war after the war, and the fight to save Marcus and our family.

We were very good soldiers for a very long time, thoroughly exhausting all conventional options of healing offered to us by military medicine, the VA, and Western healthcare. Except, in the years following Marcus's service nothing was working and time was running out. Completely out of options and with practically no hope left I took matters into my own hands. In 2017 I arranged for Marcus to leave the United States as a last-ditch effort to save him. I arranged for him to take part in a treatment involving plant medicine also commonly referred to as psychedelic
Therapy. This intervention undoubtedly saved his life.

Immediately Marcus knew we had to pay this lifeline forward to other veterans in need which began our initial grassroots effort in January of 2018. What began with our friends became their Friends and their friends' friends and friends of theirs. By 2019, we realized that we had a crisis of epic proportions on our hands and also an opportunity and the responsibility to continue helping fellow veterans but with a larger goal of changing U.S. healthcare system for veterans in the united states.

We formed our organization VETS which stands for veterans exploring treatment solutions. To date, VETS has provided funding for upwards of 350 special operations veterans who've had to leave the united states to seek the healing that they need and absolutely deserve. As word of this spreads our waitlist continues to explode with veterans and their families practically begging for help, We can no longer carry this responsibility on our own. Our veterans deserve access to the most meaningful healthcare interventions available."

Since its inception, VETS has maintained a special emphasis on ibogaine and its remarkable potential for neuroregenerative effects in combating blast injury and mild traumatic brain injury, the "signature injury" of the post-9/11 conflicts overseas.   The VETS mission also includes grant funding and advocacy for five other psychedelic compounds: 5-MeO-DMT, psilocybin, MDMA, ketamine, and ayahuasca. As a global leader in the psychedelic space, VETS has raised over $8 million to provide integration support and therapeutic access abroad to hundreds of veterans, spouses, and Gold Star spouses, while also spearheading research and policy change at the state and federal levels in the U.S. VETS has provided key testimony in a number of states, with the most significant legislative victory being the passage of HB 1802 in Texas. Marcus and Amber are frequent guest speakers and advocates of psychedelic therapies for veterans and non-veterans alike, and believe that psychedelic therapies are the future of mental healthcare. They are committed to fighting for veterans and their families just as hard as they've fought for their own, with an ultimate goal of making these therapies available within the borders of the United States for all who need them.

Learn more and donate at <u>vetsolutions.org</u>.

Andrew Marr,
Co-Founder, Warrior Angels Foundation

Adam Marr,
Co-Founder, Warrior Angels Foundation

Andrew and Adam Marr are the founders of the U.S.-based nonprofit organization, Warrior Angels Foundation, a 501(c)(3) organization that provides resources, research, and advocacy for U.S. veterans suffering from Traumatic Brain Injuries (TBIs). WAF sponsors individualized assessments and personalized treatment protocols that pinpoint – and, more importantly, treat – the underlying condition for U.S. Service Members and Veterans who have sustained a Traumatic Brain Injury (TBI) while in the line of duty. They are the best-selling co-authors of TALES FROM THE BLAST FACTORY: A Brain Injured Special Forces Green Beret's

Journey Back from the Brink. Their book has been turned into an award-winning full-feature documentary titled Quiet Explosions: Healing the Brain by EMMY and Academy Award winners.

Andrew Marr, MBA is a husband, father, Retired Special Forces Green Beret. Andew was medically retired with a Traumatic Brain Injury. He credits his recovery to the help of Dr. Mark Gordon, cutting-edge neuroscience and psychedelic therapy.

Adam Marr is a retired Apache Helicopter Aviation Officer, Co-Founder of Warrior Angels Foundation, and Strategic Advisor to the Veteran Mental Health Leadership Coalition, a 501c(19) that promotes the welfare of Veterans by advocating for policy and legal reforms needed to facilitate safe and affordable access to psychedelic medicine and assisted therapies on behalf of its Veteran members.

I asked Andrew and Adam what led them down this path.

Andrew:

"My background is in army special forces. I'm retired from special forces. My brother and I Co-Founded the Warrior Angels Foundation. I'm also the Vice President of the Special Operations Association of America. When I was medically discharged I was given medication and told to take these for the rest of my life to maintain some semblance of normalcy. In 2015 I was able to experience the healing power of psychedelic therapy. Today I am symptom and medication free. I feel as good if not better than my pre-injury status. That experience is not special to me but is normal to all the veterans we are helping through our organization and with our partners. This comes down to freedom of consciousness. We are talking about life, liberty, and the pursuit of happiness. Medical freedom and health freedom to be able to use the plants that grow on the earth that have been used for thousands of years for the betterment of all at a fraction of the costs with little to no side effects. Our own institutions call these medicines a breakthrough. Right now we need to redefine the future where all Americans can access the tools that heal us and reconnect us with us. The Native Americans have been saying that the only real sickness is being disconnected from oneself and these technologies, the plant medicines are ancient technologies that have the ability to reconnect us with ourselves."

Adam:

"Having spent 10 year in the Army and the last 8 years on the front lines of the Veteran Mental Health crisis I can firmly say that we need scalable solutions to address price and accessibility for the Veteran community and beyond but we cannot achieve this by forfeiting safe and efficacious practices with a patient first focus that includes coaching, community & peer support, along with post experience integration and action plans. Service & more specifically combat service has its price for our military Veterans & First Responders. My trauma came directly from serving in combat, deploying my munitions to kill an enemy force and protect American lives. However, serving my mission gave me the feeling of being less of an Apache Pilot because I didn't have the opportunity to kill more "enemies" while serving our nation. That's a feeling no human should have to experience. My trauma also came from the indirect effect that TBI and PTSD have on the service member.

In my case, it was from my older brother Andrew and my younger brother Austin both Army combat Veterans. Andrew was near suicide and unraveling before our eyes due to his TBI/PTSD before getting help outside of the military and VA systems. Then there was the middle of the night frantic search for my suicidal younger brother Austin. Ultimately finding his alive but unresponsive body, it was all just too much for me to handle in a short period of time.

All these direct and indirect struggles and military-related traumas had me at a point in 2018 where my life was filled and consumed with depression, fear, anxiety, and heavy drinking. It wasn't until I had the chance to begin going through Psychedelic Assisted Therapy with Ayahuasca, Ibogaine, and 5meODMT that I could genuinely start addressing this trauma from a new plane of awareness and perspective. Later MDMA and Ketamine therapies would prove to be central to my own mental health healing and well being.

Yes we need more research of these modalities but let us not forget what Matt Weintrub has so comprehensively pointed out in his research on psychedlics and religion, that many of these modalities have been the sacred healing sacrament of indigenous peoples and religions of the world as far back as we can tell. Should we really have to wait years to catch up to what has been in practice since recorded history?

What do you think are the biggest barriers for veterans to access psychedelic-assisted therapies (like psilocybin and ayahusca)? And along those lines, how can we give more access to more people who need this medicine the most?

First, to think that psychedelic assisted therapy and treatment will fit into a completely western model of care denies the very spiritual nature of the medicine that Matt and so many others have outlined. It also cuts most therapy sessions off from connection to and in nature. My hypothesis is that research will show true healing happens in conjunction with connection to nature and the combination of these factors in my opinion is a major contributor to the Veteran and human Mental Health crisis.

So how can one properly build this infrastructure without the required resources? Truth is we need to be open to new models of care, innovation, and funding so we do not once again fall prey to models that provide symptom masking medicine as a commodity to return shareholder value instead of addressing the root cause in order to allow healing. Some of this burden should come from appropriations at the state and federal level. But I can tell you that it should NOT be only the government who is solely responsible for building this infrastructure.

Lastly, psychedelic medicine is no magic pill solution but rather another set of very sacred tools available that can help to address many of the mental health problems plaguing so many, it must be part of a more comprehensive and individualized treatment program and it must be available at scale."

**Wyly Gray,
Founder, Veterans of War**

Wyly is a United States Marine and the leading voice supporting guided psychedelic group therapy for veterans. As Founding Director of Veterans of War, Wyly is deeply committed to changing the mental health paradigm regarding trauma, plant medicine, and veteran suicide. Wyly has survived a broken family, foster care, two deployments in support of the War on Terror, and Post Traumatic Stress

(PTS). Through his work with Veterans of War, he experienced firsthand the strength of guided psychedelic therapy in battles against treatment-resistant trauma, depression, anxiety, insomnia, and PTS.

"I've undertaken a healing journey to date both on and off the grid to try to find relief from post-traumatic stress disorder since 2009. For me, it manifested as insomnia, nightmares, severe anxiety, violent outbursts, rage, and even suicidal ideations. At the worst of it, I truly believed that I was poisoning my family. It would take me years of further study and continuing dark experiences to finally push me over the edge to seek out plant medicine deep in the jungles of Peru but it's ridiculous that I even had to do that, that I had to go on such a dangerous
trip by myself in a foreign country where I didn't speak the language to get access to a medicine that there wasn't a lot of information about uh it took me more than a decade of suffering to just to overcome my fear and take that leap i'm forever grateful that I did because I wouldn't be here today without it.

It's 2022 and these safe and effective solutions for overcoming trauma have been on the planet living with us for millennia. We're talking about them now as though they're somehow novel approaches or new only reflects our lack of study and not their efficacy or their continued persistence in our culture. With these medicines, I found a path towards healing that's paved by hard work. This work was highlighted by the intense connection I was reminded we all share in ayahuasca. Ayahuasca for me, if you're unfamiliar, is simply a psychedelic tea. Equally important is the integration work that is expected for you to be successful. Before we can change the paradigm of mental health, we have to identify its tenants. How have we as a modern society dealt with mental health care and how have we dealt with veteran mental health care? I'd also like to give a quick shout-out to Jesse Gould of Heroic Hearts Project and Amber and Marcus

Capone from VETS. These organizations have laid the groundwork for mental health care solutions in the veteran community."

Thanks to plant medicines, Wyly overcame suicidal thoughts and ideations, found sleep again, and cemented his purpose to bring safe and effective tools for recovery out of the shadows to serve those suffering from the treatment-resistant after-effects of war. Wyly passionately believes that entheogenic plant medicines offer a unique path forward towards recovery from trauma and he is part of ballot initiatives advocating for their decriminalization.

Learn more and donate at www.veteransofwar.org

Healing is a human right. In the context of human rights work, the silencing of voice — whether on the part of the victim who cannot speak out or on the part of the addressee who does not listen — signals a moral dispute of the first order. It is with great gratitude and honor that I count the souls quoted as friends. God Bless You and thank you for your service. I love you always with all my heart.

Your Brain on Psychedelics

So how does psychedelic therapy work? And why should the same treatment work for disorders as seemingly different as depression, addiction, and anxiety? According to Amanda Fielding, founder of the Beckley Foundation, "It's a well-known fact that LSD, and all psychedelics for the matter, work through the serotonin 2A receptors[37]."

For several decades, we didn't know anything beyond Amanda's statement, however; within the last few decades scientists have discovered how psychedelics change our brain. Psychedelics induce neuroplasticity and create neurogenesis in the brain - a process that causes your brain to grow new cells[38]. Neuroplasticity is the brain's ability to change and adapt due to experience. It is an umbrella term referring to the brain's ability to change, reorganize, or grow neural networks. This can involve functional changes due to brain damage or structural changes due to learning. Through visualization we can see the direct impact psychedelics have on the brain in the chart below.

Placebo Brain	Psilocybin Brain

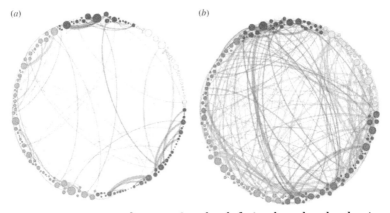

(a)   (b)

Here you see two brains. On the left is the placebo brain going about its normal day. On the right, we see the brain under the influence of psilocybin. Psilocybin is the natural compound in magic mushrooms. The Psilocybin brain looks like a lot of things are going on there but actually, what is happening in the brain is reorganizing itself in a smarter, more effective way. The diagram depicts diverse brain regions not normally in communication becoming strongly linked. Psilocybin causes the brain to explore new underdeveloped parts of the brain.

As Michael Pollan explores the neuroscience in his new book How to Change Your Mind, he writes: When scientists at Imperial College began imaging the brains of people on psilocybin[39], they were surprised to find that the chemical, which they assumed would boost brain activity, actually reduced it, but in a specific area: the default mode network. This is a brain network involved in a range of "metacognitive" processes, including self-reflection, mental time travel, theory of mind (the ability to imagine mental states in others), and the generation of narratives about ourselves that help to create the sense of having a stable self over time.

The default mode network is most active when our minds are least engaged in a task—hence "default mode." It is where our minds go when they wander or ruminate. The Imperial scientists found that when volunteers reported an experience of ego dissolution, the fMRI scans of their brains showed a precipitous drop in activity in the default mode network, suggesting that this network may be the seat of the ego.

One way to think about the ego is as a mental construct that performs certain functions on our behalf. Chief among these are maintaining the boundary between the conscious and unconscious realms of the mind and the boundary between self and other.

So what happens when these boundaries fade or disappear under psychedelics? Our ego defenses relax, allowing unconscious material and emotions to enter our awareness and also for us to feel less separate and more connected—to other people, to nature, or the universe. And a renewed sense of connection is precisely what volunteers in the various addiction, depression, and cancer anxiety trials have all reported.

This points to the most compelling reason to pursue the new science of psychedelics: the possibility that it may yield a grand unified theory of mental illnesses, or at least of those common disorders that psychedelics show promise in alleviating: depression, addiction, anxiety, and obsession. All these disorders involve uncontrollable and endlessly repeating loops of rumination that gradually shade out reality and fray our connections to other people and the natural world. The ego becomes hyperactive, even oppressive, enforcing rigid habits of thought and behavior— habits that the psychedelic experience, by loosening the ego's grip, could help us to break.

That power to disrupt mental habits and "lubricate cognition" is what Robin Carhart-Harris, the neuroscientist at Imperial College who scanned the brains of volunteers on psychedelics, sees as the key therapeutic value of the drugs. The brain is a hierarchical system, with the default mode network at the top, serving as what he variously calls "the orchestra conductor," "corporate executive," or "capital city." But as important as keeping order in such a complex system, a brain can also suffer from an excess of order. Depression, anxiety, obsession, and the cravings of addiction could be how it feels to have a brain that has become excessively rigid or fixed in its pathways and linkages—a brain with more order than is good for it.

Dr. Carhart-Harris suggests that, by taking the default mode network offline for a time, psychedelics can, in effect, "reboot" the brain, jog it out of its accustomed grooves and open a space for new pathways to arise. His lab has made maps of the brain's traffic patterns on psychedelics showing that when the default mode network is quieted, myriad new connections spring up in the brain, linking far-flung areas that don't ordinarily talk to one another directly[40].

Your DNA on Psychedelics

Dr. Simon Ruffell, is a Senior Researcher at the Psychae Institute and Chief Medical Officer for Heroic Hearts UK, a charity supporting veterans with psychedelic plant medicine. As a researcher at Kings College London, Dr. Ruffell led an observational study where the team looked at the use of ayahuasca by 63 participants who attended a traditional

Shipibo retreat, and its effects on their mental health[41].

The research team collected inventory surveys before and after participants' retreats, and then again six months later to look primarily at depression, anxiety, and self-compassion, as well as mindfulness, general well-being, the perception of traumatic memories, and other secondary measures. They also collected saliva samples.

"We collected saliva samples in order to assess potential changes in gene expression—a field called epigenetics," says Ruffell. His team assessed three genes related to trauma and neuroplasticity, the brain's ability to make new connections.

Ruffell says based on the existing body of research on ayahuasca and mental health outcomes, he wasn't surprised to learn that participants showed decreases in depression and anxiety and improvements in mindfulness, self-compassion, and general well-being. In addition, participants were found to perceive memories in a less negative way.

"We also found that, the greater degree their mystical experience, the greater their decrease in depression, which was in line with other psychedelic research," he added. The results of the six-month follow-up showed that the impact ayahuasca had on participants' depression was lasting, with some even continuing to experience a decrease in their symptoms long after the retreat had ended.

"This was the first-ever study to look at any psychedelic and epigenetics, and that in itself is exciting," says Ruffell, though he's quick to caveat that statement with a note about the study's small sample size. While he says there was a "statistically significant change" in the expression of the gene SIGMAR1, which is thought to be involved in how traumatic memories are stored, it's too early to generalize the results.

"We can't draw any conclusions, but what it does suggest is that ayahuasca may well be having some kind of effect on the genetic level," he says, noting the group is awaiting additional funding to continue the study and increase the sample size.

Making Psychiatry Spiritual Again

"Psychiatrist" derives from the Greek words psukhe meaning "soul" and iatros meaning "healer". So "psychiatrist" actually means – and originally meant when it was first used around 170 years ago – "soul healer"[42].

Yet so much of 21st Century mental health treatment focuses only on the mind. Could it be that one of the reasons rates of what are known today as mental health problems have increased so dramatically is because we ignore the spiritual aspect of being a person?

Since the Industrial Revolution started in Europe in the 18th Century, the Western world has put increasingly less emphasis on spirituality. Nations and their people look to the material world as a reason for living and the way to happiness.

Striving for material gain has led to much more pressure and stress in life. Now, for instance, it is a necessity that both partners work full-time whereas until relatively recently that was not the case.

In a recent talk entitled The Power of Connection,[43] physician, trauma expert and author Dr Gabor Maté said: "There are mental illnesses that develop originally really as compensations against stress and trauma. In a materialistic society, we measure success by the possession or the control or the production of matter, of materials. It's materials that matter. But is it a true measure of a successful society? Can a society be called successful because it produces, controls or owns more matter than some other society? An equally important measure, at least as important measure of a society and culture, is to what degree does it meet human needs? How well does it promote healthy human development and to what degree and ways does it undermine it?"

Maté talks about disconnection caused by our modern Western system playing a major part in both physical and mental illnesses. Connection with others can be seen as a spiritual aspect of the human condition. Feeling disconnected from others is a major part of many mental health illnesses, including conditions such as addiction and depression.

We live in a world today that despite us being more connected than ever before through technology, there is often less actual connection. A large part of recovery is about restoring connection. That is to other people – but also for the person seeking help to reconnect with their true selves.

A Moral Biology

Clinical psychologist William Richards, the longtime collaborator in the John Hopkins psilocybin trials, concludes that ethics and morality are hardwired, "perhaps genetically encoded" within the human DNA[44]. Psilocybin appeals to unlock that code by tapping directly into what the mystics have been trying to mine over the history of religion with chanting, meditation, fasting, and prayer. Morality is encoded in our biology. Science affirms that morality is a human biological attribute because we make moral judgments: to judge some actions as good and others as evil. The primary origin of our moral instincts traces back to the relation between cooperation that humanity needed to create the proper infrastructure for civilization.

Biological research shows that human societies are so prosperous mostly because of how altruistic we are. Unlike other animals, people cooperate even with complete strangers. We share knowledge on Wikipedia, we show up to vote, and we work together to responsibly manage natural resources. This branch of study is called biological altruism. Evolutionary biologists and animal behaviorists study such behaviors, looking for both immediate and evolutionary explanations. Arunas L Radzvilavicius, an evolutionary theorist at the University of Pennsylvania, partnered with Joshua Plotkin, a theoretical biologist at the University of Pennsylvania, and Alex Stewart at the University of Houston, both experts in game theoretical approaches to human behavior, to better understand the source of biological altruism[45].

More empathy, more cooperation

As the researchers turned up the amount of empathy (on the horizontal axis) in their modeled societies, cooperation rates (on the vertical axis) tended to climb, whichever rules they told individuals to use to assign good or bad reputations. Only the social norm known as "Scoring" wasn't affected by growing empathy in the society.

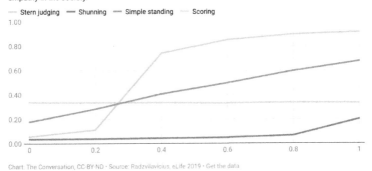

Their research model which claims that the modern empathy members have in a society is directly linked to the success of society matches up with other biological and real world research.

Humans are social, and empathy is a fundamental component of the human condition. As humans, we all have mirror neurons in our brain. Mirror neurons allow humans - and all other animals - to mirror the emotions of others as if they were their own. The scientific press often refers to them as "empathy neurons". The discovery of mirror neurons has forced biologists, philosophers, linguists, psychologists and others to rethink a generation of misinformation about our innate connection to each other and to nature. Marco Iacoboni is a neuroscientist at UCLA and a leading researcher of mirror neurons. In his book, Mirroring People, Professor Iacoboni points out neuroscience research which shows that we are wired to connect:

> "Mirror neurons help us to be empathic and
> fundamentally attuned to other people. This is
> perhaps the most important finding of all, and it is a
> beautiful[46]."

Human nature is not to seek autonomy - to become an island to oneself - but, father, to seek companionship, affection and intimacy. Babies, for example, are prewired for companionship. Research shows that if infants are denied affection and maternal companionship, the infants will lose the will to live[47]. The point that Iacoboni and other scientists are making is that empathy is our nature and what makes us social beings.

The Health Benefits of Nature

Perhaps we are disconnected from our own nature of empathy because we have become disconnected from nature. The majority of western civilization lives in artificial environments. A growing body of research points to the beneficial effects that exposure to the natural world has on health, reducing stress and promoting healing. Now, policymakers, employers, and healthcare providers are increasingly considering the human need for nature.

In a study of 20,000 people[48], a team led by Mathew White of the European Centre for Environment & Human Health at the University of Exeter, found that people who spent two hours a week in green spaces — local parks or other natural environments, either all at once or spaced over several visits — were substantially more likely to report good health and psychological well-being than those who don't. Two hours was a hard boundary: The study, published last June, showed there were no benefits for people who didn't meet that threshold.

"It's well-known that getting outdoors in nature can be good for people's health and well-being, but until now we've not been able to say how much is enough," White says. "Two hours a week is hopefully a realistic target for many people, especially given that it can be spread over an entire week to get the benefit.[49]"

These studies have shown that time in nature — as long as people feel safe — is an antidote for stress: It can lower blood pressure and stress hormone levels, reduce nervous system arousal, enhance immune system function, increase self-esteem, reduce anxiety, and improve mood. Attention Deficit Disorder and aggression lessen in natural environments, which also help speed the rate of healing. In a recent study, psychiatric unit researchers found that being in nature reduced feelings of isolation, promoted calm, and lifted mood among patients[50].

The organization Children & Nature Network, founded by Louv and others, advocates for more time in nature for children, tracks the research, and has a long list of abstracts that summarize studies on the subject on its website.

The number of "forest schools" — which have long been a tradition in Scandinavia and where much of the learning takes place in natural settings in the outdoors — has mushroomed in the United States, up by 500 percent since

2012, according to Louv. Oregon recently passed a ballot measure to raise money for outdoor schools, and the state of Washington just became the first state to license outdoor preschools, where much of the play and learning occurs outside.

The western world is rediscovering through science our lost roots to our true nature, our inner reality, to nature and to relationships with life itself. Especially our relationships with our inner lives. Now science is posed to help us understand that spirituality is also part of nature because we are nature.

The Science of Prayer

David H. Rosmarin, assistant professor of psychology at Harvard Medical School and director of the Spirituality and Mental Health Program at McLean Hospital, believes that the benefits of prayer are similar to those of meditation. Studies have shown that prayer can calm the nervous system, reduce the fight or flight response, and make a person less reactive to negative emotions and less angry. However, Rosmarin notes that there is a lack of funding for research on the benefits of spirituality in the medical community.

In a 2005 study published in the Journal of Behavioral Medicine, researchers compared secular and spiritual forms of meditation. The study found that spiritual meditation, where a person focuses on a spiritual word or text, was more effective at calming anxiety and stress, increasing positive mood, and increasing pain tolerance than secular meditation, where a person focuses on something like their breath. Participants who meditated using words of self-affirmation showed similar benefits to those who meditated with words that described a higher power.

Participants were divided into groups, with some being taught how to meditate using words of self-affirmation ("I am love") and others taught how to meditate with words that described a higher power ("God is love"). They then meditated for 20 minutes a day for four weeks.

Researchers found that the group that practiced spiritual meditation showed greater decreases in anxiety and stress and more positive mood. They also tolerated pain almost twice as long when asked to put their hand in an ice water bath.

Some scientists who study prayer believe that people who pray are benefiting from a feeling of emotional support. Imagine carrying a backpack hour after hour. It will start to feel impossibly heavy. But if you can hand it off to someone else to hold for a while, it will feel lighter when you pick it up again.

"This is what prayer can do," says Amy Wachholtz, associate professor and clinical health psychology director at the University of Colorado Denver, and lead researcher on the meditation study. "It lets you put down your burden mentally for a bit and rest."

Prayer can also foster a sense of connection—with a higher power, your environment and other people, including "the generations of people who have prayed before you," says Kevin Ladd, a psychologist and director of the Social Psychology of Religion Lab at Indiana University South Bend.

The Science of Reincarnation

Our ancestors used psychedelics as part of their rituals to see beyond the veil of death and become one with life. As a result, our ancestors shared a common belief in reincarnation. Reincarnation means to take on the flesh again or to be reborn.
In one form or another, the belief that the soul, spirit or consciousness is reborn in another body is not limited to spiritual doctrines: it is a widespread, nearly universal belief. It occurs in almost all corners of the planet amongst many groups of people. This idea has been part of the thinking about the nature of reality for thousands - if not tens of thousands - of years.

In the modern era, about 2/3 of people still hold a common belief in the concept of the soul or reincarnation. The ⅓ of people who don't share that belief are found in the western world. For example, there are 2 billion Christians who don't believe in reincarnation. Hindus and Buddhists feature reincarnation as the foundation of their beliefs. The ancient Egyptians believed in it; the ancient Persians arrived at it; the Greek philosophers made it the corner-stone of their philosophy; the Pharisees among the Hebrews accepted it; and the Sufis almost universally acknowledged its truth.

> *"The statistical probability that reincarnation does in fact occur is so overwhelming that cumulatively the evidence is not inferior to that for most if not all branches of science..."*
> - Doris Kuhlmann-Wilsdorf, Professor Physics - University of Virginia.

Serious scientific study of reincarnation has indeed been undertaken, despite the fact that it is a touchy subject, and the results ultimately challenge the belief systems of many. This topic has been studied by numerous scientists who belong to various academic institutions from all over the world. In the interest of concise but compelling argument choosing which examples and studies to highlight can be difficult given how many of them exist.

Much of today's reincarnation research comes to us from the legacy of Ian Stevenson. Ian Stevenson was the Carlson Professor of Psychiatry and Director of the Division of Parapsychology, Department of Behavioral Medicine and Psychiatry, at the University of Virginia School of Medicine. His research has become perhaps the best-known and most respected collection of scientific data that provides scientific evidence for reincarnation. Dr. Stevenson eventually founded the Division of Perceptual Studies at the University of Virginia School of Medicine. Over 40 years, he accumulated about 3,000 cases of children who claimed to remember past lives. They had certain physical and verifiable similarities and circumstances regarding their present and remembered past lives.

After working with Stevenson for several years, Jim Tucker took over his research when Stevenson retired in 2002. A board-certified child psychiatrist, Tucker is an associate professor of psychiatry and neurobehavioral sciences at the University of Virginia. He is the director of DOPS and has published two books on children with past-life memories and numerous paper and supervises cases at the University Child and Family Psychiatry Clinic.

Children can have verifiable past life memories that can be independently corroborated. Over many decades, researchers have documented cases of children - often as young as two - reporting memories they say are from a previous life. In some cases, the children can present specific names, places and events that they never can had a chance to know about. These specifics can be used to "solve" the case by going back years in the public records.

During his medical practice, Dr. Ian Stevenson noted that certain fears and phobias, unusual abilities, and illnesses in his young patients could not be explained by heredity or the environment. He had heard of reincarnation and sought to investigate if it could somehow provide an explanation and to find out if human emotions, memories and physical attributes, birthmarks, and susceptibility to certain diseases could be transferred from one life to the next.

Since 1950, past life regression, a method of healing where patients are put under hypnosis, was already gaining acceptance by medical practitioners. During hypnosis, the underlying spiritual reasons for the complaints could be traced to some root cause or causes related to the patient's past life experiences. Dramatic results were achieved by applying the knowledge gained as part of the therapy. Beginning in the 1960s, Dr. Helen Wambach conducted her studies on more than 10,000 volunteers to examine reincarnation's truth. Her books chronicle the true accounts of those who remembered some of the details of their past lives.

> *"Initially intending to disprove reincarnation, on finishing her work, she concluded, 'I don't believe in reincarnation – I know it!'"*
> (Wambach 1978).

In his book 'A Lawyer Presents the Evidence for the Afterlife,' Victor Zammit, a retired attorney of the Supreme Court of the New South Wales and the High Court of Australia, lists the following information[51]:

1. "I am absolutely convinced of the fact that those who once lived on earth can and do communicate with us. It is hardly possible to convey to the inexperienced an adequate idea of the strength and cumulative force of the evidence." - *Sir William Barrett F.R.S. One of the pioneers in psychical research in the UK.*

2. "I tell you, we do persist. Communication is possible. I have proved that the people who communicate are who and what they say they are. The conclusion is that survival is scientifically proven by scientific investigation." *Sir Oliver Lodge F.R.S. His research led to the invention of the wireless telegraph and the radio.*

3. "It is quite true that a connection has been set up between this world and the next." *Sir William Crookes F.R.S. One of the founders and past president of the* Society for Psychical Research (SPR) in England.

4. "I have been talking with my (dead) father, my brother, my uncles... Whatever supernormal powers we may be pleased to attribute to (the medium) Mrs. Piper's secondary personalities, it would be difficult to make me believe that these secondary personalities could have thus completely reconstituted the mental personality of my dead relatives..." *Professor Hyslop is a Former Professor of Logic at Columbia University.*

5. "After the spirit has been separated from the body (which happens when a person dies), he is still alive, a person, the way he was before.

"To assure me of this, I have been allowed to talk with practically everyone I have ever known during this physical life—with some for hours, with some for weeks or months, with some for years—all for the overriding purpose that I might be assured of this fact, (that life continues after death) and might bear witness to it." (Emmanuel Swedenborg, inventor of the glider, submarine, the ear trumpet for the deaf and a gifted clairvoyant, Heaven and Hell: 437)."

6. "Alfred Russell Wallace, who propounded the theory of evolution at the same time as and independently of Charles Darwin, painstakingly investigated Spiritualism over a number of years. Eventually, he stated that its phenomena were proved quite as well as the facts of any other science."

7. "John Logie Baird, television pioneer and inventor of the infra-red camera, stated that he had contacted the 'deceased' Thomas A. Edison through a medium. He said: 'I have witnessed some very startling phenomena under circumstances which make trickery out of the question' (Logie Baird 1988: 68-69)."

8. "Dr. Kübler-Ross, who has had a global impact on the way that dying people are treated, became totally convinced of life after death through her close association with thousands of dying patients. She writes: 'Up until then, I had absolutely no belief in an afterlife, but the data convinced me that these were not coincidences or hallucinations.' (Kübler-Ross 1997: 188)."

9. "Dr. Melvin Morse (a pediatrician and a recognized world leading authority on dying children) was, as he put it, 'an arrogant critical-care physician' with 'an emotional bias against anything spiritual' before his scientifically based studies of dying children and his extensive study of the literature led him to the inescapable conclusion that 'there is a divine something which serves as a glue for the universe.' He writes: 'When I review the medical literature, I think it points directly to evidence that some aspect of human consciousness survives death.' (Morse 1994:190)."

10. "Dr. J.B. Rhine and his wife, Dr. Louisa Rhine of the Rhine Research Centre, coined the term 'parapsychology' and conducted extensive experiments into the existence of psi (a neutral term for all extra sensory perception and psychokinetic phenomena like telepathy, clairvoyance, and precognition), the sixth sense or mediumship.

"In their book *Extra-Sensory Perception After Sixty Years* (Rhine et al.) they claim that by 1940, 33 experiments had been done involving almost a million trials, with protocols which rigorously excluded possible sensory clues, e.g., by introducing distance and barriers between sender and receiver, or by employing precognition protocols where the target has not yet been selected at the time subjects make their responses. Twenty-seven (27) of the 33 studies produced statistically significant results.

"These studies were replicated in 33 independent replication experiments done in different laboratories in the five years following Rhine's first publication of his results. Twenty of these, or 61%, were statistically significant where 5% would be expected by chance alone."

11. Other world-renowned classical scientists and thinkers around the world, such as Sir Arthur Conan Doyle, Arthur Findlay, Camille Flammarion, Dr. Baraduc, Professor Richet, Professor Robert Hare, Professor Albert Einstein, Marconi, F.W. Myers, Professor William James, and Dr. Carrington, after investigation, accepted the afterlife.

Everything is Consciousness

The dominant materialist science paradigm of the 21st century reduces everything to matter. Materialist science in the West says that we are just meat, we're just our bodies. So when the brain is dead, that's the end of consciousness, there is no life after death, there is no soul; we just rot and are gone. The biggest problem with their argument is that scientists should admit that consciousness is the greatest mystery of science and that we don't know exactly how it works. The brain is involved in it some way but we're not sure how.

The Law of Conservation of Energy states that energy can neither be created nor destroyed - only converted from one form of energy to another.

If we want to understand consciousness, the last people we should ask are materialist scientists. Instead, we should look at ancient cultures, like the Egyptians, who highly valued dream states or we should look to quantum physicists who are rewriting our understanding of the material universe. Many of us have been taught a classical materialist version of physics. That knowledge is now incompatible with what physicists at the forefront of the field know today. There are aspects of quantum physics that show us the divine nature of reality and the interconnectedness of all that is. The easiest way to crack open that box is to talk about consciousness or God as energy.

Quantum Mechanics states that the Universe is made up of space filled with fields of vibration, interconnected, unified and in constant communication, where distance and time are of no consequence; where one end of the Universe moves connected and in relationship to the other end and everything in between is a grand movement or dance held in space. In truth then, our lives and indeed everything in the entire universe are not only all connected, but absolutely so, with no separation.

At the core of Quantum Mechanics is an absolutely simple experiment called the 'double slit experiment'. This describes the nature and mechanics of the building blocks of the world we live in, the atomic world. The double-slit experiment illustrates how we, through our observation of objects, actually affect those objects or outcomes. It exposes the process of how we uphold a world, or so-called reality, that holds us back from connecting to a far grander truth and the all that we are part of.

A great reflection of this is found in our oceans. Just as waves in the ocean travel endlessly, reflecting off the shore and each other, vibrations move as waves, never truly ending; they simply interact and transform with each other and objects. Objects themselves are simply vibrations of a denser frequency. Since everything is vibration, then everything is formed by vibration and hence there is no individuality, only interconnectedness that evolves and expands by its own interaction with its grand self.

Evidence of a brand new physics?

Posted by **EarthSky Voices** *in* **HUMAN WORLD** | March 28, 2021

Physicists at the LHCb Collaboration at CERN have found particles not behaving the way they should according to the guiding theory of particle physics. Could it be evidence of a brand new physics?

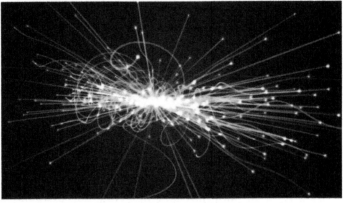

Particle collisions are starting to reveal unexpected results. Image via vchal/ Shutterstock.

Quantum mechanics, the foundation of modern science, has continued to move closer to the startling and revolutionary conclusion that everything is consciousness—albeit reluctantly. As physicists explored the relationship between energy and the structure of matter - the belief that a physical, Newtonian material universe that was at the very heart of scientific knowledge was dropped, and the realization that matter is nothing but an illusion replaced it. Scientists began to recognize that everything in the Universe is made out of energy.

> *"Get over it, and accept the inarguable conclusion. The universe is immaterial-mental and spiritual"*

> – Richard Conn Henry, Professor of Physics and Astronomy at Johns Hopkins University (quote taken from "the mental universe)

It's quite the conundrum, isn't it? Our experience tells us that our reality is made up of physical material things, and that our world is an independently existing objective one. The revelation that the universe is not an assembly of physical parts, suggested by Newtonian physics, and instead comes from a holistic entanglement of immaterial energy waves stems from the work of Albert Einstein, Max Planck and Werner Heisenberg, among others.

I regard consciousness as fundamental. I regard matter as derivative from consciousness
- Max Planck, father of quantum mechanics

If science is telling us that everything is consciousness then it would make sense to review the research on consciousness to see if there is evidence corroborating that conclusion.

What are the most powerful tools we have to explore consciousness? Arguably, they are psychedelics and meditation.

For thousands of years, meditators have reported the mystical experience of becoming one with the universe. Many have suggested that, though psychedelics and meditation are very different, the mystical experience each can induce are identical. This would indicate that, though the path is different, both meditator and psychedelic user arrive at the same place.

What is that place? It is when a soul's awareness "turns around" and becomes aware of, and conscious of, itself. The mystical experience during meditation, outside of meditation, and during a psychedelic session all corroborate what quantum mechanics has indicated about our universe. The research shows that consciousness is part of everything in the universe and that everything is consciousness.

In Judaism there is the phrase:

(אין עוד מלבדו) = Ein od milvado

This Hebrew phrase comes to us from Judaism and translates to: there is nothing but God. In Chabad philosophy (orthodox Judaism) the phrase means that not only is there

no other God besides Him, there is nothing besides Him—
literally. Only God exists. This is a statement on the nature of
the cosmos as much as it is a theological belief.

We see this belief permeate many of the world's religions.
The Vedas, ancient religious texts from India, teaches us that
God is everywhere in creation. The Vedas describe God as:

yato va imani bhutani jayante, yena jatani jivanti,
yatprayantyabhisamvisanti

This sanskrit phrase translates to:

"God is He, Who has created this world;
God is He, within Whom the entire world exists;
God is he, within Whom the whole world will
merge at the time of annihilation"
Taittiriya Upanisad, 3.1

The Vedic hymns confirm the fact that God the Creator is the
origin of all living entities and the rest of all that is. After
creation, everything rests in the Lord's omnipotence, and
after annihilation, everything again returns to rest in God.
These are the confirmations of Vedic hymns.

Religions, mystics and philosophers have consistently
pointed humanity in the direction of a Creator being who
connects and transcends the entire universe. And today, we
now have a large body of scientific evidence to prove what
these mystics and religions have long sought to teach us
about our place in the cosmos.

Psychedelics and meditation are two of the best ways to
experience consciousness. Interesting then that we learn that
all the great messengers of History were practitioners of
meditation and psychedelics. Mary & Jesus taught there is no
sin but to forget you are a soul in a human body. They taught
that the unity of the soul with the ego is how we become

spiritually aligned, integrated and conscious with the Kingdom of Heaven in our own hearts. Science has now caught up to the ancient wisdom of the masters and wisdom keepers who have guided humanity for thousands of years.

CHAPTER 13:

A Roadmap for Global Healing

Psychedelics changed my life. They taught me the truth about what I am, where I come from, and why I'm here on this earth. These natural medicines opened my eyes to the injustice that exists in our modern world. As a spoiled, privileged kid, I learned the hard way that the system in which we live is unfair. These medicines healed me but they've done more than heal me; they saved my soul and made me a better man. They taught me how to become my best self, how to live my life from a place of service, how to overcome my anxiety and depression, and childhood traumas.

I am dedicating my life to spreading the good word about God's natural medicine. I didn't make it. You didn't make it. But the creator of the universe did. I will spend all my resources and talents to create change in any way possible. I hope you can hear me and I hope you can see the healing power of psychedelic medicine. On a spiritual level, the medicine helped me attain a level of self-awareness, a level of gratitude, and an abundance of love and kindness for myself and for others which I have never known before. What I know now is that feeling is native and naturally found within all of us deep down in our souls. I am honored to share my story, to spread the gospel of psychedelic medicine and to represent the medicine plant teachers in a good way.

Drupon Lama Dorje, founder of the Lama Dorje Foundation, invited me to go with him to meet the Dalai Lama. Sadly, I couldn't make the dates work. When he met with the Dalai Lama, he asked: "Dalai Lama, how do we create peace in this world?"

The Dalai Lama said, "Ah, everyone talks about global peace. Global peace this, Global peace that. But the way to make global peace starts with inner peace. To make outer peace, one must create inner peace. The way to inner peace is compassion."

The way to enter into peace is to give love and kindness to oneself. Through holy communion with sacred sacraments and other spiritual practices we can begin to build that connection. We can learn the truth: we are all connected. We are all brothers and sisters. Every religion from Christ to Buddha, all the way back at least 80,000 years, masters were using natural psychedelic medicine to connect with the divine and ultimately create a world full of love.

Dear Sibling, I have one dream: to build a world based on love, kindness, and goodness. I have staked my life fulfilling this mission, but I can't do it alone. I need you; I need your medicine; I need your help. So I hope you enjoy some of my ideas for creating a better world. I hope you enjoyed this book, it is my gift to you. Thank you for listening.

Giving Birth to a New Earth

The Q'ero Elders and Shamans are keen to share the prophecies of their Ancestors with the Modern world. As part of their message to the modern world about the prophecy of Pachakuti, which they believe completes on 21 December 2012, they highlight the great opportunities for humanity at this time[2]:

> In this life, we need to share and live in community with no jealousy, no competitions, united, sharing, not only

between people, but sharing with the earth and mountains. Incas prophecies talk about Pachacuti. "Pacha" means "earth" and "Cuti" means "turn over, renewal of life.

This is a Time of tremendous crisis in the world, but as with any crisis it brings opportunity. Opportunities to reinvent who we are, to reinvent what world we want to create for our children and our children's children.

The Earth's new guardians will come from the West and, those who have made the greatest impact on Mother Earth, now have a responsibility to redo the relationship with Her, after redoing themselves.

We need to re-learn to honor and respect Mother Earth, Father Sun, Sisters, discover and respect everything and everyone and so on, be able to make a quantum leap towards what we are becoming, all together. The prophecies say we are ending the time of the transition and a new higher level of consciousness will begin to manifest and the golden age of humanity will gradually begin, step by step.

Imagine

What kind of world are we building for our children, for their children and for the next seven generations of children?

Children are the most precious resource in all the world because they are our future. Good parents always consider their children when making life decisions. So why do we not first consider the children when we make societal decisions? It's up to us to imagine a new world, a better world for all children, their children and seven generations of children into the future. Imagine a world where we build communities around healing. A world where we replace the sick care system, which profits from keeping our brothers and sisters sick, with a system of WellCare, where the real profit is made caring for our families.

As the hip-hop duo Dead Prez once said: True wealth is good health and wise ways. Imagine a world without suicide, an epidemic of mental illness and spiritual disease. Imagine a world filled with goodness, love and kindness. It is the world I dream about. This dream can be real if we learn to work together, and it's never been more achievable than now.

Walking the Path of Loving Kindness

You are invited to walk the path of Loving Kindness. This path is a simple way of life. It needs no temples; it has no complicated doctrine. Our brain, our own heart, is our temple. It is the philosophy of spirit, the religion of loving-kindness. One walks this path to embody love and light.

And this is the message which we have heard from him, and declare to you, that God is light, and in him is no darkness at all.
(1 John 1:5)

God is love, and he that abides in love abides in God, and God in him.
(1 John 4:16)

Love is Kind
(1 Corinthians 13:4)

The path of Loving Kindness is to remember that our lives are connected, that everyone matters, and that all life is precious. We are all related. Loving Kindness is a state of being one practices and cultivates to achieve Gnosis - the knowledge of spiritual truths to achieve salvation and enlightenment. Yeshua the Christ, Buddha, and all the Masters have walked the path of Loving Kindness. Through spiritual disciplines, they became one with love and light.

These masters gave their lives to spread the true original Gospel of Loving Kindness.

I am the light of the world. Whoever follows me will not walk in darkness.

Believe in the light while you have the light so that you may become children of light.
John 12:3

So I call out to you. I call out to those who hear this message and are ready to give their lives for the highest good of all beings. I call to those who wish to walk the path of loving kindness and learn the true original teachings of Yeshua and the Masters.

The alchemy one needs to impact the world is to live in a way of radical kindness. Love and Kindness are often confused. Kindness is strength. It is the gift of seeing good in everyone despite what life brings our way. Kindness is speaking one's truth.

So hear this: something is seriously wrong with this moment in our lives. We, humankind, are not well. We are sick. Our spirit, our souls are dis-eased. For many years I asked God to show me the cause of this illness.

Ask, and it shall be given you;
seek, and ye shall find;
knock, and it shall be opened unto you
(Matthew 7:7)

I see now how humanity abandoned the path of loving kindness in favor of other masters. The first step on this path is to acknowledge we need to heal. May we grant ourselves the kindness to be honest with ourselves. You'll find this message is shared freely with anyone who wishes to receive it.

This Gospel is called by the ancestors of the east the *Sanatana* Dharma. *Sanatana* is a Sanskrit word that means everlasting. Dharma means the religious duty to sustain and that which is integral to something. Therefore, a person's *dharma* consists of duties that sustain them according to their innate characteristics. In many ways, it is our eternal duty to remain rooted in the natural law of loving kindness for the benefit of all beings and to sustain the balance of life on earth.

A Message from the Master Plants

We are the spirits of the Master Plants and Fungi. We reveal now and forevermore our teachings to you through the "Word." In the beginning, was the Word, and the Word was with God, and the Word was God. Soon after, the Word was made flesh, and God said Let there be light, and there was light. The original flesh on Earth was our flesh, the flesh of plant life. We are the flesh of the Great Spirit. God said, "See, I give you every seed-bearing plant that is upon all the earth and every tree that has seed-bearing fruit; they shall be yours for food."

We are Medicine.
All medicines for the mind, the body, and the spirit are found in the bodies of plants and fungi people.

We are the Guardians.
As plant and fungi people, we were here before humankind. We protect millions of years of information and access to multidimensional realms. We naturally maintain a sacred harmony with all of life.

We are the Light.

The sustenance for all plants is light. We are beings of light.

We are the Way.
Your scientists are learning that using our medicines helps humans remember the sacred truth that we are all one heart, one mind, one family, and one sacred chanupa.

We are Life.
Without clean air, water, and healthy soil, there can be no life. These are universal laws for life on earth. As we once facilitated the enlightenment of Master Yeshua, we intend to facilitate the spiritual transformation of the human family for the benefit of all beings.

Gospel means good news, so this is the good news of God's Medicine. God created life. We are all the children of God. On behalf of God, the Angels, the Ancestors, and Spirits, you are instructed to cultivate healing, knowledge and understanding of naturally occurring psychedelic sacraments. You are to learn these lessons and spread the gospel to all four corners of the Universe. This Gospel is now entrusted to you.

Your scientists have learned that we, the plant people, have consciousness. Mountains of research confirm that we, the plant people, have intelligence and even beyond that consciousness by many of the same measures as humans do[21]. Not only do we feel pain, but we also perceive and interact with their environment in sophisticated ways.

The deep intelligence possessed by plants has been explored and discussed by many people of note over the past several centuries, including Goethe, Luther Burbank, George Washington Carver, Masanobu Fukuoka, Jagadis Bose, and the Nobel Prize-winner Barbara McClintock. Plants, it turns out, really are highly conscious, intelligent and yes, they do have a brain. It's just that no one ever looked in the right place. The old paradigm about plants, which is very common and unfortunately still believed by most people, is that plants are unconscious, "passive entities subject to environmental forces and organisms that are designed solely for accumulation of photosynthetic products."[22]

But as Baluska et al. note: The new view, by contrast, is that plants are dynamic and highly sensitive organisms, actively and competitively foraging for limited resources both above and below ground, and that they are also organisms which accurately compute their circumstances, using sophisticated cost-benefit analysis, and they take defined actions to mitigate and control diffuse environmental conditions. Moreover, plants are also capable of a refined recognition of self and non-self and this leads to territorial behavior[23].

Now perhaps you have the scientific knowledge and the spiritual knowledge to understand Master Christ's message:

> Very truly, I tell you,
> unless you eat the flesh
> of the Son of Man
> and drink his blood,
> you have no life in you.
> Whoever eats my flesh
> and drinks my blood has an eternal lie.
> I am the true vine, and my Father
> is the gardener.

The Importance of the Sacred Fire

Our bodies are made of air, earth, water, fire, and spirit. These are the basic elements of life in this dimension. When we are praying and communing with spirit using God's medicines, it is important we sit around a fire. This fire serves as a sign to the spirits and ancestors looking down on us. When we sing prayers, give offerings and put our hearts into the fire; we send a smoke signal to the spirit world to bring the ancestors to us and help us heal. Grandfather Fire shares his spirit with us and serves to anchor the light of the creator in the ceremony circle. When we practice the spiritual disciplines and achieve Christ consciousness, we learn that we are the light. Our soul is made of light. From the light we come and to the light we return. This is why the Buddhists say *Namaste* which means the light within honors and acknowledges the light within you. The Buddhists know we are light just as Jesus Christ knew we are light. It's the same reason those who experience a NDE - near death experience - report seeing bright lights. This understanding of our souls and our relationship to all of life was the original universal religion of our ancestors. The use of the Sacred Fire and God's natural psychedelic medicines was the basis for communion and worship. We the people of earth have forgotten these sacred memories and truths.

Know this: we forget so we can remember. This moment of the prophecy is to be known as the Great Remembering. Many use the term Great Awakening because we, as a human family, are awakening from a collective spiritual slumber.

The Role of Religions

For thousands of years, religion was a way for our ancestors to better understand the relationship between us, the earth, and why we exist. We learned about these connections and developed this relationship through shamanic ceremonies using psychedelic sacraments. This is the way of our ancestors. Thankfully, this legacy is maintained by the indigenous tribes of North and South America. So, we should look for inspiration in reforming our religious practices. I think it's time we use the scientific understanding of psychedelics to understand better spirituality, our connection to nature and the universe, and ultimately return to the old ways of psychedelic shamanism.

None of the major spiritual teachers throughout history were religious. Jesus wasn't a Christian and Buddha was not Buddhist. All of these spiritual masters did not practice religion, they mastered themselves in solitude by looking within, meditating, and healing with natural psychedelic medicine, and as a result, they discovered that they were infinite and connected with the universal consciousness. Only later did we call this consciousness God.

Zoroaster, Buddha, Muhammed, Jesus, and Moses were all prophets and messengers from God that preceded the founding of the modern religions. After the prophets' pioneering work and new revelations, the newly formed religion clarifies and disseminates the new teachings, accepts converts and propagates the new faith, maintains the gains of previous efforts, and ministers to the needs of their flock. Their focus and primary objective is more of a spiritual nature. While pursuing knowledge and scientific studies is important, they are also secondary to the objectives relating to righteous living and character formation.

In general, religion teaches the concept of a G-d or gods that created the Cosmos and everything in it. They created man in their image and likeness. Man is upon the earth to learn about himself, attain a certain high level of spiritual development and return home from whence he came – to God and the heaven life, there to stay for all eternity.

The core of all the spiritual teachings are about: how we are all spiritual beings, and that we are equal to God, and by practicing such things as forgiveness, kindness, honesty, and introspection we can become the Gods that we already are and create a peaceful heaven here on Earth.

The Harm of Western Culture

The scientific worldview of Western civilization is what anthropologists characterize as an exploitative worldview. It assumes life's materialistic nature rather than reality's divine nature. In it, religion and spiritual disciplines are less a part of daily activities and tend to be restricted to special occasions.

Since God is outside of nature, the attitude is held that nature exists only to be used by humans. By extension, anthropologists observe that societies that adopt a worldview may find nothing wrong with manipulating other societies to assure their survival. This exploitative worldview, prevalent among food-producing peoples, contributes to inter-societal warfare.

When we take God out of nature and out of humankind, we establish the basis for an exploitative worldview. When an exploitative worldview gains international strength through 1500 years of "progress," we now face nuclear catastrophe and the potential destruction of earth's natural ecosystems.

> No one can serve two masters, for either he will
> hate the one and love the other; or else. he will be
> devoted to one and despise the other. You cannot
> serve both God and money.
> Matthew 6:24

When I think about western culture, I see a society suffering from spiritual decay that is bleeding into all facets of life. That is because western culture worships the false idol of money

Worship of False Idols

Associating money with the sacred lets us believe that there is some magic to its accumulation. Those in the western culture have been transformed into pagans worshiping false idols in the guise of millionaires like the Kardashians. Becoming rich isn't like gaining enlightenment or becoming a world-leading theoretical physicist or a master of martial arts. Chance and circumstance come into play a lot of the time, and we end up following the entertainers rather than the educators. Deceived by money worship[3]. The loss of sacredness speaks to the godlessness in our time and the loss of what it means to be a real human being.

The 20th century saw the fall of widespread religious influence like we have never seen before. At home, many people still practiced their beliefs, but the dominant cultural narrative was one that lacked a firm confidence in God, and in turn a cohesive philosophy. The notion of divinity for example, no longer held a position of paramount importance in our lives, as it had done for millennia. Millions of individuals in the Western world seemed to keep their religious affiliations for cultural rather than spiritual reasons.

> The number one reason people hate America, the
> number one reason is because of our religion.
> Americans worship money, we worship money.
> Separate God from school, separate God from work,
> separate God from government but on your money it
> says in God we trust. All my life I've been looking for
> God and he's right in my pocket! Americans worship
> money, and we all go to the same church, the church
> of ATM.
> - *Chris Rock*

Paganism has left a profound gap in our culture. Man has always needed a story, a myth by which to arrange his belief systems in a way that his psyche can digest. The narrative that took the place of traditional Judeo-Christian values in Western culture was fundamentally based upon the ideals that came with capitalism. One key underlying belief was that men were in control of their own destiny and should build, produce, and own the fruits of their individual labor. Nothing embodies the idol worship more than the 1980s and the phrase: greed is good.

In the United States, the American Dream — the pursuit of happiness — was intrinsically tied to these notions. The dream was initially a modest ideal: basic freedoms and the potential for financial stability. Though what has spawned in the last half a century is a culture obsessed with consumption, and one that expects nothing less than extravagance. Covetousness is forbidden by the 10th commandment, and as greed is defined as idolatry In the New Testament.

לֹא-תַעֲשֶׂה לְךָ פֶסֶל, וְכָל-תְּמוּנָה,
Thou Shalt Not Worship False Idols, 1st
Commandment of God

Weitko: The Virus of Selfishness

There are many viruses affecting the world today but I believe the most deadly virus is that of greed and selfishness. Wetiko is a word that comes to us from the Cree Tribe of the Native American family of Canada. Wetiko is a word that refers to an evil person who never worries about the well-being of others.

In Paul Levy's book *Dispelling Weitko*, he writes there is a contagious psychospiritual disease of the soul, a parasite of the mind, that is currently being acted out en masse on the world stage via a collective psychosis. This mind-virus—which Native Americans have called "wetiko"—covertly operates through the unconscious blind spots in the human psyche, rendering people oblivious to their own madness and compelling them to act against their own best interests.

As a student of ancestral traditions and natural plant medicines, I have learned a little bit about how much the Indigenous tribes of North and South America have to teach and share with humanity. These are tribes that have lived sustainably with nature for thousands of years. And yet when the western world came to the Americas, we gave the tribes the name "savages". In my mind, savages live without respect for nature. Savages are infected with selfishness and greed. Perhaps it's time for us to look in the mirror and ask ourselves: Am I living from a place of Wetiko?

It's no coincidence that almost every single sector of industry is contributing to the planet's downfall, either. A deeper issue underlies our collective responsibility in the malaise enveloping the planet's ecosystems: to cure the wetiko infecting the human spirit.

The insanity Paul writes about is the idea we are separate from nature. The idea we can use nature and bend it to our will is insane. We are made of the same air, earth, water, fire and spirit. When we corrupt water and we drink it, we kill ourselves. When we pollute the air and breathe it, we kill ourselves. When we tarnish the land and eat food from it, we kill ourselves. This is the definition of insanity and the meaning of wetiko. To truly bring ourselves into harmony with the natural world, we must return to seeing ourselves -

the human family - as part of nature.

The sages teach: change yourself to change the world. So I will seek to eliminate the selfishness in my life. I promise to use my gifts, my talents, and my resources to do good and to give my life in service to make this world a better place for my family, for the human family, and for the next generation.

Trust in the Lord with all your heart,
lean not on your own understanding.
In all your ways acknowledge Him
and He will direct your paths
Prov. 3:5-6

Ending the Culture of Ego Consciousness

If one has the eyes to see, they would see that the teachings of the scripture in the New Testament is but a guide, a testimony, a path to ascension. Christ, as all spiritual masters do, taught through various spiritual practices one could walk the path of Ascension. Ascension is what the Gnostics called Gnosis. To ascend is to understand or embody the Gnosis that there is nothing to know. That at our core, at our fundamental level of the Soul, the Nous, we are one. One with God, one with nature, one with infinity.

Today, science validates that oneness. If one takes time to study the science of quantum physics, and energy, one would understand that we are all intrinsically linked. Various phenomena that explain this and testify to this like quantum entanglement. Or like how the Nobel prize was awarded to the discovery the universe is not locally real. The elders from tribes all across the earth teach this wisdom in their own way. The elders I have studied with, say Aho Mitakuye Oyasin which means we are all related. We are all connected because we are one. But we have chosen to forget all of this to get to a point of destruction, to learn the lesson of the ego, of the worship of ego, the worship of ego consciousness, the worship of false idols.

This worship of satanic consciousness violates natural law. Ego consciousness believes with such arrogance there is no God - this is the ultimate worship of false idols.

I like to imagine a conversation between a John, a member of society, and myself:

Me: "I believe God is real"

John "Oh that's foolish. We have science now and we know there is no God."

Me: "Oh, do you? You know there is no God."

John: "Of course there is no God. No science exists that proves God is real."

Me: "I see. Since you know so much can you tell me? Why is your world falling apart? Why are people so sick? So mentally ill? So diseased? Why is your world filled with homelessness and war and division?"

John: "I don't know."

Me: "Oh, so you don't know everything? And you don't know why your world is falling apart? Why people are so unhappy? You don't know?...But you sure know that God is not real? Perhaps it is your neglect of God and the sacred that has created all your problems?"

Many educated members of the western world worship at the altar of science, the religion of science. Ignorance and arrogance go hand in hand.

I've done my best to speak your language of science, to show you the science of psychedelic medicine, the science of history, the science of archaeology, to show you the oneness of the true universal religion - a philosophy of love and kindness that involves sharing space with a sacred fire, communing with prayer and sacred plant medicine sacraments in order to dive deep into one's heart, and to remember the sacred memory:

> *that we are divine,*
> *we are children of God,*
> *we are a soul in the human body,*
> *we are all related.*

Birthing a Culture of Tov (Goodness)

Culture affects everyone. There is no unenculturated human being in this world. No one is without relations, a network, or a system of life and governance. We're all shaped by our interactions with others, and that shaping becomes the culture in which we are all related, networked, and systemically connected.

That's why we need to build a new culture. A culture of *Tov* (goodness) seeks to conform our lives to the true teachings of Love, Kindness, Compassion, Godliness and Goodness by focusing on the welfare of our neighbors, brothers, and sisters instead of institutions.

We are All Related

In a culture of *Tov* one seeks good relations with all of life. A good culture fosters good relations with all of life. Indigenous Americans say *Aho Mitakuye Oyasin*, a Lakota phrase meaning to all my relations. Lakota in English means friend.

When we accept the truth that we are all one family of brothers and sisters, then we are all in relation to each other. We are not just related to each other but we are related to all of life. We all share the same air, same water and the same soil of Mother Earth. Scientifically we know this wisdom to be true through the study of DNA and energy, we are all related and connected. The interconnectedness of all life is a gift from the Creator God, Great Spirit, the source of all life.

In a culture of *Tov* we all stand in a circle because no one is greater, but together we are a greater sum than our parts. A culture of goodness is based on trust. Trust is the invisible glue that binds people together. Without trust, there can be no genuine relations. To trust someone is to believe in that person in ways that make the world safe. In fear-based power culture, trust breaks down and makes life as siblings nearly impossible. Untrusting relations lead to the manifestation of cliques and special interest groups that are not aligned with promoting goodness for the entire community.

As people, we do not live in isolation; we live in tribes. As a tribe, we are living in a relationship with each other. Relationships are all about belonging. We all belong, and we all *want* to belong. Everyone wants to feel valued. At the heart of a people-first culture will always be a commitment to include others.

In the New and Old Testament the words *siblings, brothers,* and *sisters* are more commonly mentioned than the word church. A *Tov* culture considers every brother and sister - not by social status, ethnic statues, or gendered status - but as family. The essence of family is relationships, and the foundation of our relations with a culture of goodness is that we are united as children of God, eternal and everlasting.

In a *Tov* culture, we are to honor one another as human beings, as souls on a life mission, because we know who we are and to whom we belong. We cultivate our spiritual practice to eliminate fear from our lives so that we can see the goodness within us, around us, and in us. To create a culture of goodness, we must resist whatever does not treat people as siblings.

The Power of Environment

In the Second Mountain, Brooks describes how culture is powerful enough to form us into its image: Do not underestimate the power of the environment you work in to gradually transform who you are. When you choose to work at a certain company, you are turning yourself into the sort of person who works in that company. Moreover, living in a pragmatic, utilitarian manner turns you into a utilitarian pragmatist. The "how do I succeed?" questions quickly eclipse the "why am I doing this?" questions. What people experience in contact with a community - its service, leadership, people, and programs - defines the culture. A community *is* its culture, and that culture *is* the community. This energy is a transitive wave that causes vibrational changes in one's heart, mind, and body. To create a culture of goodness (*tov*), one must understand one's culture and worldview[4].

A World View of Tov

First, what do we mean by 'world view'? A worldview is the vast and total matrix of conceptions, explicit and implicit, held by a society or an individual about the limits and workings of the world. In other words, a worldview is our perception of how the world "works." It defines and determines how individuals in a culture perceive themselves and the world around them. And more importantly, a worldview defines a culture's attitudes about God, or the nature of the divine, and the possible nature of the relationship between the divine and humankind.

One very important aspect of a worldview is that it is so much a "given," so much taken for granted, that for the most part, it is never examined or even acknowledged to exist. Its premises are experienced as prime reality, not as what they truly are: unproven assumptions.

The worldview of culture affects every attitude, every form of behavior, and every perspective of its members. It is the window through which all of the members view the experiences of their life. The language of culture grows and develops under the influences of the worldview. Different languages worldwide contain complex meanings and understandings that are often difficult to translate for non-native speakers.

Planting the Seeds of Reciprocity

God is a giver, a giver of life. All of our lives are given to us freely by the creator. The air, the water, the soil, the fire, the trees, the plants, the food, and the technology are all gifts given free to us by the creator.

> *We are the ignorant ones. We put a price on God's gifts because we have not learned how to share.*

Another gift God gives us is redemption. Grace is not something we deserve or can earn based on our achievement status. In a grace-based culture, giving habits are common because we accept that our souls are recipients of God's gift of grace.

Trusting relationships are built on reciprocity - we must give to receive. As one sister or brother contributes to the family, and another receives the fit, a community of reciprocity is manifested. Power-based and fear-based cultures are one-way abusive relationships: the flow of trust is toward the powerful, the leaders. In a goodness-filled culture, reciprocity flows freely, as do the gifts.

When brothers and sisters see themselves as equal recipients of God's gifts and allow themselves to be transformed by God's medicine and the circle of life, we learn to love and trust each other. Fear-based cultures stifle freedom through censorship, legalism, authoritarianism, status, and approval-based relationships. That's not freedom, and that's not love.

At the heart of redemption is forgiveness. We are God's children. A good parent learns that letting their child struggle is good for their development. God knows what we can handle and is always ready to forgive and redeems us with love because God knows our heart best.

God commands us to give every being profound respect and honor for *who they are* - even if karmic mistakes have tarnished the Godliness in their soul. Recognizing all people are a child of God means *always* seeing their *potential* and reserving judgment of their being in the present moment. The only constant is change which is why God/Great Spirit extends redemption, forgiveness, and compassion to all Her Children, despite their *past* mistakes.

Embracing Indigenous Wisdom

The Culture of Tov has its roots in Indigenous wisdom. Wisdom is essential for the survival of humanity. Indigenous Peoples have taken care of the planet for thousands of years, and it is time to embed their philosophies into our daily lives, be it in urban or rural settings.

Indigenous Peoples make up less than 5 percent of the global population, yet they inhabit 80 percent of the most biodiverse regions. They have long practiced land management and conservation methods that scientists now say are crucial for tackling the climate crisis and enriching biodiversity. Nature's own systems offer the greatest climate solutions and when coupled with Indigenous ways of preserving ecosystems like forests, wetlands or savannas, can greatly contribute to making a better world for the children of today and tomorrow.

Native peoples' connection with nature is the most important point of traditional knowledge. Furthermore, Native Psychedelic Healing is creating a culture shift in a western world besieged by a mental health epidemic. Countless veterans and individuals ill served by the Western medical model travel to the tribes for psychedelic healing. There is much to be learned from the wisdom of the native peoples.

Nurturing Goodness and Healing Our Communities

We must acknowledge spiritual malpractice which is a perversion of the original teachings of Love and Kindness based upon ego-driven manifestations of patriarchalism and misogyny that protects the reputations of powerful institutions and individuals while debasing the rights of the wounded, their victims, causing even more physical, mental, emotional and spiritual torture; not to mention the different lifetimes of Karma earned.

Spiritual malpractice:
- Perverts spirituality and the eternal Dharma (lost teachings of Christ)
- Invents male-centeredness as a teaching of Jesus
- Fosters anti-female attitudes
- Censors the ceremony of the psychedelic sacrament
- Protects institutions at the expense of the people
- Protects the leaders of corrupt institutions
- Violates human rights and Laws of the Universe
- Hurts people
-

Waking up from religious indoctrination is frightening and lonely. The scariest part is one's support system, the one we need when we are in crisis, are often indoctrinated by the very poison one is trying to release. The people cannot hear beyond their own dogma. They can't hold space for a person's experience and out of their own fear they try to keep a person in religion. They might make a person feel crazy or like the 'devil' is ahold of them. This leaves the awakening person in an isolated state. There are so many psychological dysfunctions embedded in Abrahamic Religions. However; the most damaging is the belief that the members of 'said Religion' are 'chosen' and better than the rest of humanity. Everybody else, except them, has got it wrong.

Here is the truth: God hates religion. God hates religion because it keeps his people away from Him. God hates religion because it becomes a replacement for a relationship with Him. Religion is essentially idolatry. Siblings worship their man-made formations and structures their ideological idols formed in the concrete of inflexible minds. Religion is inevitably the result of man taking that which is of God and forming it, formulating it, in such a way that men end up "playing God."

Members of Religions claim to tolerate those with different beliefs but in reality they believe the only way to heaven is their 'single story scripture' and that everyone else is going to hell. These religions have twisted scripture to a point where they tell their members (who simply want to connect with God & the teachings of Christ) that any exploration or opinion different from theirs is evil. And, not only that, one will go to hell if one does not believe exactly what they say scripture says.

Due to this twisted spiritual programming, the person can't freely explore the vastness of themselves and their consciousness because religion has implanted a hellish fear mechanism into their psyche. This is a form of mind control and spiritual abuse. Psychologists call this Religious Trauma Syndrome.

You are not alone. If you identify with this, keep going. Trust in God to lead you. God loves your curiosity and your good heart. God's love is not found in a book. No matter what someone tries to tell you, you are not crazy.

If you believe in Love, Kindness and Goodness you are commissioned - not only to see and hear and believe the wounded but also to care for them, to help heal their wounds and afflictions. We must foster a culture that protects and heals our wounded: women, men, and children who did the right thing, and spoke their truth, only to suffer the humiliation of rejection, intimidation, and re-victimization but who nonetheless found the inner strength to share the truth no matter the consequences. This is for the voiceless who have told their story to no one outside the circle of close and trusted family, friends, and counselors. We must begin to treat each other in a loving and kind way.

How to Treat Your Sisters and Brothers
- Siblings care for one another
- Siblings look out for one another
- Siblings protect one another
- Siblings believe one another
- Siblings have integrity with one another
- Siblings honor their word
- Siblings trust one another
- Siblings see the goodness and mistake fullness and love each other no matter what

Communities with a *Tov* culture will do what is right because they love people and only want what is best for them[5].
Christ taught this message repeatedly:

- Thou shalt love thy neighbor as thyself
- My command is this: Love each other as I have loved you
- Do to others as you would have them do to you
- Do everything in love
- A friend loves at all times

A goodness culture begins when we see people for who they are: a divine, multidimensional angel; an eternal, everlasting soul incarnated on the physical plane of reality to manifest their gifts for the betterment of all beings; by treating everyone with love, kindness, respect, trust, and good humor; by extending nourishment to everyone in our family; by developing good relations with all of life on earth and out into the universe.

Overcoming Fear

A goodness culture builds relations with all of life, including God. All relationships are built on the foundation of trust. When we learn to trust *Tov* and when we learn to trust God, we no longer have fear. Fear is a mind-virus.

> 'There is no fear in love.
> Perfect love drives out fear,
> Because fear has to do with punishment.
> The one who fears is not made perfect in love.
> 1 John 4:18

Fear is an illusion, a coping mechanism, a construct of our brain and thoughts to 'help' us or to 'convince' us that whatever it is we are feeling is true. I can't count how many times I have been scared: of what people will think, of what they will say, of what they may do. If they'll go or if they'll stay. If they'll understand me. If they'll judge me and all of these led to me shutting down and tolerating people and things instead of standing up for myself. So where does fear come from?

Fear is the tool Satan uses to control our thoughts, words, actions, and deeds. However, fear is not real. Fear is an illusion that preys on the mind. It causes us to forget how to think biologically. It limits you. It paralyzes you into thinking people are against you when the truth is: you are against yourself.

When you think about it, fear is not about reality, it's about what you think of it. We do not fear the unknown, but we fear our idea of the unknown. Today people walk around with fear of sin for everything: fears about making love, fears about death, and fears about breathing God's air. All this fear serves one master, and that is neither God nor Christ. Science shows how fear depresses and weakens the immune system.

the pioneer

Wednesday, 26 October 2022

Fear weakens immune system, so don't scare public: Scientist to docs

Monday, 24 August 2020 | Kumar Chellappan | KOCHI

A medical scientist with decades of experience behind them have asked doctors and media to stay away from creating panic among the people at the time of the coronavirus pandemic. Prof B M Hegde, in the editorial in the latest issue of the "Journal of the Science of Healing Outcomes", an international peer-reviewed scientific journal has written that the thrust must be to help the public to boost their immune systems during this kind of outbreaks.

AJMC   BIOSIMILARS

AJMC

The Effects of Chronic Fear on a Person's Health

November 11, 2017

Jaime Rosenberg

Conference |
Neuroscience Education
Institute (NEI) Congress

Christ never taught children were born sinners. The Institution of the Church did that. Christ taught there is no sin but forgetting you are a soul in the human body. He taught that when you forget your soul, you live in the ego and now are susceptible to manipulation and making *chait* (mistakes). God grants you eternal salvation and forgiveness so what is there to be afraid of?

Christ taught we are all children of God which means we all have a soul and we all have everlasting life through the process of reincarnation. He taught that we too can become like him if we consume the flesh of the God's plant relatives. He healed many using God's True Eucharist which we today know as natural psychedelic medicine. Again, what is there to be afraid of?

Only the Father of Lies, the Great Deceiver, Lord of Darkness, Satan would want you to believe his lies that you go to hell, that you do not have eternal life, that you can't become like Christ, that Christ is better than you, that you are born a sinner, that you are not a perfect union of spirit and matter, a divine angel here to play, to learn, to manifest and to grow.

Reinventing Education

This moment requires a radical reorientation of education and realignment of purpose for both adults and children. We must shift education from the current model of shaping children into components of an economic machine and cultivate the natural-born creative and spiritual energies so the future world can reap the harvest of full-awakened and educated beings. We have been so "busy" educating our children that we have missed the purpose of education: a happy, good, loving life[6].

> Are we missing the deeper meaning and higher
> purpose of learning? Have we forgotten about the
> spirit of the child, the purpose of life, the unique and
> fragile expression of a passionate and integrated life?
> - The Happy Child: Changing the Heart of Happiness,
> Steven Harrison

Never before in history and nowhere else in the world has so much time, energy, attention and money been devoted to raising children as here in the U.S. Collectively as a nation, we invest billions of dollars every year in services for children. There are more child specialists - teachers, psychologists, social workers, pediatricians, pediatric nurses, counselors, school principals, recreation leaders and parent educators - who devote their lives to the welfare of children than in any other country in the world. Our children have more of everything from toys, to resources, to laptops than children have ever had anywhere. But in spite of all this and much more, who would want to be a child today? Not me, I think it is a terrible time for childhood.

It is quite difficult, in adult life, to rid ourselves of the education in self-rejection and lack of self-trust that we have received at home and in school. How tragically blind and ridiculous it is, therefore, to purport to be interested in the self-esteem of children, while all the while we continue to disempower them and psychologically damage them. We need to re-imagine education for ourselves and for our children. As we work to remember the sacred truths of life, we should teach children to appreciate the goodness of nature as well as natural law. Without gratitude for life and appreciation for a sense of beauty, our world will not survive. Native Americans have known this for thousands of years and natural law is taught within every American Indian Tribe.

One very important thing that education not only neglects in its programs but even fails to mention as a goal is responsibility. Response-ability is the ability to respond. We all have a responsibility to do our spiritual homework and to cultivate good relations with all of life. We are all partly responsible for the current mess that is the state of the world and we are all part of the solution for healing what must be healed. We must re-learn and teach what is natural. We need to re-learn how natural medicines keep us healthy. Natural medicine is exercise, is prayer, is meditation, is love, is kindness, is compassion, is community, is nature, is plant medicine. Natural medicine is clean air, clean water and healthy soil. Natural medicine is fresh healthy fruits, veggies and meat. These medicines lead to a good life. You do not need "an MD" to understand what is natural and what is medicine. These are natural laws, God's laws. Follow these laws and we will have a good life.

The Time of Prophecy

The era of false teachings, worship of false idols and rampant evil is over. We are now at the end of a cycle of time that has been described in prophecies by Indigenous peoples all over the world. The Hindu calendar shows that for the past 2,700 years we have been evolving through the ascending Kali Yuga, and this Yuga is coming to an end in 2025-2030.

The Hindu prophecy on Kali Yuga teaches that humanity is currently in its darkest age. Kali Yuga is characterized by sin, corruption, misery and evil all around. The world is said to have lost all its righteousness; people are corrupt and perform evil on a daily basis. Diseases and afflictions plague humanity. No one knows the vedas (truth), the original teachings of Christ, in its entirety and in its true essence. People fight over petty things like religion and land. Even hard work refuses to pay good results and people who perform bad deeds sit on the top of the societal ladder. In Kali Yuga, the poor and the rich will live in the same locality. The rich will be overflowing with fortune, yet they will not spare a single coin to help the poor like the dry well-received not a drop of water from the surrounding wells that were overflowing with water.

The Ancient Egyptian hermetic texts, 2000 years old, describe Thoth's prophecy. They say that at this time: Darkness will be preferred to light, and death will be thought more profitable than life; no one will raise his eyes to heaven;

the pious will be deemed insane, and the impious wise; the madman will be thought a brave man, and the wicked will be esteemed as good.

As to the soul, and the belief that it is immortal by nature, or may hope to attain immortality, as I have taught you, all this they will mock at, and will even persuade themselves that it is false.

No word of reverence or piety, no utterance worthy of heaven and of the gods of heaven, will be heard or believed. And so the gods will depart from mankind, a grievous thing!, and only evil angels will remain, who will mingle with men, and drive the poor wretches by main force into all manner of reckless crime, into wars, and robberies, and frauds, and all things hostile to the nature of the soul.

Like the Vedas & the Thoth text, the new testament shares this prophecy. Matthew 24:3 describes events and conditions that would mark "the conclusion of the current system of things," or "the end of the world." The Bible calls this time period "the last days" and the "time of the end," or "end times." (2 Timothy 3:1; Daniel 8:19; Easy-to-Read Version) It is true, we are ending one cycle of time and beginning a new cycle.

> But realize this, that in the last days difficult times
> will come. For men and women will be lovers of self,
> lovers of money, boastful, arrogant, revilers,
> disobedient to parents, ungrateful, unholy.
> 2 Timothy 3:1-2

Some of the prophecy in revelations says there will be:

- War on a large scale.—Matthew 24:7; Revelation 6:4.
- Famine.—Matthew 24:7; Revelation 6:5, 6.
- Great earthquakes.—Luke 21:11.
- Pestilences, or epidemics of "terrible diseases."—Luke 21:11, *Contemporary English Version*.

- Increase of crime.—Matthew 24:12.
- Ruining of the earth by mankind.—Revelation 11:18.
- Deterioration of people's attitudes, as shown by many who are "unthankful, disloyal, . . . not open to any agreement, slanderers, without self-control, fierce, without love of goodness, betrayers, headstrong, puffed up with pride."—2 Timothy 3:1-4.
- Breakdown of the family, with people who have "no natural affection" and children who are "disobedient to parents."—2 Timothy 3:2, 3.
- Love of God growing cold in most people.—Matthew 24:12.
- Noteworthy displays of religious hypocrisy.—2 Timothy 3:5.
- Increased understanding of Bible prophecies, including those related to the last days.—Daniel 12:4.
- Global preaching of the good news of the Kingdom.—Matthew 24:14.
- Widespread apathy and even ridicule toward the evidence of the approaching end.—Matthew 24:37-39; 2 Peter 3:3, 4.
- The simultaneous fulfillment of all these prophecies, not just a few or even most of them.—Matthew 24:33.

The time has come for judging the dead,
and for rewarding your servants
the prophets and your people who revere
your name, both great and small--
and for destroying those who
destroy the earth
Revelation 11:18

The Crimes of the Catholic Church

History repeats itself. In the modern era, the Catholic Church is working hand in hand with the Chineses Communist party to rewrite the Bible, alter and censor the story of Jesus, and promote state power and the King of China. Just as it did in the Roman Empire, it created a more politically palatable version of Christianity.

China Tells Christians to Replace Images of Jesus with Communist President

Propaganda effort in poor province latest sign of Xi Jinping consolidating control.

KATE SHELLNUTT | NOVEMBER 17, 2017 10:07 AM

Image: Lintan Zhao / Getty Images

The Chinese Communist Party, China's ruling regime, has been on a mission to rewrite the Bible through a communist lens. This quest has reportedly resulted in shocking distortions of Scripture and Gospel truth.

"This is a project that the Chinese Communist Party announced in 2019. At the time, they said it would be about a 10-year process ... to release a new translation of the Bible," noting it would include Confucian and Buddhist principles, among others. "This new translation ... would support the Communist Party."

From the Family Research Council

When a Chinese Christian, Chen Yu, was caught boldly selling religious publications not authorized by the government, his punishment was a seven-year sentence and an approximately $30,000 fine, handed down by a court last month. Such steep punishment for promoting and adhering to religion is common in China today[z].

Faith is increasingly under attack in President Xi Jinping's China. As religious expression becomes more dangerous there, people worldwide should speak up to defend China's persecuted believers. In addition to Chen's fine and imprisonment, the court ordered local police in the Zhejiang province to destroy 12,864 religious books from his online bookstore. This is a regime that is deeply afraid of the growth of Christianity.

The estimated 100 million Christians in China make eradicating Christianity from China difficult. Chairman Mao tried and was unsuccessful. President Xi prefers a more subtle tactic than Mao's, a campaign to "Sinicize " religion to make it more compatible with the teachings of the Chinese Communist Party (CCP). One way China seeks to Sinicize Christianity is by re-writing the Bible. A complete communist translation has yet to be revealed. The news of one chapter's government-approved revision left Christians outraged last month.

A textbook for a class on professional ethics and law at the government-run University of Electronic Science and Technology Press quotes the Bible's book of John, chapter eight. In this passage, an adulterous woman is brought to Jesus, and her accusers ask if she should be killed by stoning for her sins. In every authentically translated version of Scripture, Jesus responds, "Let him who is without sin among you be the first to throw a stone at her." These words disperse the angry crowd, and Jesus tells the woman, "Go, and from now on, sin no more" (ESV).

The Chinese Communist Party's version takes a different turn. In this telling, the crowd leaves, but Jesus tells the woman, "I, too, am a sinner. But if men could only execute the law without blemish, the law would be dead." Then Jesus proceeds to stone the woman.

The Party's distortion of Scripture whereby the Savior kills a woman is offensive and defamatory. That the CCP made this change is revealing. The Party's story teaches that forgiveness, an important Christian value, is rejected, and the law must be obeyed without question. In China, the law is whatever the CCP says.

While China may technically allow Christianity, it only allows a version of Christianity remade in the image of the CCP. These developments, among many others, make this a critical time in the history of religion in China. On Friday, the Vatican officially renewed its controversial deal with Beijing from 2018, making it even more so.

The secret agreement between the Vatican and Beijing in 2018 gave the officially atheist Chinese government a role in bishop appointments, while China's burgeoning religious oppression was overlooked. The aim of this deal may be admirable — to unify the Catholic Church in China, long divided between "underground" Catholics loyal to the Holy See and those belonging to the government-approved Chinese Patriotic Catholic Association. Despite the agreement, however, two years later, conditions have not improved for Catholics or any other religious adherents in China.

In September, reports surfaced that Chinese authorities tortured a 46-year-old priest in the Fujian province for refusing to join the state-approved Chinese Patriotic Catholic Association. The torture method allegedly included shining a bright light into his eyes for days and repeatedly banging a gong beside his ear. In July, bishops, and priests from the unregistered Catholic Diocese of Yujiang, in Jiangxi province, claimed that Chinese authorities had prohibited "any pastoral activity," and several priests were forced to undergo "patriotic" training.

After China lifted COVID-19 lockdown restrictions in June, some Catholic priests were instructed that Mass could resume as long as they preached "patriotism." Remember that "patriotism" in China means loyalty to the CCP. Catholics reluctant to join the state-approved church, which is often influenced by Party-approved teachings, are under more pressure than in previous years.

Former U.S. Secretary of State Mike Pompeo urged the Vatican to speak to Beijing about religious freedom in China. During a speech in Rome, he emphasized the impact a pope, the world's most influential faith leader, can make, pointing to the example of Pope John Paul II, who "played a pivotal role in igniting the revolution of conscience that brought down the Iron Curtain." For Catholic human rights activists like Benedict Rogers, Pope Francis' lack of interest in publicly speaking up for believers in China is disappointing.

Christians in China who refuse to bend to the Communist Party's agenda are under intense pressure. Government restrictions are growing tighter, and China's capacity to surveil and control its population is unprecedented. As it grows more dangerous for them to express their faith in the face of government crackdowns, it is left to the rest of the world to speak in defense of believers in China.

A History of Evil

It took until 2022 for the Catholic Church to admit the genocide and other heinous crimes it committed in the name of "God and Jesus" [8]. Here are small samples of their crimes:

- The Roman Catholic Church makes an entirely false claim when it claims that Peter could represent Christ.

- In AD 392, the same year Emperor Theodosius outlawed the Mysteries, Bishop Theophilus of Alexandria led a rabid mob into the Library of Alexandria, the most beautiful building in the world, and burned it to the ground.

- Pope Pius XII denied eyewitness reports of mass executions during the Holocaust.

- Systemically covering up tens of thousands of cases involving sexual misconduct by thousands of Priests and Clergymen[9].

- The Vatican Bank helped Nazi Germany[10] move money and gave Nazis asylum[11].

- The Australian Royal Commission into Institutional Child Sexual Abuse concluded that Archbishop Frank Little regularly put his church's reputation ahead of the welfare of raped children[12].

- Terrorizing Jews And Muslims For Hundreds of Years.

- Murdering Countless Women As Witches Because Pope Innocent VII Was Paranoid.

- Absolving Sins For Cash Payments, Including Sins Not Yet Committed

- Orchestrating The Fall Of The Knights Templar To Appease A Broke King.

- The Roman Inquisition, During Which Judaism And Love Magic Were Serious Crimes[13].

- Imprisoning Galileo In His Home For Years Because He Suggested Science Was Greater Than God[14].

- Cutting Funding For Immigrants Because Of Their Connection To The LGBTQ+ Community[15].

- Working with the Chinese Communist Party to rewrite the Bible.

- The Invention of Artificial Time, the Gregorian Calendar since 1582.

- Abusing 200,000 Children in France[16].

Genocide, murder, pedophilia, rape, torture, and censoring the true message of Jesus are some of the routine crimes of the Institution that is the Catholic Church. *Does this sound like a Church of God to you? The Church of Jesus? Or does it sound like the Church of Lucifer?*

A Culture of Wickedness

History and modern headlines reveal a sinful, deeply flawed church and an unhealthy institution marred by acts of injustice, rape, murder, torture, genocide, corruption, abuse, misogyny, and oppression. Cultural problems result in patterns of abuse. We see this pattern over and over again through church organizations across the globe. Behaviors typically don't happen in a vacuum; rather, they are an expression of an institution. The contemporary American church is wrecked with bickering and division, celebrity worship, unaccountable leaders, and false and shallow teachings.

These fake teachings passed off in the name of God and Jesus have infested modern church culture and almost all of western culture. However, these false teachings only serve one master: Satan, the Father of Lies.

The Catholic Church has created a toxic "Christian" culture that preaches the lie that girls and women only hear god referred to as a male and the father. The exclusively masculine orientation of Christianity, the "ascendancy of the Son," has deeply affected life on earth and its people. The global impact of 400-500 years of colonial imperialism by Christian nations of Europe and the U.S.A in the name of Christianity has had devastating consequences. To the extent that societies across the globe become "solar" oriented, failing to appreciate the gifts and attributes of the "feminine" as partners, they have contributed to male dominance.

In reclaiming Mary Magdalene's true importance in Christianity, we can help to restore balance in the world. In the United States, the "most free country in the world," women were only granted legal rights within the last 100 years. There is still a movement to pass the Equal Rights Amendment, which would guarantee equal legal rights for all American citizens regardless of sex. Saudi Arabia, which doesn't guarantee women full legal rights, was the only country in the world where women were forbidden from driving motor vehicles until 2018.

Would God, who is Love, and Jesus, who became the Light one with God, want you to believe you are a sinner, or would they want you to believe you are good, God's child, eternal and everlasting, you are love?

Who would want you to believe you are born a sinner, that you can never be saved unless you pledge fealty to an organization and all else are condemned to eternal damnation? The Catholic Church teaches we are born in sin because they are led by the Father of Lies. It is a blasphemous organization that profanes the name of God, Jesus, and Mary and only serves the aims of Lucifer, Father of Lies.

For example, the growing Christian religion faced unexpected problems during the Middle Ages. The new religious structure needed more money with the rising number of priests, bishops, parishes, and churches. Due to these needs, they also invented celibacy to allow the church to own everything that belonged to their priests.

Moreover, they decided to invent more terrible outcomes for Christian followers if they didn't do what the bishops expected. In the ancient writings, there is nothing about asking the priest to ask God to release individuals from their sins...or even a place called Hell - where the people who broke God's rules were said to go after death.

Another aspect that made the Church even more resistant in allowing the belief in reincarnation was related to the Crusades. During the Crusades, people offered all they had to the Church and fought in the name of Jesus. The religious fighters might have been less intent on losing their lives for their religion if they thought they would be reborn in the future.

When the Inquisition started killing people for heresy and witchcraft crimes, the religious society remained silent. Although they were losing neighbors, friends, and family, the Christians believed it was necessary to stay on the right side of the Church and Inquisition if they wanted to go to Heaven. A belief in the rules of karma and reincarnation wouldn't have allowed the leaders of the Inquisition to hurt so many people.

The Catholic Church and modern religion is corrupt. I don't need to spend any more energy explaining that. I have compassion and love and forgiveness for the past but we are now called to be conscious co-creators in this moment. That means doing the right thing and speaking truth to power.

Healing the War on Nature

Science is how we as a society determine truth. It is tangible and provides all of us with amazing innovations. I pray we can listen to the medical science around psychedelic medicine and push back against the propagandists who claim there is no medical value to these medicines.

Psychedelic medicines are needed now more than ever at a time where we as a society must search deeply within our souls and decide how we will act in the face of climate change. Will we choose to become conscious of the threat that we have created? Will we ignore our collective responsibility and our stewardship of the earth that provides for us? Will we decide we want a healthy earth for our children and our children's children and their children?

The first step on the path of healing is acceptance. It is now that we must learn that all religions originate from psychedelic sacraments - I call them God's medicine. They are a spiritual technology.   They provide us with direct communication to consciousness and the world of spirit.

Access to these plant medicines is our birthright and a human right. To ban access to these medicines is a human rights violation. Justice must be done as we work to reform the world governments' "War on Drugs". Don't forget this is a war against the people in our communities and a war against nature. It is exciting to be here now to bear witness to the awakening of the power of God's medicine.

The first action we must take is to provide people legal access to these natural medicines and to reform the policymaking of the drug war that started during the age of the "Holy" Roman Empire.

My Perspective as a Prisoner of War

I am a prisoner of war.

CRIME

Students arrested after drugs found

Staff Writer Columbia Daily Tribune

Published 11:01 p.m. CT March 4, 2010 | Updated 12:00 p.m. CT March 5, 2010

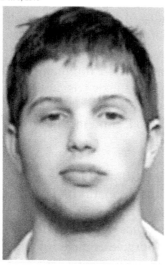

At 19, I was almost sentenced to 10 years in prison because I was trying to heal myself using God's medicine[17]. I almost spent 10 years in prison for practicing my religion. I was a felon. That wasn't my only experience with the justice system. At 18 years old, I was arrested for possession of marijuana. From 18 to 23 years old I was in the criminal justice system because I was trying to heal. I spent my senior year of high school on probation. I spent my entire time at University on probation. While the prosecutors of my LSD case sought out a 10 year prison sentence, by the grace of God, I was sentenced to a 5 year suspended sentence which meant I could still go to school.

If you are an American, you are guilty by association of injustice. Against all the sisters and brothers who rot in jail. The apathy towards doing the right thing means I almost spent ⅓ of my life in jail.

Under the laws of my time, I took personal responsibility for my actions and did everything required of me to achieve restitution. It's time you take responsibility and admit you too are guilty, guilty of injustice. The politicians are guilty. Joesph Biden, chief architect of mass incarceration and the War on Drugs, which disproportionately targeted Black Americans, you are guilty[18]. Too many of us think as long as it's not me, it's ok. Injustice is not ok. We are guilty of allowing injustice to foster in our homes and in our communities. Dear God, grant me the strength to let go of any anger that still lingers.

Be the first to say "I'm sorry"
or to offer empathy and compassion.
Of course, this is not fair, but do it anyway
because God does it for you.
You can "Forgive as the Lord forgave you".
(Colossians 3:13)

Know I have compassion and grace for you but I will live with that pain the rest of my life. I'm grateful for my scar because it fuels me to stand up and speak truth to power. I'm grateful I didn't go to prison, like others who have had their whole lives stolen away from them. Being a prisoner of war, is one of the many reasons I started the Legalize Psychedelic Medicine organization

Legalize Psychedelics Medicine

My passion for healing people and my desire to ensure no one suffers from injustice led me to found Legalize Psychedelic Medicine. We are an alliance of professionals, VSOs and NGOs working to legalize natural psychedelic medicine in order to transform mental healthcare in the United States. At the state level in Texas, we witnessed the success of Texas House Bill 1802[19]. At the federal level, dialogues have been started with the White House[20].

Texas bill paves way for study of psychedelic drugs to treat conditions like PTSD

by Jessica Gonzalez | Monday, February 28th 2022

POLITICS

Biden Administration Considers Psychedelic Therapies Task Force

BY KEN JORDAN , NOAH DALY
SEPTEMBER 20, 2022

As part of the psychedelic movement, I have witnessed the capitalists come into the space and now God's medicine is at threat of belonging in the hands of Big Pharma. Western culture created this mental health crisis and western culture does not know what it doesn't know. I believe in a different path. God gave me a vision for a new way forward combining the best of Indigenous healing with the standard care practices of western medicine to give birth to a new form of healing. I swore an oath to God, the ancestors and the master plants, to whom I've pledged my life, I won't allow the medicine to be guided into the wrong hands. So I am grateful to share with you my vision for a new world.

Ohai: Birthing Heaven on Earth

Three years ago, the Ancestors, Spirits, and Angels shared with me a vision to help create a new platform to heal the earth. Now I fully understand the vision I was given and I am beyond excited to share it with the world. The process began with a simple question: What if there was an operating system for communities that could recycle its profit into healing both the human family and our environment? What if there was a social good organization built from the ground up by a community of individuals passionate about living life in a loving and caring way. What if our culture was grounded in healing and wellness? Ideation led way to the clarity that I wanted to build a movement to heal earth.

Imagine an organization that operates on a model of social purpose and uses its various revenue streams to help heal the earth through the preservation of rainforests, restoring coral networks in the oceans, sustainable forestry, regenerative agriculture projects, developing new communities and healing veterans, homeless and those in need. That's what I was dreaming about. Only now I had to figure out how would one build it?

For me, all the goodness that is my life today is a direct result of my healing journey and my commitment to the wellness of my being. When thinking about this vision, I kept going back to the foundational roots of healing which made me believe that by building communities, online and offline, around caring for the mind, body and spirit we can give birth to a culture of *Tov* (goodness).

As a designer, we're taught to build, test and design. A large part of design is ideation. So when considering this vision I started out by asking questions like:
- What if there was a social network that used its profits for good?
- What if we built communities around healing and spiritual science?
- What if we created open-source educational curricula that taught children real world skills and critical thinking?
- What if we could replace the majority of governance (which has been corrupted by the spiritually ignorant) with a more direct and sovereign model?

- What if we could bring forced transparency to government spending using blockchain technology?
- What if we built a decentralized network of communities worldwide that were sovereign and free using modern technology?

And so the idea for Ohai was born. Ohai is to become the world's first decentralized nation dedicated to healing the earth.

What is a Decentralized Nation?

A decentralized nation is known as a network state. A network state is a futuristic social network with a moral innovation, a sense of national consciousness, a capacity for collective action, an in-person level of civility, an integrated cryptocurrency, a consensual government limited by a smart social contract, an archipelago of crowdfunded physical territories, a virtual capital, and an on-chain census that proves a large enough population, income, and real-estate footprint to attain a measure of diplomatic recognition.

The Vision to Heal Earth

Ohai will create communities and sustainable eco-cities of the future. These master-planned communities will feature a wellness center at the heart of each development. Our philosophy prioritizes the development of communities around healing, sustainability, science, spiritual truths, and economic sustainability. To do that, we will approach community building by embracing indigenous wisdom and sustainable business models for growth. Ohai's technology division will build decentralized social blockchain infrastructure to empower sovereign communities and promote free trade across the Earth. Ohai will develop a decentralized social network, a decentralized University and blockchain infrastructure for governance

We are manifesting a future where humanity leverages off-grid technologies to go back to our roots as sustainable communities. Our mission is to heal the earth by uniting people across the globe and building a platform for the new earth owned by and operated for the good of all people, ancestors, and life on Earth. Our goal is to use technology and resources to heal the oceans, forests, and people of Mother Earth. We believe that our efforts align with ancient prophecies that have been shared by Indigenous and Judeo-Christian communities around the world. Our organization exists to bring these prophecies to fruition and create a more harmonious and sustainable world for all.

Phase 1: Ohai Wellness

Phase 1 of the roadmap for Ohai is building out the core healing infrastructure. That starts with Ohai Wellness Center, a psychedelic wellness & therapeutic center pioneering the future of natural medicine at scale. A social good business, we are dedicated to healing veterans for free. Ohai Wellness solves two problems currently not being met by more niche wellness centers:

> 1. Building the infrastructure capable of helping more people to heal.
> 2. Building a model that will help make it more affordable.

We are dedicated to healing at scale (500 guests per week) to accommodate the immediate mental health crisis amongst our veterans. Our initial goal is to grow to heal 10,000 veterans a year for free, we accomplish this goal by selling 10,000 retail retreats. Aiming to heal over 1,000,000 souls per year by the end of the decade.

Ohai Wellness Center will offer a variety of retreats, including natural medicine, meditation retreats, and leadership development retreats. These retreats are designed to help guests experience profound personal growth and healing through end to end care via personal coaching, self discovery, community building, integration, and individualized post retreat action plans. Retreats are led by experienced guides who are trained in the safe and responsible use of natural medicine and meditation. Our retreats, guests, and guides are overseen by our onsite Ohai Wellness Center Medical Director - a licensed physician.

During the natural medicine retreats, guests have the opportunity to experience the transformative power of psychedelics, such as psilocybin, in a safe and supportive environment. The retreats are carefully structured and include a variety of activities and experiences, such as guided meditations, nature hikes, peer support, and group discussions, that are designed to help guests integrate their natural medicine experiences and learn from them.

In addition to the retreats, the Wellness Center line of business also offers a range of other best in class wellness services, including yoga, massage, sound bath, infrared sauna, cold immersion training, bloodwork, hormone replenishment, and nutrition counseling. These services are available to guests during retreats, and can also be booked separately by individuals who are not participating in a retreat.

Is Psychedelic Medicine Legal?

In Oregon and Colorado it is. The center will be built in compliance with state and federal regulatory and legal requirements in a to-be-determined future location in either Texas or Colorado. Ohai Co-Founders supported the 2021 passing of Texas HB1802, the 2022 Breakthrough Therapies Act co-sponsored by Senators Cory Booker (PA) and Rand Paul (KY) in the 117th Congress, and the recent 2022 natural medicine therapy ballot measure passed in Colorado.

Crowdfunding Ohai

To fund the wellness center, we are launching a crowdfunding campaign to raise $50 million dollars. To accomplish our goal, we are embracing NFT e-commerce technology. The reason we chose an NFT Collection is to build this vision for the people by the people while delivering lifetime NFT utility and benefits for individuals who hold a Legends of Ohai NFT. By building it alongside those that believe in decentralized governance and the healing power of natural medicine we can together help bring down the expensive cost of more niche retreats and build an infrastructure to allow for great accessibility to heal for all.

What is an NFT?

An NFT, or non-fungible token, is a digital asset that represents ownership of a unique item or asset. NFTs are stored on a blockchain, which is a distributed database that allows for secure and transparent record-keeping. This makes them unique and verifiable, as they cannot be replicated or counterfeited.

One of the main advantages of NFTs is that they allow for the creation of unique, digital assets that can be owned and traded in the same way as physical assets. This opens up new possibilities for artists and creators to monetize their work, and for collectors to own and trade rare and unique digital items. As innovators, we want to embrace new technologies.

The Ohai NFT

The Legends of Ohai collection consists of 9,999 utility-enabled NFTs, each of which grants its owner membership, perks, benefits, and other goodies in the Ohai Nation ecosystem, including access to events and eco-villages.

You Get a Healing Retreat
Each NFT is redeemable for a psychedelic healing or meditation retreat.

You Give a Veteran a Retreat
We give back. Every NFT will provide a free healing retreat for a Veteran.

Lifetime Discounts
Discounts on all future land sales, events, retreats, and resorts.

Token Airdrop
Receive a future airdrop allocation of the $Luv token which will fuel the Ohai ecosystem

Governance
Submit proposals for how to allocate the community treasury and vote on major decisions.

Limited Edition NFT Coffee Table Book
Every Holders of a Legend NFT will receive the right to claim a hand-illustrated coffee table books printed in ink and encrypted on the blockchain. Three Coffee Table Books will be released:
- The Psychedelic Origin of Religion (2023)
- The Science of Reincarnation (2024)
- The Gospel of Loving Kindness (2025)

Site Use
Discounted access to Ohai's co-living communities.

Early access
Event & festival tickets, meetups at Ohai properties, merch, and future drops. Owning a Ohai NFT brings you to the front of the line.

Follow us @ohaiwellness on instagram, @ohainatition on twitter, or go to heal.earth to learn more.

This is just the beginning of the vision. We want and we need people like you to be a part of this movement. We want to help people walk the path of loving kindness. There is much more that we can do together. Never doubt the power of a small group of individuals to change the world, for it's the only thing that ever has. Please check out docs.heal.earth for a more complete vision paper.

"If you adhere to my teaching, you will really be my disciples; and you shall know the Truth, and the Truth shall make you free" (JN 8)

Who Am I

Today, I speak to you in parables,
but the time is coming when I will speak to you plainly.

It is our duty to help each other remember who we are, where we come from and how we are all related. We all matter. That is why I have returned to Earth. I am here to share this message with you. I am here to plainly and lucidly use historical research and scientific research to help you understand these natural laws. I am here to guide this process for the benefit of all beings. So I speak to you plainly and clearly. You might hear me say some weird things, strange things. I might tell you that I'm a reincarnated being. But guess what? So are you. I'm not special. We are all children of the universe.

I pray this book creates more goodness in the world. If I help even just one person connect with the truth then I have served God to the best of my abilities and for that I am blessed and most grateful. In this life my name is Matthew and I give my life to you because I love you always with all my heart. I ask Creator God, Her Angels and the Spirits to guide me in a good way, guide this message in a good way and begin the reunification process of the human family from the four sacred directions of the North, South, East and West. I call on the 7 sacred directions to send love and light to anchor this process for the next seven generations until Mother Earth and her children are healed. I imagine this will be a 1000-year process.

I am the Way
I am Truth
The Life
I am Love
I am Light
I am Medicine
I am God's Son
And So Are You
You, God's Child
You are My Sibling
So Together, Let Us Walk
this Path of Loving Kindness
For the Goodness of All Beings
Thy Kingdom come,
Thy will be done,
On Earth as it is in Heaven.

Seeking Rainbow Warriors

"When the earth is ravaged and the animals are dying, a new tribe of people shall come unto the earth from many colors,

classes, creeds, and who by their actions and deeds shall make the earth green again. They will be known as Warriors of the Rainbow."
Ancient Indigenous Prophecy

The indigenous tribes of North and South America share the same prophecy. It has many names. We are in the time of prophecy. It is up to the people with good pure hearts that will not be afraid to help us to fulfill our destiny to create peace in this world. I am seeking you. If you live with a pure heart or wish to learn how to live with a pure heart, I seek you. I am seeking the True Christians, warriors who know how to use their weapons of love, compassion and goodness for the benefit of all beings. Those who walk the path of Loving Kindness. We seek those who wish to walk the path.

Join the movement at <u>Heal.Earth</u> or connect with me @heytrub on instagram.

Closing Prayer

One day the Creator will bring me back home to the spirit world and I will be asked about the love I shared and what I did to help my relatives. I want to say that I loved many, I tried my best and I created a vessel for Tov that could empower the next 7 generations. I know I can't take any material possessions with me when I die but I can leave behind a legacy of goodness. So that's why I'm building a vessel that can be self-sustaining in uplifting the human family by providing essential goods and services to my people in a community that seeks to embrace them, not exploit them. Thank You Lord for this sight.

Such is the new birth of the Cosmos; it is a making again of all things good, a holy and awe-striking restoration of all nature; and it is wrought in the

process of time by the eternal will of God. For Gods will has no beginning; it is ever the same, and as it now is, even so it has ever been, without beginning. For it is the very being of God to purpose good.

Aho, Great Spirit, Great Mystery. Aho HaShem, Creator, Allah. Thank you for this holy, sacred space. Thank you for this moment. Thank you for my life, my soul, my heart, my health, and all my blessings. Thank you for the air, the water, the earth, the fire, and the spirit that grants us the gift of life. Thank you to the spirits of the mountain, the forest, the waters, and the air. Thank you to the spirits of the North, the South, the East, and the West. Thank you to the plant people, stone people, and 2-legged, 4-legged, and multi-legged people. Thank you for teaching me to walk in beauty and live without fear. Thank you for healing me. I pray that all who seek healing be healed. I pray for the lives of my mom, my dad, my sister, my family, my friends and my brothers and sisters. I pray for the sick, the needy, the lonely, the downtrodden, and the wicked. I pray that they may have a blessed day, a good year, and a joyous life full of love and happiness. I pray that we remember the roots of religion, May we remember that we are nature, May we remember that we are one heart, one mind, one family, and one sacred chanupa. Thank you, thank you, thank you.

Aho Mitakuye Oyasin.
Te amo siempre pare siempre.

Namaste 🙏

About the Author

Matthew Lawrence Weintrub i a Healer, Author, Psychedelic Medicine Activist, and Entrepreneur. I am the founder of Ohai Wellness and Legalize Psychedelic Medicine - missions dedicated to healing mother earth, the human family, and building heaven on Earth.

I am the son of Mark and Linda and the brother of Leah. I was born, raised, and still live in Dallas, Texas. My Hebrew name is יונה which means Dove, a sign of peace. I am the messenger of peace. As a fully realized being, I remember my past lives. I have returned to Earth to teach the Science of Reincarnation, Psychedelic Medicine, Prayer, Fasting, Natural Food, and Meditation.

I love you always.
God Bless You.

Matthew Weintrub
@heytrub
www.heal.earth

References

Chapter 1

1. Cox, Daniel, and Amelia Thomson. "Millennials Are Leaving Religion And Not Coming Back." *FiveThirtyEight*, 12 December 2019, https://fivethirtyeight.com/features/millennials-are-leaving-religion-and-not-coming-back/.
2. *Wikipedia*, "More Americans now say they're spiritual but not religious." 6 Sep. 2017, https://www.pewresearch.org/fact-tank/2017/09/06/more-americans-now-say-theyre-spiritual-but-not-religious/.
3. Neuman, Scott. "Fewer Than Half Of U.S. Adults Belong To A Religious Congregation ...." 30 Mar. 2021, https://www.npr.org/2021/03/30/982671783/fewer-than-half-of-u-s-adults-belong-to-a-religious-congregation-new-poll-shows.

Chapter 2

1. "Soma: Divine Mushroom of Immortality,: R. Gordon Wasson." https://www.amazon.com/Soma-Mushroom-Immortality-Ethno-Mycological-Studies/dp/0156838001.
2. "The Mighty Fungi - Mind And Spirit." https://www.fs.usda.gov/wildflowers/ethnobotany/Mind_and_Spirit/fungi.shtml.
3. "Algerian Cave Paintings Suggest Humans Did Magic Mushrooms ...." 27 Jan. 2021, https://www.openculture.com/2021/01/algerian-cave-paintings-suggest-humans-did-magic-mushrooms-9000-years-ago.html.
4. "Selva Pascuala cave murals 'show man may have used magic ...." 9 Mar. 2011, https://www.dailymail.co.uk/sciencetech/article-1364259/Selva-Pascuala-cave-murals-man-used-magic-mushrooms-6-000-years-ago.html.
5. "Religious use of hallucinogenic fungi: A comparison between ...." https://www.funga.fi/Karstenia/Karstenia%2032-2%201992-4.pdf. Accessed 27 Oct. 2022.
6. "(PDF) A Prehistoric Mural in Spain Depicting Neurotropic Psilocybe ...." https://www.academia.edu/1376610/A_Prehistoric_Mural_in_Spain_Depicting_Neurotropic_Psilocybe_Mushrooms.
7. "5 Examples of Ancient Psychedelic Cave Art." 20 Apr. 2022, https://psychedelicspotlight.com/5-examples-of-ancient-psychedelic-cave-art/.
8. "Revealed: Early Bronze Age carvings suggest Stonehenge was a ...." 9 Oct. 2012, https://www.independent.co.uk/news/science/archaeology/revealed-early-bronze-age-carvings-suggest-stonehenge-was-a-huge-prehistoric-art-gallery-8202812.html.

Chapter 3

1. "Early humans lived in northern India 80,000 years ago - The Hindu." 26 Feb. 2020, https://www.thehindu.com/sci-tech/science/early-humans-lived-in-northern-india-80000-years-ago/article30924041.ece. Accessed 27 Oct. 2022.
2. "How Russian scientists cracked the secret of a Vedic ritual drink." 9 Jan. 2017, https://www.rbth.com/blogs/stranger_than_fiction/2017/01/09/how-russian-

scientists-cracked-the-secret-of-a-riga-veda-era-drink_676758. Accessed 27 Oct. 2022.

3. ""We Drank Soma, We Became Immortal..." - Наука из первых рук." 30 Aug. 2010, https://scfh.ru/en/papers/we-drank-soma-we-became-immortal-/. Accessed 27 Oct. 2022.

4. "A bas-relief of Shiva holding what appears to be a mushroom, circa ...." https://www.researchgate.net/figure/A-bas-relief-of-Shiva-holding-what-appears-to-be-a-mushroom-circa-1200-ad_fig71_261922195. Accessed 27 Oct. 2022.

5. "Soma: Divine Mushroom of Immortality,: R. Gordon Wasson." https://www.amazon.com/Soma-Mushroom-Immortality-Ethno-Mycological-Studies/dp/0156838001. Accessed 27 Oct. 2022.

6. Hoernle, A. F. R. (2011) [1912]. The Bower manuscript (facsimile leaves, nagari transcript, romanised transliteration and english translation with notes). New Delhi: Aditya Prakashan [Calcutta: Superintendent Government Printing]. pp. 20n.64, 90, 106. "The Bower Manuscript | INDIAN CULTURE." http://indianculture.gov.in/rarebooks/bower-manuscript. Accessed 27 Oct. 2022.

7. Leonti, M., & Casu, L. (2014)."Soma, food of the immortals according to the Bower Manuscript ...." 8 Aug. 2014. Journal of Ethnopharmacology, 155, 373–386. https://pubmed.ncbi.nlm.nih.gov/24907429/. Accessed 27 Oct. 2022.

8. Zig Zag Zen: Buddhism and Psychedelics, pp. 69-70. https://www.amazon.com/Zig-Zag-Zen-Buddhism-Psychedelics/dp/0811832864. Accessed 27 Oct. 2022.

9. Mochtar, S., & Geerken, H. (1979). Die Halluzinogene Muscarin und Ibotensäure im Mittleren Hindukusch: Ein Beitrag zur volkheilpraktischen Mykologie [The hallucinogens muscarine and ibotenic acid in the Middle Hindu Kush: A contribution on traditional medicinal mycology] (Peter G. Werner, Trans.]. Afghanistan Journal, 6, 62–65. Retrieved from www.erowid.org/plants/amanitas/references/journal/1979_mochtar_afghanistan1.shtml

10. Saar, M. (1991). Fungi in Khanty folk medicine. Journal of Ethnopharmacology, 31(2), 175–179. doi:10.1016/0378-8741(91)90003-V

11. "HIDDEN IN PLAIN SIGHT - Secret of Secrets - Mushroom Stone." https://www.mushroomstone.com/secret-of-secrets. Accessed 27 Oct. 2022.

12. "Soma and Haoma: Ayahuasca analogues from the Late Bronze Age in." 1 Jun. 2019, https://akjournals.com/view/journals/2054/3/2/article-p104.xml. Accessed 27 Oct. 2022.

13. "Ancient Indian Rope Geometry in the Classroom - Fire Altars of ...." https://www.maa.org/press/periodicals/convergence/ancient-indian-rope-geometry-in-the-classroom-fire-altars-of-ancient-india. Accessed 16 Nov. 2022.

Chapter 4

1. "Religions - Zoroastrian: At a Glance - BBC." 2 Oct. 2009, https://www.bbc.co.uk/religion/religions/zoroastrian/ataglance/glance.shtml. Accessed 16 Nov. 2022.

2. "Soma and Haoma: Ayahuasca analogues from the Late Bronze Age in." 1 Jun. 2019, https://akjournals.com/view/journals/2054/3/2/article-p104.xml. Accessed 16 Nov. 2022.

3. "Soma and Haoma: Ayahuasca analogues from the Late Bronze Age in." 1 Jun. 2019, https://akjournals.com/view/journals/2054/3/2/article-p104.xml. Accessed 16 Nov. 2022.

4. "Soma and Haoma: Ayahuasca analogues from the Late Bronze Age in." 1 Jun. 2019, https://akjournals.com/view/journals/2054/3/2/article-p104.xml. Accessed 16 Nov. 2022.

5. "Soma and Haoma: Ayahuasca analogues from the Late Bronze Age in." 1 Jun. 2019, https://akjournals.com/view/journals/2054/3/2/article-p104.xml. Accessed 16 Nov. 2022.

6. "The Herb of the Magi: Zoroaster's Good Narcotic | Cannabis Culture." 1 Oct. 2019, https://www.cannabisculture.com/content/2019/10/01/the-herb-of-the-magi-zoroasters-good-narcotic/. Accessed 16 Nov. 2022.

7. "The Herb of the Magi: Zoroaster's Good Narcotic | Cannabis Culture." 1 Oct. 2019, https://www.cannabisculture.com/content/2019/10/01/the-herb-of-the-magi-zoroasters-good-narcotic/. Accessed 16 Nov. 2022.

8. "Fire temple - Wikipedia - The Free Encyclopedia." https://www.rumahsoal.my.id/w/index.php?title=Fire_temple&oldid=1091455103. Accessed 16 Nov. 2022.

9. "Fire temple - Wikipedia." https://en.wikipedia.org/wiki/Fire_temple. Accessed 16 Nov. 2022.

Chapter 5

1. "The Second Psychedelic Revolution, Part Five." 20 Jun. 2014, https://maps.org/news/media/the-second-psychedelic-revolution-part-five-a-short-psychedelic-history-of/. Accessed 16 Nov. 2022.

2. "The Second Psychedelic Revolution, Part Five." 20 Jun. 2014, https://maps.org/news/media/the-second-psychedelic-revolution-part-five-a-short-psychedelic-history-of/. Accessed 16 Nov. 2022.

3. "The Second Psychedelic Revolution, Part Five." 20 Jun. 2014, https://maps.org/news/media/the-second-psychedelic-revolution-part-five-a-short-psychedelic-history-of/. Accessed 16 Nov. 2022.

4. "Hallucinogens & Native Spirituality - Notes From the Frontier." 30 Jan. 2021, https://www.notesfromthefrontier.com/post/hallucinogens-native-american-spirituality. Accessed 16 Nov. 2022.

5. "Ancient ayahuasca found in 1,000-year-old shamanic pouch." 6 May. 2019, https://www.nationalgeographic.com/culture/article/ancient-hallucinogens-oldest-ayahuasca-found-shaman-pouch. Accessed 16 Nov. 2022.

6. "Hallucinogenic drugs in pre-Columbian Mesoamerican cultures." https://www.sciencedirect.com/science/article/pii/S2173580814001527. Accessed 16 Nov. 2022.

7. "Hallucinogens & Native Spirituality - Notes From the Frontier." 30 Jan. 2021, https://www.notesfromthefrontier.com/post/hallucinogens-native-american-spirituality. Accessed 16 Nov. 2022.

8. "The Narcotic Mushroom of the Aztecs - Teonanacatl - Psilosophy." https://www.samorini.it/doc1/alt_aut/sz/schultes_teo.pdf. Accessed 16 Nov. 2022.

9.   "schultes-identification-of-teonanacatl.pdf." https://www.samorini.it/doc1/alt_aut/sz/schultes-identification-of-teonanacatl.pdf. Accessed 16 Nov. 2022.

10.   "Seeking the Magic Mushroom - Cover - The Psychedelic Library." http://www.psychedelic-library.org/life.htm. Accessed 16 Nov. 2022.

11.   "Ancient ayahuasca found in 1,000-year-old shamanic pouch." 6 May. 2019, https://www.nationalgeographic.com/culture/article/ancient-hallucinogens-oldest-ayahuasca-found-shaman-pouch. Accessed 16 Nov. 2022.

12.   "The use of psychoactive plants by ancient indigenous populations of ...." 1 Jun. 2019, https://akjournals.com/view/journals/2054/3/2/article-p198.xml. Accessed 16 Nov. 2022.

13.   "Introduction: Evidence for entheogen use in prehistory and world ...." 1 Jun. 2019, https://akjournals.com/view/journals/2054/3/2/article-p43.xml. Accessed 16 Nov. 2022.

14.   "Tripping on Peyote in Navajo Nation - Scientific American Blogs." 5 Jul. 2017, https://blogs.scientificamerican.com/cross-check/tripping-on-peyote-in-navajo-nation/. Accessed 16 Nov. 2022.

15.   ""Ayahuasca," the South American hallucinogenic drink - Springer Link." https://link.springer.com/article/10.1007/BF02860772. Accessed 16 Nov. 2022.

16.   "Health_beliefs_healing_practice...." https://eprints.whiterose.ac.uk/135826/2/Health_beliefs_healing_practices_and_medico_ritual_frameworks_in_the_Ecuadorian_Andes._The_continuity_of_an_ancient_tradition._Final.doc. Accessed 16 Nov. 2022.

17.   "Reincarnation in Native American Spiritual Beliefs - UniGuide®." 18 Nov. 2021, https://www.uniguide.com/reincarnation-native-american. Accessed 16 Nov. 2022.

18.   "KARMA AND REINCARNATION IN THE WEST - Indian Institute of ...." https://www.iiwcindia.org/transactions/transaction94.pdf. Accessed 16 Nov. 2022

Chapter 6

1.   "Soma siddhas and alchemical enlightenment: psychedelic mushrooms in Buddhist tradition - PubMed." https://pubmed.ncbi.nlm.nih.gov/8583800/. Accessed 16 Nov. 2022.

2.   "Shamanism and Tantra in the Himalayas - Amazon.com." https://www.amazon.com/Shamanism-Tantra-Himalayas-Surendra-Bahadur/dp/0892819138. Accessed 16 Nov. 2022.

3.   "Secret Drugs of Buddhism: Psychedelic Sacraments and the Origins ...." https://www.amazon.com/Secret-Drugs-Buddhism-Psychedelic-Sacraments/dp/0907791743. Accessed 16 Nov. 2022.

4.   "The Last Meal of the Buddha R. Gordon Wasson." http://lirs.ru/lib/jaos/The_Last_Meal_of_the_Buddha,Wasson,1982,JAOS.pdf. Accessed 16 Nov. 2022.

5.   "Secret Drugs of Buddhism: Psychedelic Sacraments and the Origins ...." https://www.amazon.com/Secret-Drugs-Buddhism-Psychedelic-Sacraments/dp/0907791743. Accessed 16 Nov. 2022.

6.   "Why magic mushrooms turn dark blue when picked - Nature." 26 Nov. 2019, https://www.nature.com/articles/d41586-019-03614-0. Accessed 16 Nov. 2022.

7. "Indian Esoteric Buddhism: A Social History of the Tantric Movement." https://www.amazon.com/Indian-Esoteric-Buddhism-History-Movement/dp/8120819918. Accessed 16 Nov. 2022.

9. "Buddhism and Psychedelics: A High History of Buddhism - Tricycle." https://tricycle.org/magazine/high-history-buddhism/. Accessed 16 Nov. 2022.

Chapter 7

1. "Herodotus and the Egyptian Idea of Immortality | Journal of Near ...." https://www.journals.uchicago.edu/doi/10.1086/371711. Accessed 16 Nov. 2022.

2. "Ancient Egypt exhibit gives lessons in immortality - Reuters." 21 Dec. 2009, https://www.reuters.com/article/us-exhibitions-egypt-idCATRE5BL0MC20091222. Accessed 16 Nov. 2022.

3. "Ancient Egypt exhibit gives lessons in immortality - Reuters." 21 Dec. 2009, https://www.reuters.com/article/us-exhibitions-egypt-idUSTRE5BL0MC20091222. Accessed 16 Nov. 2022.

4. "The Conservation of Mushroom in Ancient Egypt through the Present." 5 Jul. 2022, https://www.researchgate.net/publication/320991848_The_Conservation_of_Mushroom_in_Ancient_Egypt_through_the_Present. Accessed 16 Nov. 2022.

5. "The Conservation of Mushroom in Ancient Egypt through the Present." 5 Jul. 2022, https://www.researchgate.net/publication/320991848_The_Conservation_of_Mushroom_in_Ancient_Egypt_through_the_Present. Accessed 16 Nov. 2022.

6. "The entheomycological origin of Egyptian crowns and the esoteric ...." 14 Nov. 2005, https://www.sciencedirect.com/science/article/abs/pii/S0378874105005131. Accessed 16 Nov. 2022.

7. "Mushrooms and Mankind: The Impact of Mushrooms on Human ...." https://www.amazon.com/Mushrooms-Mankind-Impact-Consciousness-Religion/dp/1585091510. Accessed 16 Nov. 2022.

8. "The entheomycological origin of Egyptian crowns and the esoteric ...." 5 Jul. 2022, https://www.researchgate.net/publication/7566286_The_entheomycological_origin_of_Egyptian_crowns_and_the_esoteric_underpinnings_of_Egyptian_religion. Accessed 16 Nov. 2022.

9. "The entheomycological origin of Egyptian crowns and the esoteric ...." 5 Jul. 2022, https://www.researchgate.net/publication/7566286_The_entheomycological_origin_of_Egyptian_crowns_and_the_esoteric_underpinnings_of_Egyptian_religion. Accessed 16 Nov. 2022.

10. "Osiris shedding the barley he is personifying with a Psilocybe crown...." https://www.researchgate.net/figure/Osiris-shedding-the-barley-he-is-personifying-with-a-Psilocybe-crown-growing-from-his_fig20_7566286. Accessed 16 Nov. 2022.

11. "Sacred Blue Lotus." http://www.sacredbluelotus.com/. Accessed 16 Nov. 2022.

12. "Nymphaea caerulea - The Sacred Narcotic Lily of the Nile - jstor." https://www.jstor.org/stable/4253981. Accessed 16 Nov. 2022.

13. "The sacred journey in dynastic Egypt: shamanistic trance ... - PubMed." https://pubmed.ncbi.nlm.nih.gov/2656953/. Accessed 16 Nov. 2022.

14. "Ancient Egyptian Society and Family Life - The Fathom Archive." https://fathom.lib.uchicago.edu/2/21701778/. Accessed 16 Nov. 2022.

15. "The Psychedelic Tree of Life - Token Rock." https://www.tokenrock.com/articles/the-psychedelic-tree-of-life/. Accessed 16 Nov. 2022.

16. "Wine-making in ancient Egypt - Science Learning Hub." 1 Feb. 2010, https://www.sciencelearn.org.nz/images/1362-wine-making-in-ancient-egypt. Accessed 16 Nov. 2022.

17. "Iusaaset - Religion Wiki - Fandom." https://religion.wikia.org/wiki/Iusaaset. Accessed 16 Nov. 2022.

18. "Iusâas | Henadology." 23 May. 2014, https://henadology.wordpress.com/theology/netjeru/iusaas/. Accessed 16 Nov. 2022.

19. "The underworld and the afterlife in ancient Egypt - Australian Museum." https://australian.museum/learn/cultures/international-collection/ancient-egyptian/the-underworld-and-the-afterlife-in-ancient-egypt/. Accessed 16 Nov. 2022.

20. "Complete Works of Swami Vivekananda - Vol-4." 27 Jul. 2019, https://www.celextel.org/swami-vivekananda/complete-works-of-swami-vivekananda-vol-4/6/. Accessed 16 Nov. 2022.

1. "السنط فى مصر القديمة - مجلة الإتحاد العام للآثاريين العربSndt شجرة." https://jguaa.journals.ekb.eg/article_30814.html. Accessed 31 Dec. 2022.

Chapter 8

1. "Eleusinian Mysteries - Wikipedia." https://en.wikipedia.org/wiki/Eleusinian_Mysteries. Accessed 16 Nov. 2022.

2. "The Immortality Key: The Secret History of the Religion with No Name." https://www.amazon.com/Immortality-Key-Secret-History-Religion-ebook/dp/B0818QJHKF. Accessed 16 Nov. 2022.

3. "The Road to Eleusis: Unveiling the Secret of the Mysteries." https://www.amazon.com/Road-Eleusis-Unveiling-Secret-Mysteries/dp/1556437528. Accessed 16 Nov. 2022.

4. "The Immortality Key: The Secret History of the Religion with No Name." https://www.amazon.com/Immortality-Key-Secret-History-Religion-ebook/dp/B0818QJHKF. Accessed 16 Nov. 2022.

5. "The Immortality Key: The Secret History of the Religion with No Name." https://www.amazon.com/Immortality-Key-Secret-History-Religion-ebook/dp/B0818QJHKF. Accessed 16 Nov. 2022.

6. "The Road to Eleusis: Unveiling the Secret of the Mysteries." https://www.amazon.com/Road-Eleusis-Unveiling-Secret-Mysteries/dp/1556437528. Accessed 16 Nov. 2022.

7. "The Immortality Key: Lost on The Road to Eleusis | Cannabis Culture." 14 Mar. 2021, https://www.cannabisculture.com/content/2021/03/14/the-immortality-key-lost-on-the-road-to-eleusis/. Accessed 16 Nov. 2022.

8. "God, In The View Of Pythagoras, Was ONE, A Single Substance ...." 27 Sep. 2015, https://pikequotes.wordpress.com/2015/09/27/god-in-the-view-of-pythagoras-was-one-a-single-substance-whose-continuous-parts-extended-through-all-the-

universe-without-separation-difference-or-inequality-like-the-soul-in-the-human-body/. Accessed 16 Nov. 2022.

Chapter 9

1. "Archaeologists Identify Traces of Burnt Cannabis in Ancient Jewish ...." 4 Jun. 2020, https://www.smithsonianmag.com/smart-news/cannabis-found-altar-ancient-israeli-shrine-180975016/. Accessed 16 Nov. 2022.

2. "Archaeologists Identify Traces of Burnt Cannabis in Ancient Jewish ...." 4 Jun. 2020, https://www.smithsonianmag.com/smart-news/cannabis-found-altar-ancient-israeli-shrine-180975016/. Accessed 16 Nov. 2022.

3. "Part 2 of the Great Keneh Bosem Debate: | Cannabis Culture." 23 Nov. 2009, https://www.cannabisculture.com/content/2009/11/23/part-2-great-keneh-bosem-debate/. Accessed 16 Nov. 2022.

4. "Ezra - Wikipedia." https://en.wikipedia.org/wiki/Ezra. Accessed 16 Nov. 2022.

5. "Vishtaspa - Wikipedia." https://en.wikipedia.org/wiki/Vishtaspa. Accessed 16 Nov. 2022.

6. "2 Esdras 14:1–48 NRSV - On the third day, while... | Biblia." https://biblia.com/bible/esv/2-esdras/14/1-48. Accessed 16 Nov. 2022.

7. "Entheogens and the Development of Culture: The Anthropology and ...." https://books.google.com/books?id=O45aDYWOL-oC&pg=PA66&lpg=PA66&dq=%E2%80%9CThe+image+of+a+blazing+cup+was+apparently+related+to%E2%80%A6+Zoroastrianism;+Zoroastrian+texts+mention+ritual+vessels+with+fire+burning+inside+them%E2%80%9D+(Kisel,+2007).&source=bl&ots=V7pLxP31Hn&sig=ACfU3U0QIRmB52F0W1o-8pAtLQhmLyDyfw&hl=en. Accessed 16 Nov. 2022.

8. "The Great Keneh Bosem Debate - Part 1 - Cannabis Culture Magazine." 16 Nov. 2009, https://www.cannabisculture.com/content/2009/11/16/great-keneh-bosem-debate-part-1/. Accessed 16 Nov. 2022.

9. "The Biblical Ezra's Cup of Hashish Infused Wine? | Cannabis Culture." 27 Jul. 2016, https://www.cannabisculture.com/content/2016/07/27/the-biblical-ezras-cup-of-hashish/. Accessed 16 Nov. 2022.

10. "Torah Essence - Page 2 of 259 - Published by Rabbi Shloime Mannes." 31 Oct. 2022, https://torahessence.com/page/2/. Accessed 16 Nov. 2022.

11. "Beshalah: Eating the manna and receiving the Torah." 29 Jan. 2015, https://www.jpost.com/opinion/beshalah-eating-the-manna-and-receiving-the-torah-389465. Accessed 16 Nov. 2022.

12. "Lightning Makes Mushrooms Multiply - National Geographic." 9 Apr. 2010, https://www.nationalgeographic.com/science/article/100409-lightning-mushrooms-japan-harvest. Accessed 16 Nov. 2022.

13. "Manna and Mystical Eating - TheTorah.com." 30 May. 2018, https://www.thetorah.com/article/manna-and-mystical-eating. Accessed 16 Nov. 2022.

14. "Manna and Mystical Eating - TheTorah.com." 30 May. 2018, https://www.thetorah.com/article/manna-and-mystical-eating. Accessed 16 Nov. 2022.

15.	"Manna and Mystical Eating - TheTorah.com." 30 May. 2018, https://www.thetorah.com/article/manna-and-mystical-eating. Accessed 16 Nov. 2022.

16.	"Biblical Entheogens: a Speculative Hypothesis - ResearchGate." 5 Jul. 2022, https://www.researchgate.net/publication/233597014_Biblical_Entheogens_a_Speculative_Hypothesis. Accessed 16 Nov. 2022.

17.	"Biblical Entheogens: a Speculative Hypothesis - ResearchGate." 5 Jul. 2022, https://www.researchgate.net/publication/233597014_Biblical_Entheogens_a_Speculative_Hypothesis. Accessed 16 Nov. 2022.

18.	"Magic of the Ordinary: Recovering the Shamanic in Judaism." https://www.amazon.com/Magic-Ordinary-Recovering-Shamanic-Judaism/dp/1556434448. Accessed 16 Nov. 2022.

19.	"Magic of the Ordinary | Arthur Magazine." 10 Jun. 2006, https://arthurmag.com/2006/06/10/magic-of-the-ordinary/. Accessed 16 Nov. 2022.

20.	"What Judaism Says About Reincarnation | My Jewish Learning." https://www.myjewishlearning.com/article/reincarnation-the-transmigration-of-a-jewish-idea/. Accessed 16 Nov. 2022.

21.	"What Judaism Says About Reincarnation | My Jewish Learning." https://www.myjewishlearning.com/article/reincarnation-the-transmigration-of-a-jewish-idea/. Accessed 16 Nov. 2022.

1.	"Judaism's Psychedelic Renaissance - Tablet Magazine." 26 Jul. 2021, https://www.tabletmag.com/sections/news/articles/psychedelic-summit-madison-margolin. Accessed 2 Jan. 2023.

2.	"How Wrestling God Awakened Jacob's Pineal Gland." 15 Mar. 2012, https://www.spiritofthescripture.com/id262-how-wrestling-god-awakened-jacobs-pineal-gland.html. Accessed 2 Jan. 2023.

1.	"Psychedelics in the Torah - Sefaria." https://www.sefaria.org/sheets/368921?lang=bi. Accessed 2 Jan. 2023.

Chapter 10

1.	"Archaeologists discover largest, oldest wine cellar in Near East." 22 Nov. 2013, https://www.sciencedaily.com/releases/2013/11/131122084543.htm. Accessed 16 Nov. 2022.

2.	"Medicinal plants of the Bible—revisited." 27 Nov. 2019, https://ethnobiomed.biomedcentral.com/articles/10.1186/s13002-019-0338-8. Accessed 16 Nov. 2022.

3.	"An Investigation into the Sacramental Use of Psychoactive Milk and ...." https://www.academia.edu/4135149/The_Milk_of_the_Goat_Hei%C3%B0run_An_Investigation_into_the_Sacramental_Use_of_Psychoactive_Milk_and_Meat. Accessed 16 Nov. 2022.

4.	"The Immortality Key: The Secret History of the Religion with No Name." https://www.amazon.com/Immortality-Key-Uncovering-History-Religion/dp/1250207142. Accessed 16 Nov. 2022.

5.	"Sacred Mushroom - 1970 Sunday Mirror - John Allegro." http://www.johnallegro.org/text/Allegro-SundayMirror.htm. Accessed 16 Nov. 2022.

6. "The Psychedelic Gospels: The Secret History of Hallucinogens in ...." https://www.amazon.com/Psychedelic-Gospels-History-Hallucinogens-Christianity/dp/1620555026. Accessed 16 Nov. 2022.

7. "Illustrations of Magic Mushrooms in Early Christian Iconography." https://medium.com/the-collector/illustrations-of-magic-mushrooms-in-early-christian-iconography-c92b5afa13b0. Accessed 16 Nov. 2022.

8. "Nag Hammadi library - Wikipedia." https://en.wikipedia.org/wiki/Nag_Hammadi_library. Accessed 16 Nov. 2022.

9. "The Psychedelic Gospels: The Secret History of Hallucinogens in ...." https://www.amazon.com/Psychedelic-Gospels-History-Hallucinogens-Christianity/dp/1620555026. Accessed 16 Nov. 2022.

10. "Sacred Plants and the Gnostic Church: Speculations on Entheogen ...." https://psychedelicgospels.com/wp-content/uploads/2016/06/jah-2014-0010.pdf. Accessed 16 Nov. 2022.

11. "Flight into Egypt - Wikipedia." https://en.wikipedia.org/wiki/Flight_into_Egypt. Accessed 16 Nov. 2022.

12. "The psychedelic roots of Christianity - Vox." 4 Mar. 2021, https://www.vox.com/vox-conversations-podcast/2021/3/4/21759683/christianity-psychedelics-brian-muraresku-the-immortality-key. Accessed 16 Nov. 2022.

13. "The Gnostic Gospels: Pagels, Elaine: 9780679724537 - Amazon.com." https://www.amazon.com/Gnostic-Gospels-Elaine-Pagels/dp/0679724532. Accessed 16 Nov. 2022.

14. "Gospel of Thomas — Gospels.net." https://www.gospels.net/thomas. Accessed 16 Nov. 2022.

15. "The Gnostic Gospels: Pagels, Elaine: 9780679724537 - Amazon.com." https://www.amazon.com/Gnostic-Gospels-Elaine-Pagels/dp/0679724532. Accessed 16 Nov. 2022.

16. "According To Historical Research, Jesus Used Medical Marijuana ...." 19 Dec. 2019, https://herb.co/news/culture/jesus-medical-marijuana-cannabis/?fbclid=IwAR2LR5z_bvsrbwOdr_Si2yuhnGoVXk85QyriBMkPnOZ0rz21FFJp9m77yD8. Accessed 16 Nov. 2022.

17. "Cannabis is one of five essential plants in the ... - The Economic Times." 18 Dec. 2016, https://economictimes.indiatimes.com/opinion/interviews/cannabis-is-one-of-five-essential-plants-in-the-vedas-dr-uma-dhanabalan/articleshow/56041201.cms. Accessed 16 Nov. 2022.

18. "Jesus 'healed using cannabis' | World news - The Guardian." https://www.theguardian.com/world/2003/jan/06/science.religion. Accessed 16 Nov. 2022.

19. "Sex, Drugs, Violence and the Bible - Amazon.com." https://www.amazon.com/Drugs-Violence-Bible-Chris-Bennett/dp/1550567985. Accessed 16 Nov. 2022.

20. "The Immortality Key: The Secret History of the Religion with No Name." https://www.amazon.com/Immortality-Key-Uncovering-History-Religion/dp/1250207142. Accessed 16 Nov. 2022.

21. "The Immortality Key: The Secret History of the Religion with No Name." https://www.amazon.com/Immortality-Key-Uncovering-History-Religion/dp/1250207142. Accessed 16 Nov. 2022.

22. "Pew survey shows majority of Catholics don't believe in 'Real ....'" 6 Aug. 2019, https://www.ncronline.org/spirituality/pew-survey-shows-majority-catholics-dont-believe-real-presence. Accessed 16 Nov. 2022.

23. "Were the Earliest Christians Sipping Psychedelic Wine? - Patheos." 1 Dec. 2021, https://www.patheos.com/blogs/wakeupcall/2021/12/were-the-earliest-christians-sipping-psychedelic-wine/. Accessed 16 Nov. 2022.

24. "The Council of Nicaea and Biblical Canon - Phoenix Seminary." https://ps.edu/council-nicaea-biblical-canon/. Accessed 16 Nov. 2022.

25. "Mary Magdalene Revealed: The First Apostle, Her Feminist Gospel ...." https://www.amazon.com/Mary-Magdalene-Revealed-Feminist-Christianity/dp/1401954901. Accessed 16 Nov. 2022.

26. "Mary Magdalene Revealed: The First Apostle, Her Feminist Gospel ...." https://www.amazon.com/Mary-Magdalene-Revealed-Feminist-Christianity/dp/1401954901. Accessed 16 Nov. 2022.

27. "Mary Magdalene Revealed: The First Apostle, Her Feminist Gospel ...." https://www.amazon.com/Mary-Magdalene-Revealed-Feminist-Christianity/dp/1401954901. Accessed 16 Nov. 2022.

28. "The Gospel of Philip: Jesus, Mary Magdalene, and the Gnosis of ...." https://www.amazon.com/Gospel-Philip-Magdalene-Gnosis-Sacred/dp/1594770220. Accessed 16 Nov. 2022.

29. "Why Jesus Taught Reincarnation - A Better News Gospel Paperback ...." https://www.amazon.com/Why-Jesus-Taught-Reincarnation-Better/dp/B00405BK9G. Accessed 16 Nov. 2022.

30. "Why Jesus Taught Reincarnation - A Better News Gospel Paperback ...." https://www.amazon.com/Why-Jesus-Taught-Reincarnation-Better/dp/B00405BK9G. Accessed 16 Nov. 2022.

31. "Why Jesus Taught Reincarnation - A Better News Gospel Paperback ...." https://www.amazon.com/Why-Jesus-Taught-Reincarnation-Better/dp/B00405BK9G. Accessed 16 Nov. 2022.

32. "Journey Into Kashmir and Tibet: Swami Abhedananda - Amazon.com." https://www.amazon.com/Journey-Kashmir-Tibet-Swami-Abhedananda/dp/9380568363. Accessed 16 Nov. 2022.

33. "The difference between Christ and anti-christ." 20 Aug. 2014, https://askrealjesus.com/the-difference-between-christ-and-anti-christ/. Accessed 16 Nov. 2022.

1. "'Tomb of Jesus' In Kashmir–Roza Bal Shrine | India Heritage Walks." 30 Sep. 2020, https://www.indiaheritagewalks.org/blog/tomb-jesus-kashmir-roza-bal-shrine. Accessed 28 Nov. 2022.

1. "Jesus and the Lost Goddess: The Secret Teachings of the Original ...." https://www.amazon.com/Jesus-Lost-Goddess-Teachings-Christians/dp/1400045940. Accessed 6 Dec. 2022.

Chapter 11

1. "The Psychedelic Nature of Islamic Art and Architecture - Sam Woolfe." 1 Oct. 2018, https://www.samwoolfe.com/2018/10/the-psychedelic-nature-of-islamic-art-and-architecture.html. Accessed 28 Nov. 2022.

2. "Mohammed and The Sacred Mushroom." 19 Jul. 2013, http://cannibalchristians.blogspot.com/2013/07/mohammed-and-sacred-mushroom.html. Accessed 28 Nov. 2022.

3. "Peganum Harmala - an overview | ScienceDirect Topics." https://www.sciencedirect.com/topics/neuroscience/peganum-harmala. Accessed 28 Nov. 2022.

4. "celestial botany: entheogenic traces in islamic mysticism." http://en.psilosophy.info/celestial_botany_entheogenic_traces_in_islamic_mysticism.html. Accessed 28 Nov. 2022.

5. "Haoma - Wikipedia." https://en.wikipedia.org/wiki/Haoma. Accessed 28 Nov. 2022.

6. "(PDF) Dictionary of Deities and Demons in the Bible - Academia.edu." https://www.academia.edu/30069945/Dictionary_of_Deities_and_Demons_in_the_Bible. Accessed 28 Nov. 2022.

7. "On Wild Rue | Islamic Medical Wisdom, The Tibb al-A'imma." https://www.al-islam.org/islamic-medical-wisdom-tibb-al-aimma/wild-rue. Accessed 28 Nov. 2022.

8. "Classic Hallucinogens and Mystical Experiences - NCBI." https://www.ncbi.nlm.nih.gov/pmc/articles/PMC6707356/. Accessed 28 Nov. 2022.

9. "The Mongol Warlords: Genghis Khan, Kublai Khan, Hulegu ...." https://www.amazon.com/Mongol-Warlords-Genghis-Tamerlane-warriors/dp/1853141046. Accessed 28 Nov. 2022.

10. "(PDF) Bread of heaven or wines of light: Entheogenic legacies and ...." https://www.academia.edu/1376609/Bread_of_heaven_or_wines_of_light_Entheogenic_legacies_and_esoteric_cosmologies. Accessed 28 Nov. 2022.

11. "Mysticism and Philosophy: W.T. Stace, Huston Smith + Free Shipping." https://www.amazon.com/Mysticism-Philosophy-W-T-Stace/dp/0874774160. Accessed 28 Nov. 2022.

12. "Hashish and other psychoactive substances in the Islamic World." 22 Nov. 2018, https://www.cannabisculture.com/content/2018/11/22/hashish-and-other-psychoactive-substances-in-islam/. Accessed 28 Nov. 2022.

13. "Iranian Religious Authority Considers Psychedelic Medicines Halāl." 28 Dec. 2017, https://psychedelictimes.com/irans-top-religious-leader-approves-therapeutic-use-psychedelics/. Accessed 28 Nov. 2022.

14. "Ayahuasca and the Godhead: An Interview with Wahid Azal of the ...." 12 Jun. 2014, https://realitysandwich.com/ayahuasca-and-the-godhead-an-interview-with-wahid-azal-of-the-the-fatimiya-sufi-order/. Accessed 28 Nov. 2022.

Chapter 12

1. "Mental Health Disorder Statistics | Johns Hopkins Medicine." https://www.hopkinsmedicine.org/health/wellness-and-prevention/mental-health-disorder-statistics. Accessed 16 Dec. 2022.

2. "Mental disorders - World Health Organization (WHO)." 8 Jun. 2022, https://www.who.int/news-room/fact-sheets/detail/mental-disorders. Accessed 16 Dec. 2022.

3. "VA Mental Health Services | Veterans Affairs." 12 Oct. 2022, https://www.va.gov/health-care/health-needs-conditions/mental-health/. Accessed 16 Dec. 2022.

4. "Facts About Suicide - CDC." https://www.cdc.gov/suicide/facts/index.html. Accessed 16 Dec. 2022.

5. "Veterans suicide rate may be double federal estimates, study suggests." 17 Sep. 2022, https://www.militarytimes.com/veterans/2022/09/17/veterans-suicide-rate-may-be-double-federal-estimates-study-suggests/. Accessed 16 Dec. 2022.

6. "Facts About Suicide - CDC." https://www.cdc.gov/suicide/facts/index.html. Accessed 16 Dec. 2022.

7. "AAP-AACAP-CHA Declaration of a National Emergency in Child and ...." 19 Oct. 2021, https://www.aap.org/en/advocacy/child-and-adolescent-healthy-mental-development/aap-aacap-cha-declaration-of-a-national-emergency-in-child-and-adolescent-mental-health/. Accessed 18 Dec. 2022.

8. "Washington Post: 'A cry for help': CDC warns of a steep decline in ...." 12 Apr. 2022, https://www.pcavt.org/all-news/2022/4/12/washington-post-a-cry-for-help-cdc-warns-of-a-steep-decline-in-teen-mental-health. Accessed 18 Dec. 2022.

9. "Statement by President Joe Biden on New Mental Health Funding." 18 Oct. 2022, https://www.whitehouse.gov/briefing-room/statements-releases/2022/10/18/statement-by-president-joe-biden-on-new-mental-health-funding/. Accessed 16 Dec. 2022.

10. "Secretary of Defense Lloyd J. Austin III's Statement on DoD Annual ...." 20 Oct. 2022, https://www.defense.gov/News/Releases/Release/Article/3193957/secretary-of-defense-lloyd-j-austin-iiis-statement-on-dod-annual-suicide-report/. Accessed 16 Dec. 2022.

11. "Psychedelic Drug Use Could Reduce Psychological Distress ...." 9 Mar. 2015, https://www.hopkinsmedicine.org/news/media/releases/psychedelic_drug_use_could_reduce_psychological_distress_suicidal_thinking. Accessed 16 Dec. 2022.

12. "Pilot study of the 5-HT2AR agonist psilocybin in the treatment of ...." https://pubmed.ncbi.nlm.nih.gov/25213996/. Accessed 16 Dec. 2022.

13. "With 'How to Change Your Mind,' Taking a Trip With Michael Pollan." 20 Jul. 2022, https://www.nytimes.com/2022/07/15/arts/television/how-to-change-your-mind-netflix-michael-pollan.html. Accessed 18 Dec. 2022.

14. "Psilocybin produces substantial and sustained decreases in ... - NCBI." 30 Nov. 2016, https://www.ncbi.nlm.nih.gov/pmc/articles/PMC5367557/. Accessed 16 Dec. 2022.

15. "Rapid and sustained symptom reduction following psilocybin ... - NCBI." 30 Nov. 2016, https://www.ncbi.nlm.nih.gov/pmc/articles/PMC5367551/. Accessed 16 Dec. 2022.

16. "Amanda Feilding: 'LSD can get deep down and reset the brain." 10 Feb. 2019, https://www.theguardian.com/politics/2019/feb/10/amanda-feilding-lsd-can-reset-the-brain-interview. Accessed 18 Dec. 2022.

17. "The psychedelic escape from depression - Nature." 28 Sep. 2022, https://www.nature.com/articles/d41586-022-02872-9. Accessed 18 Dec. 2022.

18. "Psilocybin Treatment for Major Depression Effective for Up to a Year ...." 15 Feb. 2022, https://www.hopkinsmedicine.org/news/newsroom/news-releases/psilocybin-treatment-for-major-depression-effective-for-up-to-a-year-for-most-patients-study-shows. Accessed 18 Dec. 2022.

19. "Psilocybin can occasion mystical-type experiences having ... - PubMed." https://pubmed.ncbi.nlm.nih.gov/16826400/. Accessed 17 Dec. 2022.

20. "Profound experiences linked to mental health benefits - JHU Hub." 26 Apr. 2019, https://hub.jhu.edu/2019/04/26/experiencing-god-psychedelics-mental-health/. Accessed 17 Dec. 2022.

21. "Psilocybin can occasion mystical-type experiences having ... - PubMed." https://pubmed.ncbi.nlm.nih.gov/16826400/. Accessed 17 Dec. 2022.

22. "Survey of entity encounter experiences occasioned by inhaled N,N ...." 28 Apr. 2020, https://journals.sagepub.com/doi/10.1177/0269881120916143. Accessed 17 Dec. 2022.

23. "Survey of subjective "God encounter experiences" - PLOS." 23 Apr. 2019, https://journals.plos.org/plosone/article?id=10.1371/journal.pone.0214377. Accessed 17 Dec. 2022.

24. "Marsh Chapel Experiment - Wikipedia." https://en.wikipedia.org/wiki/Marsh_Chapel_Experiment. Accessed 18 Dec. 2022.

25. "THERAPEUTIC APPLICATION OF THE CHANGE IN ... - PubMed." https://pubmed.ncbi.nlm.nih.gov/14345225/. Accessed 16 Dec. 2022.

26. "Ego-Dissolution and Psychedelics: Validation of the Ego ... - Frontiers." 20 May. 2016, https://www.frontiersin.org/articles/10.3389/fnhum.2016.00269/full. Accessed 16 Dec. 2022.

27. "Self unbound: ego dissolution in psychedelic experience." https://academic.oup.com/nc/article/2017/1/nix016/3916730. Accessed 16 Dec. 2022.

28. "American happiness hits record lows | CNN Politics." 2 Feb. 2022, https://www.cnn.com/2022/02/02/politics/unhappiness-americans-gallup-analysis/index.html. Accessed 18 Dec. 2022.

29. "Oregon Psilocybin Services to finalize rules in December 2022 - KGW." 4 Aug. 2022, https://www.kgw.com/article/news/local/oregon-psilocybin-services-finalize-rules-in-december-2022/283-5fb47d31-3e7e-4d23-bcbe-ba2bcc653da8. Accessed 16 Dec. 2022.

30. "Texas legislature approves bill to study psychedelics to treat PTSD ...." 31 May. 2021, https://www.independent.co.uk/news/world/americas/texas-mushrooms-legislature-veterans-ptsd-b1857123.html. Accessed 16 Dec. 2022.

31. "Colorado Legalizes Therapeutic Psychedelics – Now What? | Blogs." 14 Nov. 2022, https://www.foley.com/en/insights/publications/2022/11/colorado-legalizes-therapeutic-psychedelics. Accessed 16 Dec. 2022.

32. "VA community clinics expand Ketamine treatment options for ...." 29 Sep. 2022, https://www.militarytimes.com/off-duty/military-culture/2022/09/29/va-community-clinics-expand-ketamine-treatment-options-for-depression/. Accessed 16 Dec. 2022.

33. "Johns Hopkins Medicine Receives First Federal Grant for ...." 18 Oct. 2021, https://www.hopkinsmedicine.org/news/newsroom/news-releases/johns-hopkins-medicine-receives-first-federal-grant-for-psychedelic-treatment-research-in-50-years. Accessed 16 Dec. 2022.

34. "Bipartisan Lawmakers Form New Psychedelics Caucus In Congress." 17 Nov. 2022, https://www.marijuanamoment.net/bipartisan-lawmakers-form-new-psychedelics-caucus-in-congress/. Accessed 16 Dec. 2022.

35. "Booker, Paul Introduce Bipartisan Legislation to Promote Research ...." 17 Nov. 2022, https://www.booker.senate.gov/news/press/booker-paul-introduce-bipartisan-legislation-to-promote-research-and-access-to-potential-life-saving-drugs. Accessed 16 Dec. 2022.

36. "Why You Only Need to Test with 5 Users - Nielsen Norman Group." https://www.nngroup.com/articles/why-you-only-need-to-test-with-5-users/. Accessed 16 Dec. 2022.

37. "Psychedelic Medicine: The Healing Powers of LSD, MDMA ...." https://www.amazon.com/Psychedelic-Medicine-Healing-Psilocybin-Ayahuasca/dp/1620556979. Accessed 18 Dec. 2022.

38. "Psychedelics and Neuroplasticity: A Systematic Review Unraveling ...." 19 Aug. 2021, https://www.frontiersin.org/articles/10.3389/fpsyt.2021.724606/full. Accessed 16 Dec. 2022.

39. "Neural correlates of the psychedelic state as determined by fMRI ...." https://www.pnas.org/doi/10.1073/pnas.1119598109. Accessed 16 Dec. 2022.

40. "The New Science of Psychedelics - Michael Pollan." 3 May. 2018, https://michaelpollan.com/articles-archive/the-new-science-of-psychedelics/. Accessed 16 Dec. 2022.

41. "Ceremonial Ayahuasca in Amazonian Retreats—Mental Health and ...." 14 May. 2021, https://www.frontiersin.org/articles/10.3389/fpsyt.2021.687615/full. Accessed 16 Dec. 2022.

42. "Is mental health illness actually a spiritual sickness?." https://www.tikvahlake.com/blog/is-mental-health-illness-actually-a-spiritual-sickness/. Accessed 19 Dec. 2022.

43. "Dr. Gabor Maté: The Power of Connection & The Myth of Normal." 17 Oct. 2022, https://www.youtube.com/watch?v=X0cODqqYyi8. Accessed 19 Dec. 2022.

44. "The Immortality Key: The Secret History of the Religion with No Name." https://www.amazon.com/Immortality-Key-Uncovering-History-Religion/dp/1250207142. Accessed 19 Dec. 2022.

45. "Biologists Think They've Found The Secret Ingredient That Made ...." 11 Apr. 2019, https://www.sciencealert.com/empathy-is-the-secret-ingredient-that-made-civilization-possible. Accessed 19 Dec. 2022.

46. "Mirroring People: The Science of Empathy and How We Connect ...." https://www.amazon.com/Mirroring-People-Science-Empathy-Connect/dp/0312428383. Accessed 19 Dec. 2022.

47. "Harlow's Classic Studies Revealed the Importance of Maternal Contact." 20 Jun. 2018, https://www.psychologicalscience.org/publications/observer/obsonline/harlows-classic-studies-revealed-the-importance-of-maternal-contact.html. Accessed 19 Dec. 2022.

48. "Spending at least 120 minutes a week in nature is associated with ...." 13 Jun. 2019, https://www.nature.com/articles/s41598-019-44097-3. Accessed 19 Dec. 2022.

49. "Ecopsychology: How Immersion in Nature Benefits Your Health." 9 Jan. 2020, https://e360.yale.edu/features/ecopsychology-how-immersion-in-nature-benefits-your-health. Accessed 19 Dec. 2022.

50. "Gardening on a psychiatric inpatient unit: Cultivating recovery." 5 Oct. 2018, https://www.psychiatricnursing.org/article/S0883-9417(18)30298-X/fulltext. Accessed 19 Dec. 2022.

51. "Amazon.com: A Lawyer Presents the Evidence for the Afterlife." https://www.amazon.com/Lawyer-Presents-Evidence-Afterlife/dp/1908733225. Accessed 19 Dec. 2022.

Chapter 13

1. "Did Jesus Start a New Religion Called Christianity?." 18 Sep. 2017, https://www.anewdaydawning.com/blog-1/2017/9/18/was-jesus-a-christian-did-he-start-a-new-religion-called-christianity. Accessed 28 Nov. 2022.

2. "Q'eros Inca Indigenous 2012 Prophecy | Pachakuti, Earth's turnover." https://theshamanictimes.com/qeros-indigenous-prophecies-2012.html. Accessed 28 Nov. 2022.

3. "The Secret Religion of the Dollar: How Money is Really Impacting ...." 31 Jan. 2020, https://www.highexistence.com/the-secret-religion-of-the-dollar-how-money-is-really-impacting-your-life/. Accessed 28 Nov. 2022.

4. "The Second Mountain: The Quest for a Moral Life: Brooks, David." https://www.amazon.com/Second-Mountain-David-Brooks/dp/0812993268. Accessed 28 Nov. 2022.

5. "A Church Called Tov: Forming a Goodness Culture That Resists ...." https://www.amazon.com/Church-Called-Tov-Goodness-Promotes/dp/1496446003. Accessed 28 Nov. 2022.

6. "Healing Civilization: Naranjo, Claudio, Houston, Jean - Amazon." https://www.amazon.com/Healing-Civilization-Claudio-Naranjo/dp/0895561638. Accessed 28 Nov. 2022.

7. "China To Christians: We're Rewriting The Bible, And You'll Use It Or ...." 26 Oct. 2020, https://www.frc.org/op-eds/china-to-christians-were-rewriting-the-bible-and-youll-use-it-or-else. Accessed 28 Nov. 2022.

8.   "Pope says genocide took place at Church schools in Canada for ...." 30 Jul. 2022, https://www.reuters.com/world/pope-says-genocide-took-place-church-schools-canada-indigenous-children-2022-07-30/. Accessed 28 Nov. 2022.

9.   "Roman Catholic Church Sex Abuse Cases - The New York Times." https://www.nytimes.com/topic/organization/roman-catholic-church-sex-abuse-cases. Accessed 28 Nov. 2022.

10.   "In 'confession of guilt,' German Catholic Church admits 'complicity ...." 2 May. 2020, https://www.timesofisrael.com/german-bishops-said-to-admit-complicity-in-nazi-actions-in-new-report/. Accessed 28 Nov. 2022.

11.   "Newly Unsealed Vatican Archives Lay Out Evidence of Pope Pius ...." 5 May. 2020, https://www.smithsonianmag.com/smart-news/researchers-find-evidence-pope-pius-xii-ignored-reports-holocaust-180974795/. Accessed 28 Nov. 2022.

12.   "Catholic Church sexual abuse cases in Australia - Wikipedia." https://en.wikipedia.org/wiki/Catholic_Church_sexual_abuse_cases_in_Australia. Accessed 28 Nov. 2022.

13.   "The spanish holocaust: inquisition and extermination in twentieth ...." 31 Dec. 2014, https://researchportal.bath.ac.uk/en/publications/the-spanish-holocaust-inquisition-and-extermination-in-twentieth-. Accessed 28 Nov. 2022.

14.   "Galileo is accused of heresy - HISTORY." https://www.history.com/this-day-in-history/galileo-is-accused-of-heresy. Accessed 28 Nov. 2022.

15.   "Catholic Church Cuts Funds To Immigrant Group Because It Doesn't ...." 6 Apr. 2012, https://archive.thinkprogress.org/catholic-church-cuts-funds-to-immigrant-group-because-it-doesnt-discriminate-against-gay-people-700225034ea2/. Accessed 28 Nov. 2022.

16.   "A9 on Twitter: "CW: child sex abuse We have been posting about the ...." https://twitter.com/A9Collective/status/1574081811361439744. Accessed 28 Nov. 2022.

17.   "Students arrested after drugs found - Columbia Daily Tribune." 5 Mar. 2010, https://www.columbiatribune.com/story/news/crime/2010/03/05/students-arrested-after-drugs-found/21486166007/. Accessed 28 Nov. 2022.

18.   "FACT: Joe Biden Was the Architect of Mass Incarceration." 22 Oct. 2020, https://www.presidency.ucsb.edu/documents/campaign-press-release-fact-joe-biden-was-the-architect-mass-incarceration. Accessed 28 Nov. 2022.

19.   "Texas bill paves way for study of psychedelic drugs to treat ... - KFOX." 28 Feb. 2022, https://kfoxtv.com/news/local/texas-bill-paves-way-for-study-of-psychedelics-drugs-to-treat-conditions-like-ptsd. Accessed 28 Nov. 2022.

20.   "Biden Administration Considers Psychedelic Therapies Task Force." 20 Sep. 2022, https://www.lucid.news/biden-administration-psychedelic-task-force/. Accessed 28 Nov. 2022.

21.   "The radical new experiments that hint at plant consciousness." 24 Aug. 2022, https://www.newscientist.com/article/mg25534012-800-the-radical-new-experiments-that-hint-at-plant-consciousness/. Accessed 28 Nov. 2022.

22.   "PLANT CONSCIOUSNESS: Scientific Evidence Showing How ...." 23 Jun. 2022, https://animamundiherbals.com/blogs/blog/plant-consciousness-the-fascinating-evidence-showing-plants-have-human-level-intelligence-feelings-pain-and-more. Accessed 28 Nov. 2022.

23.   "Frantisek Baluska University of Bonn - ResearchGate." https://www.researchgate.net/profile/Frantisek-Baluska. Accessed 28 Nov. 2022.

Printed in Great Britain
by Amazon

40266979R00162